T0212491

Communications in Computer and Information Science   **612**

Commenced Publication in 2007
Founding and Former Series Editors:
Alfredo Cuzzocrea, Dominik Ślęzak, and Xiaokang Yang

More information about this series at http://www.springer.com/series/7899

Diego Calvanese · Dario De Nart
Carlo Tasso (Eds.)

Digital Libraries on the Move

11th Italian Research Conference
on Digital Libraries, IRCDL 2015
Bolzano, Italy, January 29–30, 2015
Revised Selected Papers

 Springer

Editors

Diego Calvanese
Fac. di Scienze e Tecnologie Informatiche
Libera Univ. di Bolzano
Bolzano
Italy

Dario De Nart
Dip. di Scienze Matematiche, Informatiche
 e Fisiche
Università degli Studi di Udine
Udine
Italy

Carlo Tasso
Dip. di Scienze Matematiche, Informatiche
 e Fisiche
Università degli Studi di Udine
Udine
Italy

ISSN 1865-0929   ISSN 1865-0937 (electronic)
Communications in Computer and Information Science
ISBN 978-3-319-41937-4   ISBN 978-3-319-41938-1 (eBook)
DOI 10.1007/978-3-319-41938-1

Library of Congress Control Number: 2016943797

Printed on acid-free paper

This Springer imprint is published by Springer Nature
The registered company is Springer International Publishing AG Switzerland

Preface

Since 2005, the Italian Research Conference on Digital Libraries (IRCDL) has provided a great opportunity for Italian researchers in the field of digital libraries to present and discuss their current research activities and to envision together further developments. The 2015 edition of IRCDL continued the traditional emphasis on the multidisciplinary nature of the research on digital libraries, which has been characterizing the conference over the years.

Digital libraries are "on the move" – they experience today a significant, almost revolutionary development, which can be seen in various ways in their numerous multidisciplinary aspects, ranging from computer science to humanities in the broader sense, including research areas such as archival and library information sciences, information management systems, semantic technologies, information retrieval, new knowledge environments, and new organizational/business models. This is a tremendous challenge for the digital libraries field and there is a strong need to improve the cooperation between the many communities that share common objectives. Moreover, deep changes are affecting the world of scientific communication, where new non-linear but object-centric products are progressively taking shape, and new problem areas emerge, requiring for the integration, publication, and preservation of research data.

The aim of the IRCDL Conference series has always been to provide attendees with the opportunity to explore new ideas, techniques, and tools, and to exchange experiences also from on-going projects. The IRCDL series was launched and initially sponsored by DELOS, an EU FP6 Network of Excellence on digital libraries, together with the Department of Information Engineering of the University of Padua. Over the years, IRCDL has become a self-sustainable event that is supported by the Italian digital libraries community.

The 2015 edition of IRCDL was organized with the patronage and the sponsorship of the Faculty of Computer Science and the Library of the Free University of Bozen-Bolzano.

This volume contains the reports on the invited presentations and revised versions of a selection of the accepted papers presented at the conference. After the presentation, the papers were resubmitted by the authors in a revised version that included the suggestions received during the presentation at the conference. The peer-review process was performed under the responsibility of the Scientific Committee of IRCDL 2015.

The topics included in the papers cover many aspects of digital libraries, which were organized under the following five categories:

- Semantic Modelling
- Projects
- Models and Applications
- Content Analysis
- Digital Libraries Infrastructures.

The program of IRCDL 2015 also included two invited events: Dr. Antonio Gulli from Elsevier presented a very interesting talk on "Smart Data for the Publishing Industry," and Prof. Maristella Agosti from the University of Padua was invited to chair a Special Session devoted to the first 10 years of the IRCDL Conference series.

We would like to thank those institutions and individuals who made the conference and this volume possible. More specifically, we thank the Program Committee members and the additional reviewers, the honorary chair, the Steering Committee members, the authors, the local Organizing Committee, the Faculty of Computer Science, and the University Library of the Free University of Bozen-Bolzano.

April 2016   Diego Calvanese
                                                               Dario De Nart
                                                               Carlo Tasso

Organization

IRCDL 2015 was organized by the Faculty of Computer Science and the University Library of the Free University of Bozen-Bolzano.

Honorary Chair

Costantino Thanos   ISTI CNR, Pisa, Italy

Program Chairs

Diego Calvanese   Free University of Bozen-Bolzano, Italy
Carlo Tasso   University of Udine, Italy

IRCDL Steering Committee

Maristella Agosti   University of Padua, Italy
Tiziana Catarci   Sapienza University of Rome, Italy
Alberto Del Bimbo   University of Florence, Italy
Floriana Esposito   University of Bari, Italy
Carlo Tasso   University of Udine, Italy
Costantino Thanos   ISTI CNR, Pisa, Italy

Program Committee

Stefano Berretti   University of Florence, Italy
Marco Bertini   University of Florence, Italy
Maria Teresa Biagetti   Sapienza University of Rome, Italy
Rossella Caffo   ICCU Rome, Italy
Vittore Casarosa   ISTI CNR, Pisa, Italy
Michelangelo Ceci   University of Bari, Italy
Fabio Ciotti   University of Rome 2, Italy
Rita Cucchiara   University of Modena and Reggio Emilia, Italy
Nicola Di Mauro   University of Bari, Italy
Stefano Ferilli   University of Bari, Italy
Nicola Ferro   University of Padua, Italy
Costantino Grana   University of Modena and Reggio Emilia, Italy
Maria Guercio   Sapienza University of Rome, Italy
Donato Malerba   University of Padua, Italy
Paolo Manghi   ISTI CNR, Pisa, Italy
Simone Marinai   University of Florence, Italy
Carlo Meghini   ISTI CNR, Pisa, Italy
Maurizio Messina   Biblioteca Nazionale Marciana, Venice, Italy
Antonella Poggi   Sapienza University of Rome, Italy

Marco Schaerf	Sapienza University of Rome, Italy
Gianmaria Silvello	University of Padua, Italy
Anna Maria Tammaro	University of Parma, Italy
Francesca Tomasi	University of Bologna, Italy
Paul G. Weston	University of Pavia, Italy

Organizing Committee

Diego Calvanese	Free University of Bozen-Bolzano, Italy
Luigi Siciliano	University Library, Free University of Bozen-Bolzano, Italy
Hannes Hell	Press and Event Management, Free University of Bozen-Bolzano, Italy

Smart Data for the Publishing Industry (Invited Talk)

Antonio Gulli

Elsevier, Amsterdam, Netherlands
a.gulli@elsevier.com

Abstract. Smart Data is a central element for the Publishing Industry. A review of the rich data published by Elsevier via 9 Research platforms will be presented. Particular emphasis will be devoted to our investments in Knowledge graphs, Information Extraction, and Entity annotation. After this initial introduction, we will focus our attention on three particular applications built on top of our rich data. Authors' disambiguation is an open research problem where the goal is to match different identities attributed to the same Author during his/her life. Article fingerprinting is a rich set of information extraction techniques used for classifying articles and for building analytical tools leveraged by research institutions. News Trend detection is another rich set of matching tools used for tracking how institutions and researchers are mentioned by public and social media.

Keywords: Data publishing · Publishing industry · Information extraction

Contents

Invited Talk

10 Years of IRCDL: 2005–2014
(*Invited Paper*)

Maristella Agosti[✉]

Department of Information Engineering, University of Padua,
Via Gradenigo 6/a, 35131 Padua, Italy
maristella.agosti@unipd.it

Abstract. This paper reports on the presentation made during the "11th Italian Research Conference on Digital Libraries (IRCDL 2015)" held in Bolzano-Bozen, 29–30 January 2015, in the main building of the Free University of Bozen-Bolzano. The presentation was given during the conference special session devoted to the report on the first ten editions of Italian Research Conference on Digital Libraries (IRCDL). This paper gives an account on the general aspects of the history of IRCDL, whereas the report on the research topics and trends over time, and over the research community that has been built around IRCDL over ten years, can be found in [4].

Keywords: Italian Research Conference on Digital Libraries · IRCDL · Digital libraries · Digital libraries systems · Digital archives systems · Interoperable systems · Digital humanities

1 The Initiative

The "Italian Research Conference on Digital Libraries (IRCDL)" series of conferences was originally conceived and organized in the context of the activities of DELOS, the Network of Excellence on Digital Libraries, partially funded by the European Union under the Sixth Framework Programme from 2004 to 2007[1].

The first IRCDL conference took place in 2005, as an opportunity for Italian researchers to present recent results on their research activities related to the wide world of Digital Libraries. In particular, young researchers were (and still are) invited to submit the results of their ongoing research, which were presented in a friendly and relaxed atmosphere to facilitate constructive discussion and exchange of opinions.

Much of the credit for the IRCDL series of conferences still being very active today goes to DELOS. As a matter of fact, DELOS started its activities many years ago as a working group under the ESPRIT Programme, then continued as a Thematic Network under the 5th Framework Programme and after that

---

[1] Information on the launch of DELOS in the *ERCIM News*, No. 57, April 2004, at the URL: http://www.ercim.eu/publication/Ercim_News/enw57/thanos.html.

D. Calvanese et al. (Eds.): IRCDL 2015, CCIS 612, pp. 3–7, 2016.
DOI: 10.1007/978-3-319-41938-1_1

went on as a Network of Excellence under the 6th Framework Programme. It is generally recognized that during these years DELOS has made a substantial contribution to the establishment in Europe of a research community on Digital Libraries. At the end of 2007 the funding of the DELOS Network of Excellence came to an end. In order to keep the DELOS spirit alive, a DELOS Association was established as a not-for-profit organization, with the main aim of continuing the DELOS as much as possible activities by promoting research activities in the field of digital libraries. After some years the DELOS Association completed its scope, but the annual meetings have continued thanks to the Department of Information Engineering of the University of Padua and the other institutions that have hosted and supported IRCDL over the following years.

So IRCDL has become a self sustainable yearly meeting point for Italian researchers on digital libraries and related topics that is supported by the national community of researchers on digital libraries. Information on the several editions of the IRCDL series are available in a dedicated web page that also contains the references to the websites of all editions[2].

The Italian community that meets annually at IRCDL is an active community that contributes to the achievement of European and international projects, and through its results can inform on what is happening in general in this area and give some guidance on what the new challenges and the boundaries of the area will be. One of the main focuses of IRCDL is emphasizing the multidisciplinary nature of the research on digital libraries which not only goes from computer science to humanities but also spans several areas in the same field, ranging, for example, from archival to librarian sciences or from information management systems to new knowledge environments. This is a continued challenge for the digital libraries field and there is the need to continue contributing towards the improvement of cooperation between the many communities that share common objectives.

2   The Organization

The organization that takes care of IRCDL is a "Steering Committee" of senior researchers of Italian research and university institutions where the innovative activities on topics related to the digital libraries area at large have been addressed for years in the context of renowned projects. At present the institutions represented in the steering committee are:

- Department of Computer Science, University of Bari "Aldo Moro"
- Department of Information Engineering of the University of Florence
- Department of Information Engineering of the University of Padua
- Information Science and Technologies Institute (ISTI) "Alessandro Faedo" of the Italian National Research Council (CNR), Pisa
- Department of Computer, Control, and Management Engineering "Antonio Ruberti" at Sapienza University of Rome

---

[2] http://ims.dei.unipd.it/ircdl/home.html.

– Department of Mathematics and Computer Science, University of Udine.

The Steering Committee oversees the initiative on a voluntary basis and manages the general course of its operations, identifying each year an institute willing to organize the annual event.

The institution that takes care of the organization of the annual conference identifies the general and program chair(s) that set up a program committee of take care of all the entire process of peer review of the submitted papers, the preparation of the program and the organization of the effective event itself.

A volume of post-proceedings has been published each year. The volume contains the reports on the invited presentations and the accepted papers. The accepted papers are initially reviewed for presentation at the conference, and after the presentation the papers are resubmitted by the authors in a revised version that includes the suggestions received during the presentation at the conference. The resubmitted versions of the papers are peer reviewed by anonymous reviewers and the post-review accepted papers are revised by the authors taking into considerations the reviewers' suggestions for inclusion in the volume. From 2005 to 2009 the post-proceedings were published by Italian publishers, from 2010 to 2013 the post-proceedings were published in the "Communications in Computer and Information Science (CCIS)" series of Springer International Publishing AG, whereas the 2014 post-proceedings were published by Elsevier in the "Procedia Computer Science" series and are available as Open Access.

Information on the conference editions and the post-proceedings are also available under the name of "Italian Research Conference on Digital Library Management Systems" in the DBLP computer science bibliography, the world's most comprehensive open bibliographic data service in computer science[3].

An analysis of the papers of the first ten editions of the conference has been conducted by the researchers of the Artificial Intelligence Lab of the Department of Mathematics and Computer Science of the University of Udine. This analysis gives an account of the authors network, the most commonly presented concepts, and the network of concepts, as well as a chronological analysis of the topics of all the papers collected in the volumes of the first ten editions of IRCDL; the analysis is reported in [4].

It is also worth recalling that in 2010 the IRCDL steering committee promoted the launch of the "Italian Information Retrieval (IIR) Workshop" series, that started in 2010 with its first edition which was supported by IRCDL and organized in Padua side by side with the 2010 edition of IRCDL.

3   The Logo

Starting with the first edition of the conference series a logo for the conference was designed and used for the web site and for all publicity material. This logo is shown in Fig. 1.

---

[3] URL: http://dblp.uni-trier.de/db/conf/ircdl/index.html.

Fig. 1. The IRCDL logo. (Color figure online)

The logo is a collection of colored pencils. This choice is based on the fact that the researchers, regardless of the specific theme of interest of their research and in addition to working with a strictly scientific approach, also need to address their research topic of interest with "color" and imagination.

4   Final Considerations and the Future

In the first ten years the topics addressed by IRCDL have been mostly concerned with the representation and management of the various information resources that are of interest to diversified cultural heritage institutions – such as libraries, archives and museums both of general and specialized type – to build effective integrated collections of digital resources and to design and implement effective digital library systems. Although these systems have been designed and developed to create digital libraries and archive systems that allow users to better exploit the digital resources managed by the different systems, practices are needed to address and manage interoperability among systems at a higher level of abstraction than what is presently done and in line with what has been proposed in [2].

The future that is now unfolding before the communities involved in the evolution of digital libraries systems is really challenging because new areas need to be addressed. Two of these in particular need to be tackled as underlined in [1]:

- It is important to continue to focus on the multidisciplinary nature of research on digital libraries which not only goes from computer science to humanities but also crosses areas in the same field, ranging, for example, from archival to librarian sciences or from information management systems to new knowledge environments. This is an ongoing challenge for the digital library field and there is need to continue to contribute to improve the cooperation between the many communities that share common objectives.
- We witness a profound change that is happening in the world of scientific communication, where the object of scientific communication is no longer a linear text, although digital, but an object-centric network that consists of text, data, images, videos, blogs, etc. This change is likely to deeply modify

the nature and the role of digital libraries and their relationships with other data centric realities. So future trends in digital libraries and scientific communications must be considered together with the study of the evolution in digital scholarship, because the publication and the consumption of scientific information are witnessing radical changes producing also relevant transformations on the scholarly record [3,5].

References

1. Agosti, M., Catarci, T., Esposito, F. (eds.) Pushing the Boundaries of the Digital Libraries Field - 10th Italian Research Conference on Digital Libraries: Preface IRCDL 2014, Procedia Computer Science, vol. 38. Elsevier (2014)
2. Agosti, M., Ferro, N., Silvello, G.: Digital library interoperability at high level of abstraction. Future Gener. Comput. Syst. **55**, 129–146 (2016). http://www.sciencedirect.com/science/article/pii/S0167739X15003003
3. Appleton, G.: Future trends in digital libraries and scientific communications. In: Agosti, M., Catarci, T., Esposito, F. (eds.) Pushing the Boundaries of the Digital Libraries Field - 10th Italian Research Conference on Digital Libraries, IRCDL 2014. Procedia Computer Science, vol. 38, pp. 18–21. Elsevier (2014)
4. De Nart, D., Degl'Innocenti, D., Basaldella, M., Agosti, M., Tasso, C.: A content based approach to social network analysis: a case study on research communities. In: Calvanese, D., De Nart, D., Tasso, C. (eds.) IRCDL 2015. CCIS, vol. 612. Springer International Publishing, Heidelberg (2016). doi:10.1007/978-3-319-41938-1
5. Thanos, C.: The future of digital scholarship. In: Agosti, M., Catarci, T., Esposito, F. (eds.) Pushing the Boundaries of the Digital Libraries Field - 10th Italian Research Conference on Digital Libraries, IRCDL 2014. Procedia Computer Science, vol. 38, pp. 22–27. Elsevier (2014)

Semantic Modeling

Description Logics for Documentation

Carlo Meghini[✉]

Consiglio Nazionale delle Ricerche, Istituto di Scienza e Tecnologie della
Informazione, Pisa, Italy
carlo.meghini@isti.cnr.it

Abstract. Much of the activity in a digital library revolves around collecting, organizing and publishing knowledge about the resources of the
library, in the form of metadata records. In order to document such
activity, digital librarians need to express knowledge about the metadata records they produce. This knowledge, which we call *documentation knowledge,* may express *e.g.,* provenance, trustability, or access
restrictions of the records. Today, documentation knowledge is mostly
represented in digital libraries via RDF. We propose a new type of information system, called documentation system, as a basic component of a
digital library allowing to represent and reason about both domain and
documentation knowledge in an expressive language such as OWL.

1 Introduction

In a digital library, it is often necessary to represent and reason about two different kinds of knowledge. One kind is *domain* knowledge, which in is typically
embodied in metadata and ontologies, used by the end-users, for instance to
discover and access the resources of the library. The other kind of knowledge
concerns domain knowledge and is used by digital librarians in order to manage the resources of the library. For instance, a digital librarian might want to
describe the provenance, or the degree of trust or the access policy of a metadata
record. We call this latter kind of knowledge as *documentation* knowledge, since
documentation is one of the main reasons that brings it into life. Documentation
knowledge is a primary matter dealt with by curators in libraries and archives.
In general, it shows up in any organization that devotes resources to the documentation of artifacts, events, users, services and in general any resource that is
of value to the organization. Its scope of application is therefore quite ample.

Documentation knowledge consists of factual and ontological statements
about individuals, concepts and relations of the domain of dicourse, and as such
it can be expressed and reasoned upon using standard logics, such as OWL [10].
However, a problem arises if documentation knowledge is to be used *together
with* domain knowledge, as it happens in digital libraries. The problem is due to
the fact that the individuals of documentation knowledge are domain knowledge
statements, and in order to express knowledge about resources and about the
statements used to describe such resources *in the same language,* one needs very
powerful languages, whose expressive power goes beyond that of first-order logic.

D. Calvanese et al. (Eds.): IRCDL 2015, CCIS 612, pp. 11–23, 2016.
DOI: 10.1007/978-3-319-41938-1_2

Such languages, though, are hardly usable in digital libraries, because their negative computational properties are inadequate to digital library requirements.

The Resource Description Framework (RDF) [6] is a case in point. RDF allows to express metadata records as statements having the described resource as subject and metadata elements as properties. It also allows to express a certain amount of documentation knowledge, by allowing properties as subjects in statements. However, as soon as the expressivity of the language goes beyond that of RDF Schema [3] by including constructs from Description Logics, serious computational problems arise. Indeed, the combination of RDF with Description Logics yields the language OWL Full [7], which is undecidable in spite of the decidability of its two constituents.

In this study, we tackle the problem of representing and reasoning about both domain and documentation knowledge by means of languages significantly more expressive than RDF, but we follow a different approach than RDF. Our approach is based on the *simultaneous* usage of two different logics: the *object* logic devoted to represent domain knowledge, and the *documentation* logic (or *doc*-logic for short) devoted to represent documentation knowledge. We view the resulting information system, which we call *documentation system,* as the backbone of a digital library, used for representing and reasoning about domain and documentation knowledge both in an independent and in a joint way, the latter option offering an innovative query functionality. As such, the present study extends the model presented in [8], which also allows to represent documentation knowledge, but whose expressive power does not go beyond that of RDF.

In order to illustrate our approach in general terms, we choose the Description Logic $\mathcal{ALCO}$ [1] as the object logic, relying on the abstract syntax of DLs, which is more concise than the official OWL notation [4].

2   Motivation

Much of the activity of digital librarians revolves around *metadata records.* A metadata record can be viewed as consisting of three separate parts: a description; a described object, the *subject* of the metadata record; and the attribution of the description to the subject. A description is a set of features. For instance, a description in a metadata record may consist of two features: (1) being a book and (2) being titled "Waverley". Each one of these features may be understood as describing a set of resources. In particular, the former feature describes anything that is a book, while the latter describes anything that is titled "Waverley". Taken together, the two features form a description that describes any resource satisfying *both* of them. In Description Logics (DLs for short), descriptions are represented by concepts, and in fact the two terms "description" and "concept" are synonymous; we will follow the same convention. In the DL $\mathcal{ALCO}$, the above description may be represented by the concept Book $\sqcap$ $\exists$Title.{*Waverley*} The attribution of a description to a particular subject is the act of asserting that that subject does indeed possess *simultaneously* all the features that make up the description. This attribution produces a metadata record. In a DL, attribution is realized by concept assertion, therefore in $\mathcal{ALCO}$, the metadata record as a whole can be expressed by the following concept assertion: b : (Book $\sqcap$ $\exists$Title.$\{Waverley\}$) where b is the DL individual that stands for the subject, a book in this case. In a DL knowledge base (KB for short), such an assertion is placed in the ABox, the component of the KB holding factual knowledge. The axioms of DLs can be used for modelling ontologies, understood as vocabularies that establish, via terminological axioms, the meaning of the concepts used in descriptions [5]. A terminological axiom in our example, could be the following: $Book$ $\sqsubseteq$ ($\exists$Title.Literal $\sqcap$ $\exists$Author.Person) stating that every book has a title that is a literal, and an author that is a person. The ontology underlying an ABox is placed in the other component of a DL KB, the TBox. The discussion so far seems to indicate that DLs are adequate representation languages for the knowledge contained in a digital library. Indeed, OWL [10], the W3C recommendations that stand for DLs in the semantic web architecture [2], is known and used in digital libraries. However, there is a fundamental requirement of digital libraries that DLs are not able to capture. This requirement comes from the fact that documentation, a central activity in a digital library, may be a *recursive* process; it may not be solely confined to the domain of discourse, but it may also concern the descriptions and metadata records used for documenting the resources of the domain of discourse. For example, a digital librarian may need to represent the fact that a metadata record has a certain provenance, (*i.e.*, it has been created by a certain person, on a certain date, as a result of a certain activity), or a certain degree of trustability; or that the record is subject to a certain set of access restrictions, or to a certain billing policy. In general, the same requirements arise in every information system that deals with the documentation of the individuals of the domain of discourse, be these individuals users, devices, or events.

In order to cope with the recursiveness of documentation, we argue that a knowledge representation language is needed that offers descriptions as first class citizens, that is as individuals on their own right, endowed with an identity and a structure. In addition, the language in question should offer the machinery to attribute a description to a certain individual, which may itself be a description, thereby coping with the recursiveness of documentation. DLs, in spite of their name, fall short of this requirement. They offer a rich machinery to create descriptions, yet these descriptions are not denotable as individuals, and therefore it is not possible to state any knowledge on them, other than assertions and axioms. As such, the support that DLs offer to documentation is practically limited. The situation, however, is not unrecoverable. The machinery of DLs can be used to remedy at this inconvenient, by slightly shifting the focus of representation from the individuals, concepts and roles in the domain of discourse, to descriptions made up of these. The shift is a form of reification and leads to a logic, the doc-logic, that allows the expression of documentation knowledge, in contrast to the object-logic that is used for representing domain knowledge.

In order to show how this can be done, in the next Section we introduce a doc-logic corresponding to the object-logic $\mathcal{ALCO}$. Our doc-logic will be doc-$\mathcal{ALCO}$, more simply called as *alco*.

3   Introducing *alco*

Suppose we wish to create the above description for the Waverley, and we also want such description to be identified as the individual d. In order to achieve our goal, in *alco* we describe the structure of d as the conjunction of two concepts, which we choose to identify as d_1 and d_2. We use the *alco* role CCId (for *Concept Conjunction Identification*) for associating the identifier of a conjunction to the identifiers of the conjuncts, as follows: CCId(d, d_1), CCId(d, d_2) The role CCId binds an identifier to a concept *part*, and therefore we will call it a *binding* role.

Next, we need to state that d_1 identifies an atomic concept, say *Book*. For this, we use the *alco* role ACId (for *Atomic Concept Identification*) as follows: ACId$(d_1, Book)$ An assertion on the role ACId is in fact an assignment of an identifier to a whole concept, not just to a part of it, as in the case of binding roles; therefore will call ACId a *concept identifying role,* or more simply an *identifying role.* Of course, we could choose to use an atomic concept as an identifier of itself (*e.g.*, the *alco* individual *Book* as an identifier of the $\mathcal{ALCO}$ concept *Book*) to make a doc-KB more readable; but we prefer to use different names in order to avoid confusion. We also introduce in *alco* the role CNId (for *Concept Negation Identification*) for identifying negation concepts as follows: CNId(d, e) assigns the identifier d to the negation of the concept identified by e. Also CNId is an identifying role.

As seen in the previous section, the title feature is expressed in $\mathcal{ALCO}$ as the concept $\exists$ *Title.*{*Waverley*}, known in the DL world as *existential quantification*. In order to reduce this concept to something denotable as the individual d_2, we follow the same style followed above for concept conjunction, as follows:

- we introduce the identifying role ARId (for *Atomic Role Identification*), and use it to identify the $\mathcal{ALCO}$ role *Title* as d_3 by the assertion ARId$(d_3, Title)$;
- we introduce the identifying role SCId (for *Singleton Concept Identification*) and use it to identify the $\mathcal{ALCO}$ singleton concept {*Waverley*} as d_4 by the assertion SCId$(d_4, Waverley)$;
- finally, we introduce two identifying roles ERId (for *Role Identification in an Existential Quantification*) and ECId (for *Concept Identification in an Existential Quantification*) and use them to bind d_2 to its constituent parts by the assertions: ERId(d_2, d_3), ECId(d_2, d_4)

Now we have completed the description of d, and can create the desired meta-data record by attributing d to the book b that we want to describe. The obvious way to state the association between d and b, is to introduce the *alco* role CAss (for *Concept Assertion*) and use it as follows: CAss(d, b). The first argument of a CAss assertion is always a description identifier, whereas the second argument identifies the subject, which can be any resource. The CAss role allows to represent in *alco* an $\mathcal{ALCO}$ concept assertion. Yet, it is not adequate to document metadata record, because there is no individual that denotes the resulting metadata record in a CAss assertion. An alternative way of proceeding is to coin a name, say m, for the metadata record that we want to create, and then connect m to d and b by using appropriate role assertions, namely: $\mathsf{MRD}(m,d), \mathsf{MRS}(m,b)$. There is an obvious relation between the just introduced roles and CAss. This relation will be captured by an axiom, introduced in next Section.

So far we have simply used a rather cumbersome notation for expressing a concept assertion. However, this notation has given us identifiers for the description and the metadata record that we have created, therefore we are in the position of representing documentation knowledge about them. Suppose we want to state that d was created by *John*. The latter feature can be expressed as a description identified by e as follows: $\mathsf{ARId}(e_1, Author), \mathsf{SCId}(e_2, John), \mathsf{ERId}(e, e_1), \mathsf{ECId}(e, e_2)$ The description e can be attributed to d by stating $\mathsf{CAss}(e, d)$.

Analogously we can document the metadata record m by specifying a creation time, a creation place and an author for it. We first create a description h for the $\mathcal{ALCO}$ concept $\exists Author.\{Sue\}$, using the *alco* roles (for brevity, we do not detail h); finally, we add the assertion: $\mathsf{CAss}(h, m)$ to the ABox of the doc-KB.

In order to make *alco* a full doc-logic, we need a role for representing (at the doc-level) concept subsumptions in an object-TBox. To this end, we introduce CSAx (for *Concept Subsumption Axiom*) with the intended meaning that: $\mathsf{CSAx}(e, d)$ states that the concept identified by e is a sub-concept of the concept identified by d.

4   Semantics

As a DL, *alco* has a well-defined semantics, based on the notion of interpretation. This notion, however, turns out to license undesired situations. In this section we discuss these undesired situations, and introduce axioms for ruling them out. These axioms are intended to be in the TBox of *any* doc-KB, since they express the semantics of the *alco* roles. In order to ease the expression of the axioms, we introduce some atomic concepts:

- OInd, OACon and OARol, for representing individuals, atomic concepts and atomic roles of the object-DL, respectively; these concepts are defined as follows (as customary, $\exists R$ abbreviates $\exists R.\top$):

$$\mathsf{OInd} \equiv \exists \mathsf{SCId}^-; \quad \mathsf{OACon} \equiv \exists \mathsf{ACId}^-; \quad \mathsf{OARol} \equiv \exists \mathsf{ARId}^-$$

- Concepts denoting the different types of concept and role identifiers:

$$\mathsf{AtomId} \equiv \exists \mathsf{ACId}; \, \mathsf{ConjId} \equiv \exists \mathsf{CCId}; \, \mathsf{NegId} \equiv \exists \mathsf{CNId}$$
$$\mathsf{SomeId} \equiv \exists \mathsf{ERId}; \, \mathsf{SingId} \equiv \exists \mathsf{SCId}; \, \mathsf{RoleId} \equiv \exists \mathsf{ARId}$$

- The concept ConcId denoting concept identifiers:

$$\mathsf{ConcId} \equiv \mathsf{AtomId} \sqcup \mathsf{ConjId} \sqcup \mathsf{NegId} \sqcup \mathsf{SomeId} \sqcup \mathsf{SingId}$$

Identification axioms. These axioms capture the proper behaviour of the binding and the identifying roles. First, identifying roles must behave like functions (in OWL terms, they are functional object properties [9]).

$$(\geq 2 \text{ ACId}) \sqsubseteq \bot; \quad (\geq 2 \text{ ARId}) \sqsubseteq \bot; \quad (\geq 2 \text{ CNId}) \sqsubseteq \bot$$
$$(\geq 2 \text{ ERId}) \sqsubseteq \bot; \quad (\geq 2 \text{ ECId}) \sqsubseteq \bot; \quad (\geq 2 \text{ SCId}) \sqsubseteq \bot$$

Concerning the binding role CCId, every identifier used as a first argument in an assertion on this role, must appear as a first argument also in at least another assertion on the same role, because a conjunction has at least two conjuncts. We express this condition as follows: $(= 1 \text{ CCId}) \sqsubseteq \bot$.

Moreover, for every $\text{ERId}(d, e)$ assertion, there must be exactly one $\text{ECId}(d, e')$ assertion, for any individuals e, e'; and viceversa. In order to capture this constraint, which we call *pairing constraint*, it is not sufficient to include the axiom $\exists \text{ERId} \equiv \exists \text{ECId}$ in the TBox. This is due to the fact that a DL KB is interpreted under the Open World Assumption. As a consequence, a KB whose ABox contains *only* the assertion $\text{ERId}(d, R)$ and whose TBox contains the axiom $\exists \text{ERId} \equiv \exists \text{ECId}$ is not inconsistent; rather, the KB is understood as implicitly stating that there exists some unknown individual z such that $\text{ECId}(d, z)$ is true in every interpretation. We cannot therefore capture the pairing constraint as a TBox axiom; we will do it in a different way, illustrated in the next Section.

Finally, binding and identifying roles must all together satisfy the obvious constraint that the domain of each one of them be disjoint from the domain of each of the others, otherwise it may happen that the same identifier be used to identify two concepts of different kinds. Assuming the above mentioned pairing constraints are in place, we need to consider only one of ERId and ECId because the domains of these two roles are made equivalent by the pairing constraint. So, overall we need to declare mutual disjointness of the domain of six roles; this requires fifteen axioms, all of the same type. For brevity, we only state the five axioms stating the disjointness of atomic concept identifiers from the other types of concept identifiers:

$$(\text{AtomId} \sqcap \text{ConjId}) \sqsubseteq \bot; (\text{AtomId} \sqcap \text{NegId}) \sqsubseteq \bot; (\text{AtomId} \sqcap \text{SomeId}) \sqsubseteq \bot;$$
$$(\text{AtomId} \sqcap \text{SingId}) \sqsubseteq \bot; (\text{AtomId} \sqcap \text{RoleId}) \sqsubseteq \bot$$

Syntactic axioms. Syntactic axioms are those making sure that the syntax of the object-DL concepts is properly captured by the assertions of the doc-DL.

A basic constraint of every DL, is that the symbols used for individuals, atomic concepts and roles come from three disjoint alphabets.

$$(\text{OACon} \sqcap \text{OARol}) \sqsubseteq \bot; (\text{OACon} \sqcap \text{OInd}) \sqsubseteq \bot; (\text{OARol} \sqcap \text{OInd}) \sqsubseteq \bot$$

We also must make sure that concepts are properly formed in a doc-KB. To exemplify, if in the doc-KB there is the assertion that d identifies a negation, *i.e.*, $\text{CNId}(d, d_1)$, then d_1 must identify something, and a concept in particular. The second part of this constraint can be captured via an axiom, imposing that anything that appears as a second argument in a CNId assertion be a concept identifier, and the same for all the other concept constructors. This can be done by introducing the following axioms:

$$\top \sqsubseteq (\forall \mathsf{CCId}.\mathsf{ConcId}); \quad \top \sqsubseteq (\forall \mathsf{CNId}.\mathsf{ConcId}); \quad \top \sqsubseteq (\forall \mathsf{ECId}.\mathsf{ConcId})$$

However, the first part of the constraint, namely that there be in the KB an explicit assertion binding d_1 to a concept, cannot be formalized as an axiom, again due to the Open World Assumption. Similarly to pairing constraints, we have therefore to find a different way of expressing this kind of constraints, which we call the *syntactic constraints*.

Metadata axioms. Metadata axioms concern identifiers of metadata records. Our intended notion of a metadata record requires that a metadata record concern exactly one individual. In order to capture this intention, we introduce the following axiom: $(\geq 2\ \mathsf{MRS}) \sqsubseteq \bot$. Moreover, we need to enforce a pairing constraint for MRD and MRS, in the sense that for every assertion of the kind $\mathsf{MRD}(m, d)$, we want the KB to contain at least one assertion of the form $\mathsf{MRS}(m, i)$, for some individual i; and viceversa. For the reasons given above, also this kind of pairing constraint has to be captured in a different way. Finally, we include an axiom for capturing the previously mentioned relation between the role MRD and MRS from one side, and the role CAss from the other side. In fact, every time we use MRD and MRS for structuring a metadata record m, as in $\mathsf{MRD}(m, d)$ and $\mathsf{MRS}(m, b)$, we are implicitly asserting that the d describes b, that is, that $\mathsf{CAss}(d, b)$. In order to make this connection happen in a doc-KB, we introduce the axiom:

$$\mathsf{MRD}^- \circ \mathsf{MRS} \sqsubseteq \mathsf{CAss} \tag{1}$$

where $\circ$ is the role composition operator. Notice that this axiom leaves the freedom of inserting CAss assertions without the corresponding MRD and MRS assertions. In other words, it is possible to create concept assertions that are not metadata records, such as for instance the last assertion of the previous example.

Inference Axioms. Inference axioms are required in order to model the proper behavior of the CAss and the CSAx roles.

Concerning the CAss role and returning to our example, from the assertions $\mathsf{CAss}(d, b)$ and $\mathsf{CCId}(d, d_1)$ it should follow the assertion $\mathsf{CAss}(d_1, b)$, because d identifies a concept conjunction and d_1 identifies one of the conjuncts. By the same argument, it also should follow $\mathsf{CCId}(d, d_2)$. More generally, modelling the semantics of CAss means laying down all the rules that capture implied concept assertions, ultimately leading to the axiomatization of (object-level) instance checking in the doc-logic.

Likewise, modelling the semantics of the CSAx role amounts to axiomatize (object-level) concept subsumption in the doc-logic. In other words, the doc-logic does not only have to capture the syntax of the corresponding object-logic, but also its inference mechanism.

The proof theory of DLs provides us with sound and complete inference methods for both instance checking and submsumption. These methods can be encoded in *alco* by means of axioms and semantic conditions, exactly in the same way the syntax rules of the object-logic are encoded. As a result, the users of the doc-KB would be able to exploit the implicit domain knowledge, typically for performing ask operations. In particular, in order to check whether an individual i is an instance of an object-concept c, it suffices to identify c via an individual d and then ask whether $\mathsf{CAss}(d, i)$ logically follows from the doc-KB. The same machinery also allows to do some consistency checking, for instance checking whether an individual is an instance of the $\perp$ concept, or of a contradictory description. However, the price to be paid for achieving this goal would be very high, as the encoding of inference would make the doc-logic very complex. In what follows, we will present a much simpler method for attaining the same goal.

In order to preserve the semantics of the *alco* roles, we assume that the doc TBox does not contain any axiom concerning these roles other than those given above.

5   Strong Consistency

Suppose we want to add to the KB the assertion that b is not a book. In *alco*, the complext concept $\neg Book$ must first be created and identified, say as the individual f, by using the *alco* roles, and then f must be declared to be the negation of the atomic concept $Book$. There is already an identifier for the latter concept, namely d_1, therefore all our replacement librarian must do, is to state: $\mathsf{CNId}(f, d_1)$ so that he can finally assert that b is an instance of f, by using the *alco* role assertion: $\mathsf{CAss}(f, b)$. By adding the last two assertions to those introduced in the Sect. 3, the consistency of the doc-KB is not broken. However, the represented knowledge is clearly inconsistent from an intuitive point of view, since b is asserted to be a book and not a book at the same time.

One way to capture pairing and syntacting constraints while at the same time ruling out the last kind of inconsistency, is to try to transform a consistent doc-KB into its corresponding object-KB. In order to do so, $\mathcal{ALCO}$ concepts must be extracted from the assertions of the doc-ABox. If the doc-KB suffers from a pairing or a syntactic inconsistency, then this extraction is not possible because the assertions in the doc-ABox do not conform to the syntax of the doc-logic. Otherwise the extraction is possible, and it allows to determine, for each concept identifier d in the doc-ABox, the concept identified by d, that we denote as $\nu_D(d)$ ($\nu(d)$ for simplicity). Once the function ν is determined, the doc-KB can be transformed into its corresponding object-KB, and the obtained object-KB can be checked for consistency. If this check succeeds, then the doc-KB satisfies all the intuitive consistency criteria. This approach gives us a simple method for checking consistency of the doc-KB. A further advantage of it, is that we no longer need to model object level instance checking or subsumption as implicit CAss and CSAx assertions, respectively; we can transform the doc-KB and perform these inferences on the resulting object-KB, by relying on well-known algorithms. This is the route that we will follow in the rest of the paper. To this end, we will first define how to determine the function ν from a given doc-KB D. Based on the existence of $\nu(d)$ for each concept identifier d, we will define a stronger consistency criterion for a doc-KB. Next, we state the transformation ϕ from a doc-KB to its corresponding object-KB and define the strongest consistency criterion of a doc-KB based on the consistency of its corresponding object-KB. The domain of the function ν is the set of concept identifiers:

$$dom(\nu) = \{d \mid (T, A) \models d : \mathsf{ConcId}\}$$

and can be efficiently determined as the set of identifiers that occur as first arguments in a binding or in an identifying role assertion. For each $d \in dom(\nu)$, the value of $\nu(d)$ is recursively defined in Table 1. By iterating this recursive computation on $dom(\nu)$, the function ν can be efficiently computed.

Intuitively, if $D = (T, A)$ is a consistent doc-KB, then exactly one of the conditions on the right column of Table 1, excluding the last row, is met by the ABox A, that is:

$$\nu(d) \neq \omega \text{ for all } d \in dom(\nu),$$

in other words ν *is total on* D. Based on this consideration we define a doc-KB $D = (T, A)$ to be *fully consistent* if $\nu(d)$ is total on D.

Let us now consider how to define the transformation ϕ. The DL *alco* offers the roles CSAx and CAss for representing the terminological axioms and the assertions of the object-KB, respectively. Therefore, it is natural to use assertions on the former role in order to derive the axioms in the object-TBox, and assertions on the latter role in order to derive the axioms in the object-ABox. Formally, given a doc-KB $D = (T, A)$, we have $\phi(D) = (\mathcal{T}, \mathcal{A})$ where:

$$\mathcal{T} = \{\nu(d) \sqsubseteq \nu(e) \mid \mathsf{CSAx}(d, e) \in A\}$$
$$\mathcal{A} = \{i : \nu(d) \mid (T, A) \models \mathsf{CAss}(d, i)\}$$

Some explanations are in order concerning the translation of CAss assertions. Any such assertion has the form $\mathsf{CAss}(d, i)$ where d is a description identifier and i is either a description identifier (such as e in the example above) or an

Table 1. Assignment of object-DL concepts to identifiers

$\nu(d)$	if the doc-ABox contains
A	$\mathsf{ACId}(d, A)$
R	$\mathsf{ARId}(d, R)$
$\nu(e_1) \sqcap \ldots \sqcap \nu(e_n)$	$\mathsf{CCId}(d, e_1), \ldots, \mathsf{CCId}(d, e_n), n$ maximal
$\neg\nu(e)$	$\mathsf{CNId}(d, e)$
$\exists\nu(e).\nu(f)$	$\mathsf{ERId}(d, e)$ and $\mathsf{ECId}(d, f)$
$\{o\}$	$\mathsf{SCId}(d, o)$
ω	otherwise

individual denoting any other kind of resource (such as the book b in the example above). In the latter case, i does not have to be translated, as there would be nothing to translate it into. In the former case, i is a concept identifier and d another concept identifier that describes i. If we translate both identifiers into the corresponding concepts, the result will be an assertion like $C : D$ where both C and D are object-concepts. In our example, the translation would look like:

$$(Book \; \sqcap \; \exists Ttile.\{Waverley\}) : \exists Author.\{John\}$$

The last expression reads "John created the description *Book titled 'Waverley'*", which is precisely what we want to say. However, the above is not a valid assertion in any DL, and this is the very reason why we set out to define the doc-DL. Therefore, we have no choice but to translate only the second identifier. This will result in the concept assertion: $d : \exists Author.\{John\}$ This means that d will appear in the object-KB, but its connection with the description that it identifies (*i.e.*, $(Book \; \sqcap \; \exists Ttile.\{Waverley\})$) is lost in the object-KB. Notice that we require $\mathsf{CAss}(d, i)$ to be *not only* explicitly asserted, but also implicitly present in the KB, typically as a consequence of the creation of a metadata record. Table 2 shows the translation of the doc-KB of our example.

Table 2. Summary of the running example

doc-ABox	ν	object-ABox
$\mathsf{CCId}(d, d_1), \mathsf{CCId}(d, d_2)$	$d \mapsto \nu(d_1) \sqcap \nu(d_2)$	
$\mathsf{ACId}(d_1, Book)$	$d_1 \mapsto Book$	
$\mathsf{ERId}(d_2, d_3), \mathsf{ECId}(d_2, d_4)$	$d_2 \mapsto \exists \nu(d_3).\nu(d_4)$	
$\mathsf{ARId}(d_3, Title)$	$d_3 \mapsto Title$	
$\mathsf{SCId}(d_4, Waverley)$	$d_4 \mapsto \{Waverley\}$	
$\mathsf{CAss}(d, b)$		$b : Book \; \sqcap$
		$\exists Title.\{Waverley\}$
$\mathsf{MRD}(m, d), \mathsf{MRS}(m, b)$		
$\mathsf{ERId}(e, Author), \mathsf{ECId}(e, e_1)$	$e \mapsto \exists Author.\nu(e_1)$	
$\mathsf{SCId}(e_1, John)$	$e_1 \mapsto \{John\}$	
$\mathsf{CAss}(e, d)$		$d : \exists Author.\{John\}$
$\mathsf{ERId}(h, Author), \mathsf{ECId}(h, h_1)$	$h \mapsto \exists Author.\nu(h_1)$	
$\mathsf{SCId}(h_1, Sue)$	$h_1 \mapsto \{Sue\}$	
$\mathsf{CAss}(h, m)$		$m : \exists Author.\{Sue\}$

Based on these considerations, we say that a doc-KB $D = (T, A)$ is *strongly consistent* if D is fully consistent and $\phi(D)$ is a consistent $\mathcal{ALCO}$ KB. Moreover, we define a *documentation system* $\mathcal{S}$ to be a pair $\mathcal{S} = \langle D, O \rangle$ where D is a doc-KB and O is an object-KB, such that $O = \phi(D)$.

6   Querying a Documentation System

The two KBs in a DS can be queried individually, based on the kind of knowledge they store. As customary, we will denote the answer to an object query C_o against an object-KB O as $\text{ASK}_o(C_o, O)$, or simply $\text{ASK}_o(C_o)$, and define: $\text{ASK}_o(C_o) = \{\, i \mid O \models i : C_o \}$ Likewise, we will use $\text{ASK}_d(C_d)$ for denoting the result of asking doc-query C_d to a doc-KB and define: $\text{ASK}_d(C_d) = \{\, i \mid O \models i : C_d \}$

There is a third category of queries, which we call *mixed* queries, that can be asked to a DS. Mixed queries involve both domain and documentation knowledge, and can be of one of two kinds: (1) *mixed-object* queries, asking for the resources of the object-KB that satisfy some property expressed in the doc-KB; for instance, a mixed-object query may ask for the editions of the *Waverley* that have been described by John; (2) *mixed-doc* queries, asking for the resources of the doc-KB that satisfy some property expressed in the object-KB; for instance, a mixed-object query may ask for the metadata records of the *Waverley* that have been created by Sue. In order to express mixed queries, we need to address both the object- and the doc-KB. One way of doing so, is to use the operators ASK_o and ASK_d *within* queries. Using these two operators, the editions of the *Waverley* described by John can be expressed as follows:

$$\textit{Book} \sqcap \exists \textit{Title}.\{\textit{Waverley}\} \sqcap \text{ASK}_d(\exists \mathsf{CAss}^-.\text{ASK}_o(\exists \textit{Author}.\{\textit{John}\}))$$

This is a concept denoting the individuals in the object-KB that are known to be books titled *Waverley*, and that are known in the doc-KB to be described by a description authored by *John*. Notice the double nesting of the ASK operator, without which it would not be possible to express the query. This implies that asking a doc-KB may require asking a object-KB. Let us now consider the mixed-doc query asking for the metadata records of the *Waverley* authored by Sue. Using the same ask operators introduced above, this query can be expressed as:

$$\exists \mathsf{MRD}.(\exists \mathsf{CAss}.\text{ASK}_o(\exists \textit{Title}.\{\textit{Waverley}\})) \sqcap \text{ASK}_o(\exists \textit{Author}.\{\textit{Sue}\})$$

This is a conjunction of two concepts: the first concept denotes the metadata records whose description describes an individual known in the object-KB to be titled *Waverley*. The second concept denotes the individuals known in the object-KB to be authored by Sue.

The syntax of our query language, which we call Documentation Query Language (DQL for short), is given by the following rules:

$$C ::= C_o \mid C_d$$
$$C_o ::= \text{any object-concept} \mid \text{ASK}_d(C_d)$$
$$C_d ::= \text{any doc-concept} \mid \text{ASK}_o(C_o)$$

In order to give the semantics of DQL, the interpretations of the doc- and the object-DL are combined in a rather obvious way. For simplicity, we omit such specification, pointing out that it allows us to reduce query answering on a DS to query answering on a single KB whose TBox is given by the union of the TBoxes of the doc- and the object-KBs, and the same for the ABox. In order to show the effects of this result, let us now return to our example queries. From a semantical point of view, the former query above: $Book \sqcap \exists Title.\{Waverley\} \sqcap \mathrm{ASK}_d(\exists\mathrm{CAss}^-.\mathrm{ASK}_o(\exists Author.\{John\}))$ stated against our example DS in Table 2, is equivalent to the query $Book \sqcap \exists Title.\{Waverley\} \sqcap \exists\mathrm{CAss}^-.\exists Author.\{John\}$ stated against the union of the KBs shown in the first and third column of the table. The union contains the assertions:

$$b : Book \sqcap \exists Title.\{Waverley\} \quad \mathrm{CAss}(d, b) \quad d : \exists Author.\{John\}$$

clearly implying that b is in the answer to the query. Analogously, the latter query above: $\exists\mathrm{MRD}.(\exists\mathrm{CAss}.\mathrm{ASK}_o(\exists Title.\{Waverley\})) \sqcap \mathrm{ASK}_o(\exists Author.\{Sue\})$ stated against $\mathcal{S} = (D, O)$, is equivalent to the query $\exists\mathrm{MRD}.(\exists\mathrm{CAss}.Title.\exists\{Waverley\}) \sqcap \exists Author.\{Sue\}$ stated against $D \cup O$. The assertions:

$$\mathrm{MRD}(m, d) \quad \mathrm{CAss}(d, b) \quad b : Book \sqcap \exists Title.\{Waverley\} \quad m : \exists Author.\{Sue\}$$

are in $D \cup O$, therefore m is in the answer to the query.

7   Conclusions

We have presented documentation systems as constituents of digital libraries, using description logics to represent and reason about domain and documentation knowledge at the same time. In particular, the KB of a documentation system consists of an object-KB and of a doc-KB. In the object-TBox, it is possible to express domain ontologies as terminological axioms, whereas in the object-ABox it is possible to express metadata records as DL concept assertions. In the doc-ABox, it is possible to make assertions involving descriptions and the metadata records of the object-KB Abox, thereby representing documentation knowledge. As such, a documentation system significantly extends the expressive capabilities of current digital libraries, mostly based on RDF.

References

1. Baader, F., Calvanese, D., McGuinness, D.L., Nardi, D., Patel-Schneider, P.F. (eds.): The Description Logic Handbook: Theory, Implementation, and Applications, 2nd edn. Cambridge University Press, Cambridge (2003)
2. Berners-Lee, T., Hendler, J., Lassila, O.: The semantic web. Scientific American Magazine (2001)
3. Brickley, D., Guha, R.V.: RDF vocabulary description language 1.0: RDF schema. W3C Recommendation, WWW Consortium, February 2004
4. Gandon, F., Schreiber, G.: RDF 1.1 XML syntax. Technical report, W3C Recommendation, 10 February 2004 25 February 2014
5. Guarino, N.: Formal ontology in information systems. In: Proceedings of FOIS 1998, pp. 3–15. IOS Press, Amsterdam (1998) (Amended version)
6. Manola, F., Miller, E.: RDF Primer. W3C Recommendation, WWW Consortium, February 2004

7. McGuinness, D.L., van Harmelen, F.: OWL web ontology language overview. W3C recommendation, W3C, February 2004
8. Meghini, C., Spyratos, N., Sugibuchi, T., Yang, J.: A model for digital libraries, its translation to RDF. J. Data Semant. **3**(2), 107–139 (2014). ISSN: 1861–2032
9. Motik, B., Patel-Schneider, P.F., Parsia, B.: OWL 2 Web Ontology Language Structural Specification and Functional-Style Syntax, 2nd (edn.). W3C recommendation, W3C, December 2012
10. W3C OWL Working Group. OWL 2 Web Ontology Language Document Overview, 2nd (edn.). W3C recommendation, W3C, December 2012

Towards a Semantic Web Enabled Representation of DL Foundational Models: The Quality Domain Example

Nicola Ferro[(✉)] and Gianmaria Silvello

Department of Information Engineering, University of Padua, Padua, Italy
{ferro,silvello}@dei.unipd.it

Abstract. The convergence of Libraries, Archives and Museums (LAM) has been a topic of much discussion in the *Digital Library* (*DL*) research field, but their similarities and common points are not yet fully exploited in existing formal models for DL such as the *Streams, Structures, Spaces, Scenarios, Societies* (*5S*) model or the DELOS Reference Model.

On the other hand, Semantic Web and Linked Data technology are nowadays mostly used for interoperability at the data level but they would represent a viable option for building a semantic representation and interoperability at the level of different DL models of themselves.

To this end, we discuss a quite ambitious goal that should be part of the DL agenda that is expressing foundational models of DL by means of ontologies which leverage Semantic Web and Linked Data technologies and which link them to the ontologies currently used for publishing cultural heritage data. This would pave the way for a deeper interoperability among DL systems and lower the barriers between LAMs.

In this paper we exemplify this proposal by focusing on the quality domain which is a fundamental aspect in the DL universe and we show how this part of the DELOS Reference model can be expressed via a *Resource Description Framework* (*RDF*) model ready to be used in a Semantic Web environment for interoperability at the DL model level and not only at the data level.

1 Motivation

Over the past two decades, digital libraries have been steadily evolving and shaping the way people and institutions access and interact with our cultural heritage, study and learn [6, 7, 11–13, 22, 23, 36]. Nowadays, the reach of digital libraries goes far beyond the realm of traditional libraries and also encompasses other kinds of cultural heritage institutions, such as archives and museums.

In the context of *Libraries, Archives, and Museums* (*LAM*) unifying a variety of organizational settings and providing more integrated access to their contents is an aspect of utmost importance. Indeed, LAM collect, manage and share digital contents; although the type of materials may differ and professional practices vary, LAM share an overlapping set of functions. Fulfilling these functions

ⓒ Springer International Publishing Switzerland 2016
D. Calvanese et al. (Eds.): IRCDL 2015, CCIS 612, pp. 24–35, 2016.
DOI: 10.1007/978-3-319-41938-1_3

in "collaboration rather than isolation creates a win-win for users and institutions" [37]. Although the convergence between libraries, archives and museums has been a topic of much discussion in the digital library community, the emerging similarities between these three types of cultural heritage institutions are not yet evident in the proposed formal models, developed systems, and education of professionals [29,30].

Two main approaches are viable to bridge the gap among different cultural heritage and memory institutions and to provide comprehensive DL able to embrace the full spectrum of LAMs and interoperate together: one is somewhat "top-down" and consists in the development of full (formal) models of what DL are, as in the case of the 5S model [17] or the DELOS Reference Model [8]; the other is somehow "bottom-up" and concerns the exploitation of semantic Web technologies and linked (open) data [19,20] in order to represent and describe common entities, such as actor ontologies – e.g. *Friend of a Friend (FOAF)*[1] or BIO[2]; place ontologies – e.g. GeoNames[3]; time ontologies – e.g. the time period encoding scheme[4] in the Dublin Core Metadata Terms; event ontologies – e.g. the Event Ontology[5] or *Linking Open Descriptions of Events (LODE)*[6]; and many others.

However, there is a notable gap between these two approaches: the above mentioned ontologies are used to describe entities and resources which need to be managed by DL but they are not used to represent the concepts themselves which constitute a (formal) DL model. Therefore, they allow for semantic interoperability and integration at the data level, i.e. among the resources which are managed by different DL but they do not allow for semantic representation and interoperability at the level of different models of DL as the 5S and the DELOS Reference model are.

As an example, we could use the class **Agent** in FOAF to represent the notion of user of a DL in order to allow two systems to exchange user profiles. Nevetheless, the **Agent** class is neither related to the concept of *society* in the 5S model nor to the concept of *actor* in the DELOS Reference model, which are both concerned with the notion of users of a DL. Therefore, to exchange user profiles, two different DL systems, one built using the 5S model and the other built using the DELOS Reference model, would need, at the best, a set of (hard-coded) rules instructing them to translate their internal notion of *society/actor* into the **Agent** class. This situation somehow hampers a more profound kind of interoperability among DL systems, an interoperability which stems from a commonly shared semantic view of what a DL is rather than a lower level one, deriving from the possibility of sharing data and resources with a common semantics.

Therefore, we think that a quite ambitious goal should be part of the DL agenda, namely expressing foundational models of DL by means of ontologies

---

[1] http://www.foaf-project.org/.

[2] http://vocab.org/bio/0.1/.html.

[3] http://geonames.org/.

[4] http://dublincore.org/documents/dcmi-period/.

[5] http://motools.sourceforge.net/event/event.html.

[6] http://linkedevents.org/ontology/.

which leverage semantic Web and linked data technologies and which link them to the ontologies currently used for publishing cultural heritage data. As discussed above, this would pave the way for a deeper interoperability among DL systems and lower the barriers between LAMs. Moreover, it would open up also more advanced possibilities for the automatic processing of resources since, for example, DL systems could automatically exploit the link between the models they are build upon in order to interoperate and exchange resources. This latter aspect was also part of the original 5S model vision, which aimed at automatically instantiating and deploying a DL system from a catalog of components corresponding to the notions introduced in the model [15]; unfortunately, this vision has not been fully embodied yet, especially in wide settings, but the last decade of efforts geared towards interoperability and the today pervasiveness of semantic Web technologies may offer the opportunity of performing the next step in this direction.

The paper is organized as follows: Sect. 2 briefly summarizes the main DL models, as the 5S and DELOS Reference model are; Sect. 3 describes the details of a relevant sub-domain of those models, i.e. the quality domain; Sect. 4 provides an example of the approach discussed above in the case of the quality domain; Sect. 5 draws some final remarks.

2   Models for Digital Libraries

2.1   5S Model

The 5S [12, 16, 17] is a formal model which draws upon the broad digital library literature to produce a comprehensive base of support. It was developed largely bottom up, starting with key definitions and elucidation of digital library concepts from a minimalist approach. It is built around five main concepts: (i) *streams* are sequences of elements of an arbitrary type, e.g. bits, characters, images, and so on; (ii) *structures* specify the way in which parts of a whole are arranged or organized, e.g. hypertexts, taxonomies, and so on; (iii) *spaces* are sets of objects together with operations on those objects that obey certain constraints, e.g. vector spaces, probabilistic spaces, and so on; (iv) *scenarios* are sequences of related transition events, for instance, a story that describes possible ways to use a system to accomplish some functions that a user desires; and, (v) *societies* are sets of entities and relationships between them, e.g. humans, hardware and software components, and so on.

Starting from these five main concepts, the model provides a definition for a minimal digital library which is constituted by: (i) a repository of digital objects; (ii) a set of metadata catalogs containing metadata specifications for those digital objects; (iii) a set of services containing at least services for indexing, searching, and browsing; and, (iv) a society.

2.2   DELOS Reference Model

The DELOS Reference Model [8] is a high-level conceptual framework that aims at capturing significant entities and their relationships with the digital library universe with the goal of developing more robust models of it. The DELOS Reference Model and the 5S model address a similar problem with different approaches; the former does not provide formal definitions, but it does provide a way to model and manage the resources of the digital library realm. The 5S on the other hand is a formal model providing mathematical definitions of the digital library entities that can be used to prove properties, theorems and propositions like in [16].

So the DELOS Reference Model is similar to the 5S model in its broader goal, but instead of using a mathematical formalism, it relies on concept maps [25,26] because of their simplicity and immediacy and it highlights six main domains in the digital library universe: (i) *content*: the data and information that digital libraries handle and make available to their users; (ii) *user*: the actors (whether human or not) entitled to interact with digital libraries; (iii) *functionality*: the services that digital libraries offer to their users; (iv) *quality*: the parameters that can be used to characterize and evaluate the content and behaviour of digital libraries; (v) *policy*: a set of rules that govern the interaction between users and digital libraries; and (vi) *architecture*: a mapping of the functionality and content offered by a digital library onto hardware and software components.

These six main domains represent the high level containers that help organize the DELOS Reference Model. For each of these domains, the fundamental entities and their relationships are clearly defined. Even though the 5S model and the DELOS Reference Model are at two different levels of abstractions and make use of different languages and formalisms to represent the digital library universe, it is possible to make bridges and mappings between the two, as for example has been done for the quality domain [1].

3   Modeling Quality in Digital Libraries

Quality is a fundamental aspect in DL [2,14,16,18,24], which is often related to and affected by the interoperability and integration among DL systems [9,28,31].

The quality domain in the DELOS Reference model, shown in Fig. 1 takes into account the general definition of quality provided by *International Organization for Standardization* (*ISO*) which defines quality as *"the degree to which a set of inherent characteristics fulfils requirements"* [21], where requirements are needs or expectations that are stated, generally implied or obligatory while characteristics are distinguishing features of a product, process, or system.

A Quality Parameter is a Resource that indicates, or is linked to, performance or fulfillment of requirements by another Resource. A Quality Parameter is evaluated by a Measurement, is measured by a Measure assigned according to the Measurement, and expresses the assessment of an Actor. With respect to the definition provided by ISO, we can note that: the "set of inherent characteristics" corresponds to the pair (Resource, Quality Parameter); the "degree of fulfillment" fits in with the pair (Measurement, Measure); finally, the "requirements" are taken into consideration by the assessment expressed by an Actor.

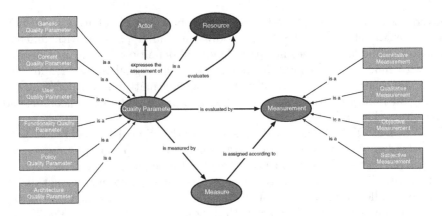

Fig. 1. Concept map of the main entities and relationships in the quality domain.

A `Resource` is any identifiable entity in the DL universe and resembles the concept of resource used in the Web [32]. In addition to this general concept, the `Resource` in the DELOS Reference Model has some additional features: it can be arranged or set out according to a resource format which, for example, allows a `Resource` to be composed of or linked to other `Resources`; it can be characterised by various `Quality Parameters`, each capturing how the `Resource` performs with respect to some attribute; it is regulated by policies governing every aspect of its lifetime; it is expressed by an information object; and, it can be described by or commented on by an information object, especially by metadata and annotations. An `Actor` is someone or something which interacts with the DL universe, being it a human being or a computing device. An `Actor` is a `Resource` and inherits all its key characteristics, even if they are specialized to better fit to the notion of `Actor`. For example, the policies represent the functions that `Actors` can perform or the information objects they have access to.

`Quality Parameters` serve the purpose of expressing the different facets of the quality domain. In this model, each `Quality Parameter` is itself a `Resource` and inherits all its characteristics, as, for example, the property of having a unique identifier. `Quality Parameters` provide information about how, and how well, a `Resource` performs with respect to some viewpoint and resemble the notion of quality dimension in [5]. They express the assessment of an `Actor` about the `Resource` under examination. They can be evaluated according to different `Measurements`, which provide alternative procedures for assessing different aspects of a `Quality Parameter` and assigning it a value, i.e. a `Measure`. Being a `Resource`, a `Quality Parameter` can be organised in arbitrarily complex and structured forms because of the composition and linking facilities, e.g. a `Quality Parameter` can be the compound of smaller `Quality Parameters` each capturing a specific aspect of the whole or it can be itself characterised and affected by various `Quality Parameters`. For example, `Availability` is affected by `Robustness` and `Fault Management`: in fact, when a function is both robust and able to recover from error conditions, it is probable that its availability is also increased. A Quality Parameter can be regulated or affected by policies. For example, the Economic Convenience of accessing a DL may be affected by its charging policy, since the latter is responsible for the definition of the charging strategies adopted by the DL. Finally, a Quality Parameter can be enriched with metadata and annotations. In particular, the former can provide useful information about the provenance of a Quality Parameter, while the latter can offer the possibility to add comments about a Quality Parameter, interpreting the obtained values, and proposing actions to improve it. In order to clarify the relationship between Quality Parameter, Measurement and Measure, we can take an example from the information retrieval field. One of the main Quality Parameters in relation to an information retrieval system is its effectiveness, meant as its capability to answer user information needs with relevant items. This Quality Parameter can be evaluated according to many different Measurements, such as precision and recall [27]: precision evaluates effectiveness in the sense of the ability of the system to reject useless items, while recall evaluates effectiveness in the sense of the ability of the system to retrieve useful items. The actual values for precision and recall are Measures and are usually computed using standard tools, such as trec_eval[7], which are Actors, but in this case not human. Quality Parameters are specialized and grouped according to the Resource under examination as follows:

- Generic Quality Parameters when the assessed Resources are a Digital Library, or a Digital Library System, or a Digital Library Management System;
- Content Quality Parameters when the assessed Resources belong to the content domain;
- User Quality Parameters when the assessed Resources belong to the user domain;
- Functionality Quality Parameters when the assessed Resources belong to the functionality domain;
- Policy Quality Parameters when the assessed Resources belongs to the policy domain;
- Architecture Quality Parameters, when the assessed Resources belong to the architecture domain.

It is important to note that the grouping described above is made from the perspective of the Resource under examination, i.e., the object under assessment. In any case, the Actor, meant as the active subject who expresses the assessment and knows the requirements a Resource is expected to fulfill, is always taken into consideration and explicitly modelled, since he is an integral part of the definition of Quality Parameter. For example, the User Satisfaction parameter is put in the Functionality Quality Parameter group because it expresses how much an Actor (the subject who makes the assessment) is satisfied when he uses a given function (the object of the assessment). On the other hand, in the case of the User Behaviour parameter, the

---

[7] http://trec.nist.gov/trec_eval/.

object of the assessment is an `Actor` together with his way of behaving with respect to some policy, while the subject who is making the assessment is another `Actor`, for example, an administrator; for this reason, this parameter is put in the `User Quality Parameter` group. `Measurements` are further categorized according to the following specializations:

- `Objective Measurements` can be obtained by taking measurements and using an analytical method to estimate the quality achieved. They could also be based on processing and comparing measurements between a reference sample and the actual sample obtained by the system. Examples of objective factors related to the perception of audio recordings in a digital library are: noise, delay and jitter.
- `Subjective Measurements` involve performing opinion tests, user surveys and user interviews which take into account the inherent subjectivity of the perceived quality and the variations between individuals. The perceived quality is usually rated by means of appropriate scales, where the assessment is often expressed in a qualitative way using terms such as bad, poor, fair, good, excellent to which numerical values can be associated to facilitate further analyses. Examples of factors related to the subjective perception of audio recordings in a digital library are: listening quality, loudness, listening effort.
- `Quantitative Measurements` are based on a unit of measurement that is expressed via numerical values. They rely on collecting and interpreting numerical data, for example, by means of the wide range of statistical methods for analysing numerical data.
- `Qualitative Measurements` are applied when the collected data are not numerical in nature. Although qualitative data can be encoded numerically and then studied by quantitative analysis methods, qualitative measures are exploratory while quantitative measurements usually play a confirmatory role. Methods of `Qualitative Measurement` that could be applied to a digital library are direct observation; participant observation; interviews; auditing; case study; collecting written feedback.

The quality domain is very broad and dynamic by nature. The representation provided by this model is therefore extensible with respect to the myriad of specific quality facets each institution would like to model. `Quality Parameter` is actually a class of various types of quality facets, e.g. those that currently represent common practice.

4   Expressing the Quality Domain via Semantic Web Technologies

In order to exploit Semantic Web technologies for enhancing the interoperability of DL we map the above defined quality domain into a RDF model. Within this model we consider a `Resource` as a generic class sharing the same meaning of resource in RDF [33] where "*all things described by RDF are called resources. [A resource is] the class of everything.*" Therefore, a `Resource` represents the class of everything that exists in the DL universe and it is related to the `rdfs:Resource` class.

The resources defined in the quality domain can be represented as *subclasses* of `Resource` and `Concept`. The main classes we take into account are: `Quality Parameter`, `Measure`, `Measurement` and `Actor` as shown in Fig. 2.

All these classes can be related to other classes defined in the *LOD cloud* by using the properties `owl:sameAs` or `schema:isSimilarTo`. For instance, the `Actor` class is the same as the `foaf:Agent` one, defined as "the class of agents; things that do stuff. A well known sub-class is Person, representing people. Other kinds of agents include Organization and Group"[8]; whereas, the `Measure` class is similar to the `basic:Measure` class in the OWL representation of ISO 19103[9] which is defined as a scaled number with a unity of measure. Also the `Quality Parameter` class can be related to an external class by means of the `schema:isSimilarTo` property; as we can see in Fig. 2 it can be related to the `observation:Parameter` class in the OWL representation of ISO 19156 (Observation model)[10].

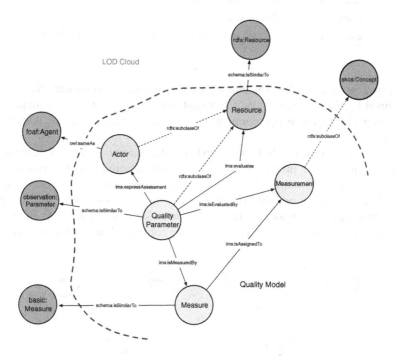

Fig. 2. The main RDF classes adopted for representing the quality model of a DL and some relationships with the LOD cloud.

---

[8] http://xmlns.com/foaf/spec/#term_Agent.

[9] http://def.seegrid.csiro.au/isotc211/iso19103/2005/basic#Measure.

[10] http://def.seegrid.csiro.au/isotc211/iso19156/2011/observation.

Measurement can be defined as a subclass of the `skos:Concept` which is defined as an idea or notion, a unit of thought. Usually, `skos:Concept` is used to define the type of relationships in a semantic environment or to create a taxonomy [34,35].

As far as the vocabulary adopted in this model is concerned, we use the namespaces and prefixes reported in Table 1; `ims` is the only vocabulary which is not inherited from other domains and all the classes described above are defined within this vocabulary.

Table 1. Namespaces and prefixes adopted in the quality model RDF specification.

Prefix	Namespace
`foaf`	http://xmlns.com/foaf/spec/
`ims`	http://ims.dei.unipd.it/
`owl`	http://www.w3.org/2002/07/owl/
`rdfs`	http://www.w3.org/2000/01/rdf-schema/
`schema`	http://schema.org/
`skos`	http://www.w3.org/2009/08/skos-reference/skos.html

In Fig. 2 we can see that the classes are related one to the other with properties defined by the `ims` vocabulary and that are the straightforward mapping of the labels of the relationships connecting the entities in the concept map drawn in Fig. 1.

As described in Sect. 3 both the `Quality Parameter` and the `Measurement` classes are specialized into several other classes defining two taxonomies. We can define these taxonomies by exploiting two properties of the `skos` vocabulary: `skos:broader` and `skos:narrower`. Given two resources, say A and B, then A `skos:broader` B asserts that B is a broader concept than A; whereas, A `skos:narrower` B asserts that B is a narrower concept than A. In Fig. 3 we show

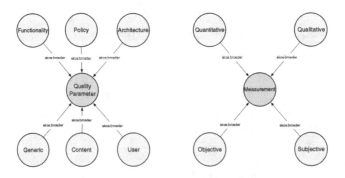

Fig. 3. The RDF representation of the taxonomies of the the `Quality Parameter` and the `Measurement` classes.

the two taxonomies defined for the `Quality Parameter` and the `Measurement` classes, where we report only the `broader` property given that `skos:broader` is `owl:inverseOf` of `skos:narrower` by definition.

We can see that this RDF representation allows us to express the quality domain of a DL by means of an RDF model, thus enabling the very interoperability promoted by the Semantic Web technologies. The model we define is easy to extend by adding new classes to the `Quality Parameter` and the `Measurement` taxonomies or connecting the classes with those defined in external vocabularies and ontologies.

5   Final Remarks

In this paper we discussed the need for a semantically-enabled representation of foundational DL models. This would allow for a deeper form of interoperability among DL systems and a better convergence in the context of *Libraries, Archives, and Museums (LAM)*. Moreover, it would open up the possibility for improved automatic processing and exchange of information resources among DL systems. In the paper, we have provided an example of what we would like to see embodied at a larger scale for full DL models, namely a semantically-enabled representation of the quality domain within the DELOS Reference model.

As future work we want to extend the unified model proposed for the quality domain to the whole DELOS Reference model by proving a general and extensible RDF model for enabling deeper interoperability among DL systems and lower the barriers between LAMs [4]. We also plan to exploit this semantically-enabled representation of the DELOS Reference model to bridge towards the common concepts shared with the 5S model, thus enabling a better understanding of DL systems built on these two different models [3,10].

References

1. Agosti, M., Ferro, N., Fox, E.A., Gonçalves, M.A.: Modelling DL quality: a comparison between approaches: the DELOS reference model and the 5S model. In: Thanos, C., Borri, F., Launaro, A. (eds.) Second DELOS Conference - Working Notes, December 2007. http://146.48.87.21/OLP/UI/1.0/Disseminate/141919105974CdqvPg4l/a2214191910598hbzOsH2

2. Agosti, M., Ferro, N., Fox, E.A., Gonçalves, M.A., Lagoeiro, B.: Towards a reference quality model for digital libraries. In: Castelli, D., Fox, E.A. (eds.) Pre-Proceedings of the First International Workshop on Foundations of Digital Libraries, pp. 37–42 (2007)

3. Agosti, M., Ferro, N., Silvello, G.: The NESTOR framework: manage, access and exchange hierarchical data structures. In: Martoglia, R., Bergamaschi, S., Lodi, S., Sartori, C. (eds.) Proceedings of 18th Italian Symposium on Advanced Database Systems (SEBD 2010), pp. 242–253. Società Editrice Esculapio, Bologna, Italy (2010)

4. Agosti, M., Ferro, N., Silvello, G.: Digital library interoperability at high level of abstraction. Future Gener. Comput. Syst. (FGCS) **55**, 129–146 (2016)
5. Batini, C., Scannapieco, M.: Data Quality. Concepts, Methodologies and Techniques. Springer, Heidelberg (2006)
6. Borgman, C.L.: What are digital libraries? competing visions. Inf. Process. Manage. **35**(3), 227–243 (1999)
7. Borgman, C.L.: From Gutenberg to the Global Information Infrastructure: Access to Information in the Networked World (Digital Libraries and Electronic Publishing). The MIT Press, Cambridge (2003)
8. Candela, L., Castelli, D., Ferro, N., Ioannidis, Y., Koutrika, G., Meghini, C., Pagano, P., Ross, S., Soergel, D., Agosti, M., Dobreva, M., Katifori, V., Schuldt, H.: The DELOS Digital Library Reference Model. Foundations for Digital Libraries. ISTI-CNR at Gruppo ALI, Pisa, Italy, December 2007. http://www.delos.info/files/pdf/ReferenceModel/DELOS_DLReferenceModel_0.98.pdf
9. Ferro, N.: Quality and interoperability: the quest for the optimal balance. In: Iglezakis, I., Synodinou, T.E., Kapidakis, S. (eds.) E-Publishing and Digital Libraries: Legal and Organizational Issues, pp. 48–68. IGI Global, USA (2010)
10. Ferro, N., Silvello, G.: NESTOR: a formal model for digital archives. Inf. Process. Manage. **49**(6), 1206–1240 (2013)
11. Fox, E.A., Akscyn, R.M., Furuta, R.K., Leggett, J.J.: Digital libraries. Commun. ACM (CACM) **38**(4), 22–28 (1995)
12. Fox, E.A., Gonçalves, M.A., Shen, R.: Theoretical Foundations for Digital Libraries: The 5S (Societies, Scenarios, Spaces, Structures, Streams) Approach. Morgan & Claypool Publishers, USA (2012)
13. Fox, E.A., Hix, D., Nowell, L.T., Brueni, D.J., Wake, W.C., Heath, L.S., Rao, D.: Users, user interfaces, and objects: envision, a digital library. J. Am. Soc. Inf. Sci. (JASIS) **44**(8), 480–491 (1993)
14. Fuhr, N., et al.: Evaluation of digital libraries. Int. J. Digit. Libr. **8**(1), 21–38 (2007)
15. Gonçalves, M.A., Fox, E.A.: 5SL - a language for declarative specification and generation of digital libraries. In: Hersh, W., Marchionini, G. (eds.) Proceedings of 2nd ACM/IEEE-CS Joint Conference on Digital Libraries (JCDL 2002), USA, pp. 263–272. ACM, New York (2002)
16. Gonçalves, M.A., Fox, E.A., Watson, L.T.: Towards a digital library theory: a formal digital library ontology. Int. J. Digit. Libr. **8**(2), 91–114 (2008)
17. Gonçalves, M.A., Fox, E.A., Watson, L.T., Kipp, N.A.: Streams, structures, spaces, scenarios, societies (5S): a formal model for digital libraries. ACM Trans. Inf. Syst. (TOIS) **22**(2), 270–312 (2004)
18. Gonçalves, M.A., Lagoeiro, B., Fox, E.A., Watson, L.T.: What is a good digital library? a quality model for digital libraries. Inf. Process. Manage. **43**(5), 1416–1437 (2007)
19. Heath, T., Bizer, C.: Linked Data: Evolving the Web into a Global Data Space. Morgan & Claypool Publishers, USA (2011)
20. Hyvönen, E.: Publishing and Using Cultural Heritage Linked Data on the Semantic Web. Morgan & Claypool Publishers, USA (2012)
21. ISO 9000: Quality management systems - Fundamentals and vocabulary. Recommendation ISO 9000: 2005 (2005)
22. Lesk, M.: Practical Digital Libraries: Books, Bytes, & Bucks. Morgan Kaufmann Publishers, San Francisco (1997)
23. Marchionini, G., Maurer, H.: The roles of digital libraries in teaching and learning. Commun. ACM (CACM) **38**(4), 67–75 (1995)

24. Moreira, B.L., Gonçalves, M.A., Laender, A.H.F., Fox, E.A.: Automatic evaluation of digital libraries with 5SQual. J. Informetrics **3**(2), 102–123 (2009)
25. Novak, J.D.: Concept maps and Vee diagrams: two metacognitive tools to facilitate meaningful learning. Instr. Sci. **19**(1), 29–52 (1990)
26. Novak, J.D., Cañas, A.J.: The Theory Underlying Concept Maps and How to Construct and Use Them. Technical report IHMC CmapTools 2006–01 Rev 2008–01, Florida Institute for Human and Machine Cognition (FI), USA (2008)
27. Salton, G., McGill, M.J.: Introduction to Modern Information Retrieval. McGraw-Hill, New York (1983)
28. Shen, R., Gonçalves, M.A., Fox, E.A.: Key Issues Regarding Digital Libraries: Evaluation and Integration. Morgan & Claypool Publishers, USA (2013)
29. Timms, K.: New partnerships for old sibling rivals: the development of integrated access systems for the holdings of archives, libraries, and museums. Archiviaria **68**, 67–96 (2009)
30. Trant, J.: Emerging convergence? thoughts on museums, archives, libraries, and professional training. Museum Manage. Curatorship **24**(4), 369–387 (2009). http://dx.doi.org/10.1080/09647770903314738
31. Vullo, G., Clavel, G., Ferro, N., Higgins, S., van Horik, R., Horstmann, W., Kapidakis, S., Ross, S.: Quality interoperability within digital libraries: the DL.org perspective. In: Castelli, D., Ioannidis, Y., Ross, S. (eds.) Pre-Proceedings of the Second DL.org Workshop - Making Digital Libraries Interoperable: Challenges and Approaches, pp. 12–24. DL.org (2010). http://www.dlorg.eu/uploads/Booklets/2nd%20Workshop%20Proceedings/Pre-proceedings-1.pdf
32. W3C: Architecture of the World Wide Web, Volume One - W3C Recommendation, 15 December 2004. http://www.w3.org/TR/webarch/
33. W3C: Resource Description Framework (RDF): Concepts and Abstract Syntax - W3C Recommendation, 10 February 2004. http://www.w3.org/TR/rdf-concepts/
34. W3C: SKOS Simple Knowledge Organization System Primer - W3C Working Group Note, 18 August 2009. http://www.w3.org/TR/skos-primer
35. W3C: SKOS Simple Knowledge Organization System Reference - W3C Recommendation, 18 August 2009. http://www.w3.org/TR/skos-reference
36. Witten, I.H., Bainbridge, D.: How to Build a Digital Library. Morgan Kaufmann Publishers, San Francisco (2003)
37. Zorich, D.M., Waibel, G., Erway, R.: Zorich: Beyond the Silos of the LAMs. Archives and Museums. OCLC Research, Dublin, USA, Collaboration Among Libraries, September 2008. http://www.oclc.org/content/dam/research/publications/library/2008/2008-05.pdf

A Semantic Model for Content Description in the Sapienza Digital Library

Angela Di Iorio[✉] and Marco Schaerf

DIAG - Department of Computer, Control, and Management Engineering
Antonio Ruberti, Sapienza University of Rome, Rome, Italy
{angela.diiorio,marco.schaerf}@uniroma1.it

Abstract. In this paper is presented the semantic model defined for descriptive metadata of resources, managed by the Sapienza Digital Library. The semantic model is derived from the Metadata Object Descriptive Schema, a digital library descriptive standard, for library applications. The semantic model can be used as top level conceptual reference model, in order to support the implementation of semantic web technologies for digital library's descriptive metadata. The semantic model is intended to be agnostic about the technology system to be adopted. The creation of resources' connections toward the linked data cloud, as well as the opportunity of exploiting the potential of services based on the ontology use, will rely on a well-defined semantic model, which has been widely tested by the implementation of a descriptive metadata profile.

Keywords: Digital libraries · MODS · Semantic modelling · Linked data · Ontologies

1 Introduction

The current scenario of Semantic Web technology challenges Organizations managing digital library systems. The increasing use of technologies oriented to the Semantic Web(SemWeb)[1] forces digital library managers to rethink the way of providing information about managed resources. The SemWeb provides a common framework which allows to share data and to re-use it across applications, enterprises, and community boundaries. Over the classic "Web of documents", the SemWeb is a technology stack[2] enabling to develop systems supporting trusted interactions over the network, and allowing computers to do more useful work. In respect to the "layer cake", the status of technologies, in the digital library management, is characterized by the wide use of the Extensible Markup Language (XML) technologies. By using semantics community-based, the digital library systems are able to exchange documents

---

[1] Semantic Web, http://www.w3.org/standards/semanticweb/.

[2] Semantic Web "layer cake", http://www.w3.org/2000/Talks/1206-xml2k-tbl/slide 10-0.html.

© Springer International Publishing Switzerland 2016
D. Calvanese et al. (Eds.): IRCDL 2015, CCIS 612, pp. 36–47, 2016.
DOI: 10.1007/978-3-319-41938-1_4

in a coherent way. At present, the Resource Description Framework(RDF) data model has started to be experimented in library communities, under the motivation of the Linked Data Initiaves(LD) and it has been especially used over the web for open values (or controlled) vocabularies [12]. In addition, different ontologies related to library domain have been developed by designated communities[3,4,5]. The semantic model, presented in this paper, aims to support the SemWeb technologies implementation, over an existing digital library management system. Derived from a community-shared metadata profile, the semantic model encompasses conceptual descriptions expressing the knowledge base of the digital library descriptive metadata. The model is the conceptual guidance for considering the best solution to be adopted, among a variety of approaches for the implementation of SemWeb technologies for descriptive metadata.

2   Background and Motivation

The technologies, composing the first layers of the SemWeb stack, are here summarized in order to show their main characteristics and informational objectives. The XML technologies[6] have been conceived for managing data, structured as a hierarchical tree. XML is widely used for application contexts where is necessary to exchange data with a structure semantically pre-defined. One of the most important historical advantage is, having provided text information with a "well-formed" structure, that is named with human-readable semantics, that are community-based. The upper layers of the SemWeb stack use the XML as official syntax. The Resource Description Framework(RDF)[7], allows to build statements about web resources in the form of a subject-predicate-object expression. The statements can be interpreted by machines, that become capable to make connections between resources over the Web. The RDF schema(RDFS)[8] provides the framework to describe application-specific classes and properties and provides a data-modelling vocabulary for RDF data. The Web Ontology Language(OWL), currently at the second version[9], is a standard for defining ontologies that are used to capture knowledge about some domain of interest. It provides classes, properties, individuals, and data values, stored as SemWeb documents. The OWL is a semantic markup language for publishing and sharing ontologies on the Web. OWL is developed as a vocabulary extension of RDF, and every OWL ontology is a valid RDF document. The OWL may be categorised into three species or sub-languages in the 1st version (OWL-Lite, OWL-DL, OWLFull), and three profiles in the 2nd version. The OWL-EL, OWL-DL, OWL-RL, as profiles of the 2nd version, have been defined for shaping the ontology

---

[3] Bibliographic Ontology Specification, http://bibliontology.com/.
[4] FaBiO, the FRBR-aligned Bibliographic Ontology, http://purl.org/spar/fabio.
[5] Semantic Publishing and Referencing Ontologies, http://www.sparontologies.net/.
[6] XML technology, http://www.w3.org/standards/xml/.
[7] Resource Description Framework, http://www.w3.org/RDF/.
[8] RDF Schema 1.1, http://www.w3.org/TR/rdf-schema/.
[9] OWL 2 Web Ontology Language, http://www.w3.org/TR/owl2-overview/.

expressiveness and coherently supporting the computability degree. The implementation of the technologies, from the RDF up to OWL, over a legacy system, that uses XML as format for exchanging information, requires to state at least a point of reference for defining semantics, in order to model the implementation of SemWeb technologies: RDF as data model, RDFS as description of RDF data, OWL as more-formal language to be used by reasoning systems. The semantic model, presented in this paper, is indeed the reference model for implementing semantic web technologies in the domain of the management of resources, that belong to a digital library. In particular, it makes transparent main concepts associated with the resources' content description, used by the digital library system. The model can be used as semantic foundation for different approaches that can be undertaken in implementing SemWeb technologies, over the existing digital library system. The following list summarizes some of the feasible implementation cases that can be undertaken:

- creating data model based on RDF/RDFS [19]
- creating vocabularies/ontologies based on RDFS or OWL [14]
- creating mapping from XML to RDF [2,20]
- creating mapping from Database Management System to RDF[10]
- creating an ontology-based data access system [4,17]

3   Use Case Overview

The Sapienza University of Rome has established its digital library by means of a research project named Sapienza Digital Library(SDL) [10]. The vision of the SDL project was to provide Sapienza's community with a digital library, supporting the use of digital material managed, owned and produced by the Sapienza University [5]. The metadata framework, supporting the digital services of the produced SDL[11], was designed for managing heterogeneous resources, digitally representing the multidisciplinary community of the Sapienza University. The SDL metadata framework is the structured container for metadata managed by the SDL services. The SDL metadata framework is conceptually based on the Open Archival Information System(OAIS) [7]) Information Package (IP). The SDL-IP has to be structurally and semantically conforming with elements defined in the SDL metadata framework. At the present time, the SDL framework uses the metadata elements of the Metadata Objects Description Schema(MODS) for describing the intellectual contents of the resources [10], the PREservation Metadata Implementation Strategies[12](PREMIS), necessary to support the long-term digital preservation, and the Metadata Encoding and Transmission Standard[13](METS), for packaging and connecting the different metadata,

---

[10] R2RML: RDB to RDF Mapping Language, http://www.w3.org/TR/r2rml/.

[11] Sapienza Digital Library, sapienzadigitallibrary.uniroma1.it.

[12] PREMIS Preservation Metadata Maintenance Activity, http://www.loc.gov/standards/premis/.

[13] Metadata Encoding Transmission Standard, www.loc.gov/standards/mets/.

belonging to the digital resources. These digital library standards, maintained by the Library of Congress[14], are defined by XML schemas[15]. The conformance with standards is based on the production of XML files validated against the pertaining XML Schema. The semantic model, presented in the Sect. 4, is focused on the descriptive metadata section of the SDL framework(see next Sect. 3.1), and is the semantic representation of the MODS profile (see Sect. 3.3). The MODS profile has been defined for the SDL implementation needs, and has aligned descriptive metadata, coming from different Sapienza's communities (libraries, museums and archives).

3.1   The SDL Descriptive Metadata

In the reference standard OAIS [7], the IP is a conceptual container of Content Information(CI) and Preservation Description Information(PDI), where the resulting package is viewed as being discoverable by virtue of the Descriptive Information. In the SDL project, during the digital resources life-cycle, the OAIS IP is considered the target package of the data management and the existence of the Descriptive Information is the pre-condition for building the SDL-IP. In the SDL implementation, the descriptive information is coded in MODS, for describing the intellectual content of the SDL-IP. The MODS uses libraries semantics, that are derived from MARC 21[16], the standard format created in 1999 (a revised version for the 21st century of the MAchine Readable Cataloguing (MARC)[17] created in 1960) and widely used by libraries information systems. The MODS semantics were used for describing the different kind of intellectual/creative works managed by the SDL. The SDL-IPs are characterized by different formats (still and moving images, texts, sounds, cartographics, etc.) and are differently structured (digital collections, books, images, videos, documents, hierarchies, maps). The intellectual/creative works, represented as SDL digital resources (SDL-IPs), can also be expressing multidisciplinary knowledge.

3.2   The MODS Standard and Linked Vocabularies

In [13] is reported how during the years, has raised the emergent need of having a standard less complex than MARC, but not as simple as the widely interoperable standard, Dublin Core Metadata Element Set (DC)[18]. In order to address these community's need, the Library of Congress developed the MODS, "a schema for a bibliographic element set that may be used for a variety of purposes, and particularly for library applications"[19].

---

[14] Standards at the Library of Congress, http://www.loc.gov/standards/.

[15] W3C XML Schema - World Wide Web Consortium, http://www.w3.org/XML/Schema.

[16] MARC 21 Format for Bibliographic Data, www.loc.gov/marc/bibliographic/.

[17] MAchine Readable Cataloguing (MARC), http://en.wikipedia.org/wiki/MARC_standards.

[18] Dublin Core Metadata Element Set, http://dublincore.org.

[19] Metadata Object Description Schema, http://www.loc.gov/standards/mods/.

The MODS XML schema includes a subset of MARC fields, using language-based tags rather than numeric ones. The official website provides guidelines primarily intended to be used for assistance in creating original MODS records, as well as converted from MARC 21 or for use in developing detailed conversion specifications. The MODS standard claims that the element set is richer than Dublin Core, more oriented to the end-user than the full MARCXML schema, and simpler than the full MARC format. These main characteristics were, in general, deemed useful for describing at a sufficient granular level, the multi-faceted materials to be managed in the SDL.

The descriptive metadata for a MODS resource aggregates titles, names, subjects and other data elements that associated with the resource, further help to describe the resource. For systems, the MODS resource description and especially its descriptive metadata aids the indexing, searching, and displaying of information about the resource. For users, a MODS resource description assists with identifying, finding, selecting, and accessing a MODS Resource. Administrative metadata provides provenance information about the descriptive metadata. It includes information, such as the individual or organization responsible for the descriptive metadata and/or the date the descriptive metadata was last modified, as well as relationships expressed in the MODS resource description.

The XML schema of MODS is deployed on 20 top elements, that are variously structured with sub-elements. Except for the administrative description of the record (`recordInfo`), all MODS elements are repeatable. No element is mandatory, and the `relatedItem` element is recursive, because it can contain all the top elements of the schema, including itself.

The web availability of different mappings[20], initiaves [11], and studies extending the use of this standard over other information science disciplines, like archivist science [3] or toward museums' artifacts [8], supports the interoperability of the semantics adopted, as well as the probability of the information loss. The SDL metadata framework exploits the MODS's ability of providing a mechanism to dereference, in documented way, the controlled vocabularies' entries, used in the XML elements. In SDL, this ability has been exploited for using entries from the Library of Congress Linked Data Service[21], from other italian LD vocabularies[22], and from vocabularies locally defined[23]. The use of MODS schema attributes, like the controlled vocabulary's source authority name (`authority`), and the identifier (`authorityURI`) and the identifier of the vocabulary's entry value (`valueURI`), allows to create authoritative connections between the MODS element value and the authority maintaining the vocabulary's term as Linked Open Vocabulary(LOV)[24].

The granularity and the flexibility of MODS, and its application in a multi-faceted environment, has required the definition of a profile for the SDL

---

[20] MODS conversions, http://www.loc.gov/standards/mods/mods-conversions.html.

[21] Library of Congress Linked Data Service, http://id.loc.gov/.

[22] Nuovo Soggettario, Biblioteca Nazionale di Firenze, http://purl.org/bncf/tid.

[23] Sapienza Digital Library vocabularies, http://sbs.uniroma1.it/sdl/vocabularies.

[24] Linked Open Vocabularies (LOV), http://lov.okfn.org/dataset/lov/.

implementation, in order to define the minimum obligation in using XML elements and attributes.

3.3   The SDL MODS Profile

The SDL MODS profile[25] encompasses metadata elements necessary to the MODS XML data coding, defines the structural and functional contexts where elements and attributes can be used, and defines the obligation constraints on the existence of specific MODS XML elements.

The principle, guiding the definition of the MODS profile, has been to maintain and to enrich as much as descriptive information about different content types, and to integrate XML elements by dereferencing URIs from LOV and the maintaining authority.

The definition of the MODS profile had followed two main reference guidelines. Firstly, the "Master List of Data Elements" is a framework of elements gathered from the profiles of the different digital library projects at the Library of Congress. The objective of the list is to work towards "compatibility of metadata usage throughout the institution, support the metadata use cases, and point to areas where metadata remediation for improved consistency or enhanced interoperability might be beneficial"[26]. Secondly, the implementation guidelines of the Digital Library Federation for the implementation of shareable MODS records[27].

The MODS profile is applied to the following content types: books, documents, images, videos, maps, hierarchical structures (like serial publications or archival collections), and digital collections.

During the project development the profile was incremented and enriched coherently to contents' descriptive needs. Each new integration of profile specifications has entailed the conformance check on the metadata relational structure, in order to verify the consistent coexistence of different materials and descriptions, inside of the same metadata framework.

Some specifications, indeed, have required the specific profiling of metadata elements with the inclusion of sub-elements and attributes, that have been set for the application context. The specifications have improved not only the granularity of the descriptive information, but also the data accuracy and the interoperability of the content re-use because the wide reference to local controlled vocabularies, and wherever possible to LOV.

Beyond the XML elements, whose semantics are defined in the MODS Schema, the profile had configured the following attributes for the local needs:

---

[25] The Sapienza Digital Library MODS profile (available by the end of January 2015), http://sbs.uniroma1.it/sdl/documentation.

[26] Metadata for Digital Content(MDC), Developing institution-wide policies and standards at the Library of Congress, http://www.loc.gov/standards/mdc/elements/MasterDataElementList-20120215.doc.

[27] Digital Library Federation/Aquifer Implementation Guidelines for Shareable MODS Records, https://wiki.dlib.indiana.edu/confluence/download/attachments/24288/DLFMODS_ImplementationGuidelines.pdf.

- @displayLabel is the label for displaying the XML element's content. In the SDL MODS profile specification, it was used for the portal implementation to show the italian label of the field.
- @xlink:href is the reference link associated with the XML element's content. In specific elements, it has been used for the portal implementation to activate the link over the XML elements content value.
- @authority, @authorityURI, @valueURI, these attributes are extensively used for referring, respectively to the authority controlled vocabulary's name, the URI/URL identifying the authority controlled vocabulary, the URI value exposed in the Linked Data Cloud.
- @xml:lang this element allows to label the XML elements' content with a language selector. It was extensively applied and coded in the existing descriptive record, and wherever it was possible, the Italian content was translated in English. The reference code used for language is the ISO-639-2[28].

The SDL MODS profile provides specifications about 28 MODS metadata elements, that are necessary to the coherent description of the SDL resources. The profile provides references to 13 controlled vocabularies, locally defined, and 21 vocabularies of third party can be used. In addition the profile provides specifications for the customization needs of the SDL portal implementation.

The Table 1 shows the occurrences of specifications that were defined for each metadata elements. The higher number of specifications occurrences is significant because reveal the susceptibility of certain elements, in respect to others for the application context. For example, four over seven titleInfo specifications are destined to the portal visualization requirements. The eight specifications of the subject element have profiled most of the sub-elements, with the specification about the controlled vocabularies to be used and in some case, with anchors necessary to the SDL browsing services. The eight specifications of the relatedItem instead reveal the extensive use of this element, for building relationships between the SDL resources. The SDL MODS profile provides reference terms for qualifying the type of relationship, occurring between resources.

Table 1. MODS metadata elements and SDL profile specification occurrences

titleInfo	7	originInfo/date	1	recordInfo	1
name	2	originInfo/place	1	note	2
abstract	4	originInfo/publisher	1	genre	2
accessCondition	2	originInfo/edition	1	subject	8
language	1	originInfo/issuance	1	relatedItem	8
typeOfResource	1	originInfo/frequency	1	part	2
identifier	1	physicalDescr./digitalOrigin	1	extension	1
location	2	physicalDescr./internetMediaType	1	targetAudience	1
tableOfContents	1	physicalDescr./form	1	classification	1
		physicalDescr./extent	2		

---

[28] ISO 639-2 Language Codes, http://id.loc.gov/vocabulary/iso639-2.html.

4   The SDL Semantic Model for Descriptive Metadata

The SDL's semantic model(SDL-SM) summarizes the concepts specified in the
SDL MODS profile. Specifically the SDL-SM represents the set of concepts

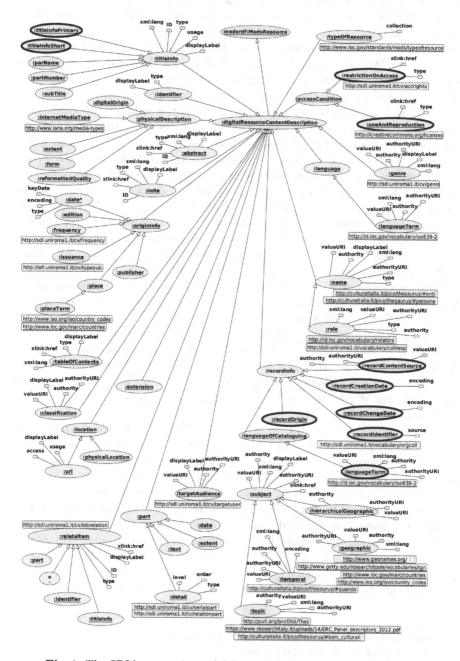

Fig. 1. The SDL's semantic model for contents' resource descriptions

underlying the knowledge domain related to the digital library descriptive metadata, about the intellectual content of digital library's resources.

The SDL-SM is meant to be agnostic about the technology system on which it will be implemented and it can be used as top level conceptual reference model, for implementing SemWeb technologies in the digital library system.

The SDL-SM can be considered as the reference model not only for developers, but also for domain experts. The pre-condition for re-using the concepts defined in this model is the acceptance of the core principles and best practices of the Semantic Web and Linked Data [6], in particular the use of specific policies for managing the SDL resource's identifiers building [9] is considered the point of reference for assigning the URI to the semantic concepts.

The Fig. 1 outlines the concepts laying down the semantics defined in the MODS XML schema hierarchy, that were used in the SDL MODS profile. The concepts are represented by the ovals and the bold line ovals represent the obligation constraints over the concepts. The repeatability constraint of concepts (only one concept is not repeatable: `recordInfo`) is distinguished by the ovals with underlined labels. Borrowing from the Description Logics the basic inference on concept expressions [1], each MODS top element is represented as a concept subsumption of the main concept `digitalResourceContentDescription` which in turn is a subsumption of the MODS `modsrdf:ModsResource` concept.

Analogously, the XML sub-elements (lower hierarchical levels), are considered as subsumptions of the concepts derived from the XML top elements of MODS. Differently from a data model design or from an ontology definition, the properties/relationships relating concepts, are placed in a subsumption hierarchy [18] leaving further definition open to the implementation choices.

The specifications, defined by the MODS profile, had leveraged on the customization of some attributes, that are relevant to the exhaustive description of the resources. The attributes used for MODS profile are represented in the figure, in Entity/Relationships diagrams notation style, for highlighting that the association of attributes to each related concept can be further modeled at implementation time.

The graphical representation of the SDL-SM respects the MODS XML schema hierarchical style, but makes evident the ambiguity points that have to be overcome in a SemWeb Technology implementation. The MODS schema has defined the use of same attributes for different XML elements[29], and indeed the figure highlights the wide re-use of the same attributes (i.e. `@displayLabel`, `@type`...) in different conceptual contexts. This graphical evidence warns that, in this case, the semantic disambiguation of the information is contained in the value of the attribute, and not in the XML schema data definition. Similarly, the homonymy of sub-elements (i.e. `@languageTerm`, `@extent`), need to be solved by inheriting the conceptual name of the higher level semantic elements. Mostly the same inheritance

---

[29] Attributes Used Throughout the MODS Schema, http://www.loc.gov/standards/mods/userguide/generalapp.html#list.

application coherently works for all sub-elements that cannot have sufficient semantic specification, like in the `role` case.

Another critical aspect to be highlighted by the semantic point of view, is the recursive functionality held by the `relatedItem` element, that requires the semantic disambiguation of the contained elements. The disambiguation can be managed by a semantic inheritance mechanism where a combination of `relatedItem`'s attribute values and contained element's names can distinguish different concepts expressed by the recursive elements. The Fig. 1 also shows the reference to the controlled vocabularies, used by the SDL MODS profile, and exhibits the association to relevant concepts. The rounded rectangles containing an URI, and in close contact with some ovals (the concepts), specify that the concept's value is derived from the controlled vocabulary deferenced by URI. The URI in pink rounded rectangles specify SDL vocabularies, while the underlined URIs in the cyan rounded rectangles specify third party vocabularies.

The SDL-SM does not provide a further ontological modelling about relationships/properties because would imply implementation-dependent choices. The modelling of relationships/properties is a customization task and it depends on the SemWeb technology to be used. For example, the production of RDF triples can mostly depend on technology environment factors, the RDF triples could come from a Relational Database mapping or managed directly by a triple store system. Similarly, the conceptual modelling of an ontology, in order to be used by reasoning systems, cannot be expressed in OWL 2 because of the high complexity of computation, but it needs to be profiled into one of the three ontology language fragments, the OWL 2 profiles(EL, QL, RL)[30].

5   Related Work and Conclusion

The initiatives that can be coherently compared, because oriented toward the SemWeb, and related to the specific library application domain of the descriptive metadata, are briefly summarized.

The draft of the MODS RDF Ontology [16] is the semantic model expression of the MODS model and is a reference for shaping MODS resources as RDF triples. The basic conceptual assumption is similar to the SDL-SM because "a MODS resource description includes descriptive metadata about a MODS resource", but the ontology (coded in OWL 1 Lite[31]) defines more prescriptive constraints. The MODS XML elements are modelled 20 classes distinguished in: 1 main class (`modsrdf:ModsResource`), 9 MODS classes as ranges for properties whose domain is `modsrdf:ModsResource`, and 10 classes imported by an external ontology. Nevertheless, mostly MODS elements are modelled in 114 `owl:ObjectProperty`, with corresponding domain and range defined by RDFS statements. The second comparable initiative is the Bibliographic Framework Initiative (BIBFRAME) [15] where the focus is the translation of MARC 21 format to a Linked Open

---

[30] OWL 2 Web Ontology Language Profiles, http://www.w3.org/TR/owl2-profiles/.

[31] OWL Lite RDF Schema Features, http://www.w3.org/TR/2004/REC-owl-features-20040210/#s3.4.

Data model. The BIBFRAME has defined a model consisting of 4 core classes (Creative Work, Instance, Authority, and Annotation), and a vocabulary structured over different categories of information. The BIBFRAME metamodel is designed to be lightweight, flexible and able to accommodate the declarative needs of existing descriptive standards(RDA[32], DACS[33], VRA[34], etc.) and yet-to-be-developed community vocabularies. To best accomodate these communities the BIBFRAME RDF Schema is intentionally underspecified in terms of constraints such as domain and range. With regard to the SDL-SM, the choice of defining a conceptual reference model based on standardized and community-based semantics, and agnostic about technology, offers more flexibility and more consistency to further conceptualizations as implementation foundation. The use of digital library metadata, in a SemWeb scenario, will trespass on the hosting system boundaries, as well as the MODS conceptual assumption, and will match to other "world" like similar ontologies as BIBFRAME or others unpredictably similar.

References

1. Baader, F.: The Description Logic Handbook: Theory, Implementation, and Applications. Cambridge University Press, Cambridge (2003)
2. Bohring, H., Auer, S.: Mapping XML to OWL ontologies. Leipzig. Informatik-Tage **72**, 147–156 (2005)
3. Bountouri, L., Gergatsoulis, M.: Interoperability between archival and bibliographic metadata: an EAD to MODS crosswalk. J. Libr. Metadata **9**(1–2), 98–133 (2009)
4. Calvanese, D., Giacomo, G., Lembo, D., Lenzerini, M., Rosati, R.: Tractable reasoning and efficient query answering in description logics: the DL-Lite family. J. Autom. Reason. **39**(3), 385–429 (2007). http://link.springer.com/10.1007/s10817-007-9078-x
5. Catarci, T., Di Iorio, A., Schaerf, M.: The Sapienza Digital Library from the holistic vision to the actual implementation. Procedia Comput. Sci. **38**, 4–11 (2014)
6. Hyland, B., Atemezing, G., Villazón-Terrazas, B.: Best practices for publishing linked data. W3C Working Group Note (2014)
7. Consultative Committee for Space Data: Reference Model for an Open Archival Information System (OAIS), Recommended Practice CCSDS 650.0-M-2 Magenta Book (2012). http://public.ccsds.org/publications/archive/652x0m1.pdf
8. Di Iorio, A., Schaerf, M.: Applicability of digital library descriptive metadata to the contemporary artworks. In: Nesi, P., Santucci, R. (eds.) ECLAP 2013. LNCS, vol. 7990, pp. 78–89. Springer, Heidelberg (2013)
9. Di Iorio, A., Schaerf, M.: The organization information integration in the management of a digital library system. In: 2014 IEEE/ACM Joint Conference on Digital Libraries (JCDL), pp. 461–462. IEEE, poster and Extended Abstract (2014)

---

[32] Resource Description & Access(RDA), http://www.rdatoolkit.org/.

[33] Describing Archives: A Content Standard, Second Edition (DACS), http://files.archivists.org/pubs/DACS2E-2013.pdf.

[34] Visual Resources Association(VRA), http://www.loc.gov/standards/vracore/.

10. Di Iorio, A., Schaerf, M., Bertazzo, M.: Establishing a Digital Library in Wide-Ranging University's context. In: Agosti, M., Esposito, F., Ferilli, S., Ferro, N. (eds.) IRCDL 2012. CCIS, vol. 354, pp. 172–183. Springer, Heidelberg (2013)
11. Europeana Libraries consortium: Europeana libraries: Aggregating digital content from Europe's libraries (2013). http://ec.europa.eu/information_society/apps/projects/factsheet/index.cfm?project_ref=270933
12. Isaac, A., Waites, W., Young, J., Zeng, M.: Library linked data incubator group: datasets, value vocabularies, and metadata element sets. W3C Incubator Group Report **25**, (2011)
13. Guenther, R., McCallum, S.: New metadata standards for digital resources: MODS and METS. Bullet. Am. Soc. Inf. Sci. Technol. **29**(2), 12–15 (2003)
14. Hogan, A., Delbru, R., Umbrich, J.: RDFS & OWL reasoning for linked data (2013)
15. Library of Congress: Bibliographic framework as a web of data: Linked data model and supporting services (2012). http://www.loc.gov/bibframe/pdf/marcld-report-11-21-2012.pdf
16. Library of Congress: The MODS RDF ontology primer (2012). http://www.loc.gov/standards/mods/modsrdf/primer.html#vocabularies
17. Noy, N.F.: Semantic integration: a survey of ontology-based approaches. ACM Sigmod Rec. **33**(4), 65–70 (2004)
18. Rector, A.L.: Modularisation of domain ontologies implemented in description logics and related formalisms including OWL. In: Proceedings of the 2nd International Conference on Knowledge Capture, pp. 121–128. ACM (2003)
19. Shadbolt, N., Hall, W., Berners-Lee, T.: The semantic web revisited. IEEE Intell. Syst. **21**(3), 96–101 (2006)
20. Van Deursen, D., Poppe, C., Martens, G., Mannens, E., Walle, R.: XML to RDF conversion: a generic approach. In: 2008 International Conference on Automated Solutions for Cross Media Content and Multi-Channel Distribution. AXMEDIS 2008, pp. 138–144. IEEE (2008)

Text Encoding Initiative Semantic Modeling. A Conceptual Workflow Proposal

Fabio Ciotti[1], Marilena Daquino[2], and Francesca Tomasi[2(✉)]

[1] Department of Literary Studies, University of Roma Tor Vergata, Rome, Italy
fabio.ciotti@uniroma2.it
[2] Department of Classical Philology and Italian Studies,
University of Bologna, Bologna, Italy
{marilena.daquino2,francesca.tomasi}@unibo.it

Abstract. In this paper we present a proposal for the XML TEI semantic enhancement, through an ontological modelization based on a three level approach: an ontological generalization of the TEI schema; an intensional semantics of TEI elements; an extensional semantics of the markup content. A possible TEI enhancement will be the result of these three levels dialogue and combination. We conclude with the ontology mapping issue and a Linked Open Data suggestion for digital libraries based on XML TEI semantically enriched model.

Keywords: Ontology · TEI · XML · Interoperability · LOD · Digital libraries

1   Introduction

Digital libraries are moving towards a radical identity redefinition. Semantic Web technologies are, in particular, contributing to increase the expressivity of the digital library as an unexplored reservoir of raw data, on which keyword as ontologies, RDF, OWL, metadata and controlled vocabularies play a crucial role. "Yet semantic technologies offer a new level of flexibility, interoperability, and relationships for digital repositories" [1].

Typically in the digital libraries and archives context XML is the meta-language of choice to encode digital documents so to ensure the maximum syntactic interchange, even between technological heterogeneous repositories. In the humanities domain the most common XML markup language is that developed by the Text Encoding Initiative (TEI), explicitly designed to represent the complex types of documents and interpretations typical of the humanistic research. TEI is a flexible and customizable schema that represents a shared approach in the community, demonstrated by the fact that the most of existent digital libraries of national textual traditions are based on this standard[1].

The TEI project originated in 1987, following a conference organized by the ACH (Association for Computers and the Humanities). During the conference, the need to define a standard for the digitization of text inspired the ACH, along with the

---

[1] http://www.tei-c.org/Activities/Projects/.

© Springer International Publishing Switzerland 2016
D. Calvanese et al. (Eds.): IRCDL 2015, CCIS 612, pp. 48–60, 2016.
DOI: 10.1007/978-3-319-41938-1_5

Association for Computational Linguistics (ALC) and the Association for Literary and Linguistic Computing (ALLC) to establish the first guidelines for the encoding and exchange of texts in electronic format. In 1999, the TEI Consortium was founded with the aim of maintaining, developing and promoting the *Guidelines*[2]. Literary texts, whether in prose, verse, or drama, find in the TEI *Guidelines* a ready set of elements for the description of all necessary phenomena suitable for interpretation: from the definition of the elements of a document's logical structure to the specification of people's names, places and dates, from the description of a manuscript to the marking of phenomena peculiar to an edition (such as the apparatus of a critical edition), from linguistic analysis to rhetorical or narrative structures. TEI is also a project in continual evolution. From version P1 in July 1990 (an initial draft, 89 tags) it has evolved to P5 (2007–2014, version 2.7.0, about 550 tags).

The XML TEI approach lets two questions emerge, in a huge debate. From one hand XML is a topic largely addressed as a reflection on a meta-language that could be exploited not only for data interchange (the data community approach) but also for text representation (the document community approach). This issue reveals a shared widespread belief among researchers: XML is semantically poor and it needs strategies for data model improving.

From the other hand TEI, that is a real standard in the humanistic domain, could be refined in a semantic perspective starting from the translation of the TEI framework (i.e. schema, community personalization, real documents) in an ontology[3]. This process is not a simple task because the conversion of the schema in OWL is just one of the levels of conceptualization. In our proposal the semantic enhancement of the existent TEI framework requires a three levels approach.

The first level is the ontological generalization of the schema. This task could not be treated as a complete automatic process. It has to be the result of a deep analysis of the original model in a class/properties dimension. But it's not a simple 1:1 relation (tei: element = tei:class; tei:attribute = tei:property) it's even a conceptual analysis of scope and content of entities.

The second level regards the domain specific approach determined by a specific community trend. In particular the information managed by some attributes values are fundamental in order to define the semantic of a model. Possible specific local additions to the general TEI schema have to be considered in order to create an ontology that could be able to describe all the XML TEI based documents.

The third level regards the real markup, i.e. the analysis of a real domain described by real documents, in order to enrich a theoretical model. This means that the ontology will require a study of marked up documents in order to manage individuals and understand the potential relations that instances could manage with other external, and potentially different at the level of semantic declaration, information.

All the described process has to be thought in a re-conceptualization of the text as a multi-levels entity. Following the FRBR approach we have to consider that each class and each property of the ontology reflect one of the levels of an analysed entity: the

---

[2] http://www.tei-c.org/Guidelines/.

[3] http://www.tei-c.org/Activities/SIG/Ontologies/index.xml.

work, the expression, the manifestation, the item. The aim of each class and each property has to be considered in potentially each of these levels: the function of classes and properties naturally changes in relation to the level that class and properties want to refer to. We have to consider that a TEI document contains information regarding not only the text but a complex granularity of contextual information that have to be likewise modeled.

The ontological approach, starting from an applied schema, let even to reflect on a deeper issue: the passage from a strictly hierarchical model (the XML TEI markup) to a network model (the ontology). The data structure has a fundamental role in semantic definition of a modelled domain. The tree model has a representational potential that could be re-thought according to the graph expressivity, compelling a semantic re-definition of text features. In the conversion of the schema into ontology we have to keep in mind that elements and attributes organized as functional modules or classes in the schema (e.g. the class of attributes for the dates) could be reorganized on real entities or real relationships (e.g. date of birth, date of an event, date mentioned in a text).

This described method will help XML TEI based digital libraries to move from a static, flat dimension towards an inter-related, interoperable and interchangeable environment. Semantic Web technologies will provide tools and methods for migrating XML TEI files in the Linked Open Data cloud. This migration will involve two other issues: the mapping of the realized ontology on classes and properties of other pertinent ontologies; the compatibility of the semantic model proposal with the LOD specification. A detailed study of TEI real cases (i.e. TEI real documents) will be also strictly necessary in order to provide the ontology refinement towards a LOD compatibility.

The paper is then organized as follow: Sect. 2 is devoted to describe the debate regarding the XML semantic enriching; Sect. 3 focuses on the specific issue of ontology creation starting from the TEI framework; Sect. 4 is devoted to ontology mapping and the LOD approach; Sect. 5 opens to next research perspectives, in order to realize a real ontology based on these conceptual reflections.

2 The XML Semantics Debate

The debate on the Markup Language semantic role has been quite lively during the last twenty years and the experience of the TEI community of practice has played an active role in this context. It is commonly acknowledged that the markup conveys semantic aspects, whether they are local 'interpretations' produced by a single scholar, or rather the expression of a general text theory.

However, this markup and, in particular, the XML markup semantic role, clashes with the fact that, as [2] already observed some time ago: "XML is a poor language for data modeling if the goal is to represent information objects in the problem domain such that they correspond transparently ("one-to-one") to the user's conceptual model of objects in this domain". XML is a powerful formalism to define the syntactic markup aspects, and, through its data model, to model some limited structural features of information objects to which it is applied. Still, it owes its semantic value almost entirely to human interpretation. Any markup restriction or semantic role accordingly needs to be expressed in natural language as instructions for human users. This is the case for ODD formalism [3], which TEI developed with the aim to combine in a single meta-XML document the custom definition of its XML schema and all its relevant documentation.

Several proposals were drawn up to provide XML with formalized and computable semantics. The work [4, 5] constitutes the first, explicit contribution in this direction.

The Authors, from the observation that semantic markup coincides with the set of inferences authorized by one of its constructs, propose a formal markup semantics based on Prolog clauses. More recent works on the topic were focused on the proposal of a RDF based model for text encoding [6]; or by exploring the potentiality of LMM, an OWL vocabulary that represents some core semiotic notions, in order to provide a better understanding of the semantics of markup [7]; or also with the idea of "transcriptional implicature" [8–10].

In these last studies the range of application possibilities offered by the definition of a formal semantics for markup is widely recognized and justified:

> … a formal description of the semantics of a markup language can bring several benefits. One of them is the ability to develop provably correct mappings (conversions, translations) from one markup language to another. A second one is the possibility of automatically deriving facts from documents, and feeding them into various inferencing or reasoning systems. A third one is the possibility of automatically computing the semantics of part or whole of a document and presenting it to humans in an appropriate form to make the meaning of the document (or passage) precise and explicit [9].

Nonetheless the same authoritative authors of this last paper observed that if the proposals for formal semantic approaches to markup have been very scarce, their practical application are even less.

The reasons for this lack of interest from the wider encoding community are manifold and complex:

- theoretical complexity in a domain already hard to understand for the average humanist scholar;
- technical and practical difficulties in the application and exploitation of the approaches proposed;
- lack of tools and applications;
- excessive "revolutionary" scope of some proposals.

In this paper, we propose a Semantic Web extension of the TEI infrastructure in order to formalize some of the semantic levels of the markup constructs it provides.

The rationales of our proposal are:

- to be based on well-established Semantic Web formalism and technologies;
- to be an extension not a replacement of current languages and practices;
- to provide a viable solution for some practical concerns that are relevant in the actual digital ecosystem in which TEI and XML live, especially interoperability and linked data.

3   TEI and Semantic Web Technologies

During the time elapsed between the first approaches to the semantics of markup language and situation today the development and the relevant spread of the Semantic Web paradigm and, more recently, Linked Data occurred. This process has made available a number of syntactically rigorous and semantically well-founded languages and data models, such as RDF/RDFS, SPARQL and OWL 2, as well as systems and software components, aimed at the semantic data processing (storage, query, and inference). As stated [11], many research and evaluation projects in the Semantic Web technologies domain produced ontologies. From the LOD (Linked Open Data) perspective, i.e. a fundamental step in the direction of the Semantic Web realization, the ontology support would provide benefits in semantic expressivity power, data interchange and machine - but also users - intelligent consumption.

Starting from this context, we propose to develop an ontological approach for TEI, that will give a formal definition to the implicit concepts underlying XML TEI text encoding.

To this purpose, it is appropriate to distinguish between three different iteratives semantic levels expressed by the markup and its content:

1. Generalization on TEI Schema (in order to define a broad ontological description of entities involved in text encoding). A top-down approach: from the schema to the ontology (see Sect. 3.1).
2. Intensional TEI markup semantics (defined by a particular user of community of practice). A bottom-up approach: from the community to the ontology revision (see Sect. 3.2).
3. Extensional semantics of the markup content. A bottom-up approach: from real documents to ontology for refinement (see Sect. 3.3).

The rationales for this proposal are both theoretical and operational. In the DH community a great relevance has been given to the notion of model and modelling, so that we often can find assertion like "text encoding is a form of modeling". The very problem with the model/modeling notions is that they are umbrella terms, relating to an ample and diverse sort of conceptual objects and practices. In general, we can summarize the roles assigned to modeling in scientific activity in three areas:

- representation/communication: models ensure that a community of practice shares the fundamental concepts of a domain;
- explanation/prediction: models relates facts and concepts providing explanations and possibly predictions of the behavior of a system;
- multiple views/perspectives mediation: models mediate between the different perspectives that can arise within a single community of practice and between different but proximal communities of practice.

Ontological modeling formalizes the common sense concept of model giving it a precise logical semantics a definite functional role in each of these areas. Creating formal models based on explicit conceptualization and logical foundation grants that all the discourses are firmly grounded to a common "setting" of the domain.

Formal ontologies license the application of computational inferences and reasoning to express explanation and make predictions. And finally Semantic Web modeling provides methods to compare and eventually merge different ontologies and, being based on the Open World Assumption, ensures the functionality of the model even if it is incomplete or conceived as a work in progress.

In order to formalize a complex taxonomy and a hierarchy for relations, following conceptual steps later described, more than one methodology have to be used iteratively in ontology engineering.

- Firstly when generalizing on entities involved in text encoding domain, a hybrid approach, which also take in account well-known models in humanistic communities, can be useful to define a shared controlled vocabulary, describing only entities of interest for the communities themselves, without too much detail of description in the first phase.
- When dealing with elements representing parts of a text, meaning both material and abstract entities, and relations among them, a top-down approach in conceptualization is recommended, in order to clearly distinguish different semantic layers of a document, i.e. a work, for referencing its context information; the expression of a work (i.e. the text) as an entity with part of speech, abstract divisions, and as subject of interpretations; its manifestation (i.e. the material representation of text) for describing concrete features of material support and characters.
- Finally, in revising hierarchy of concepts and formalizing properties among classes, also a bottom-up approach can be useful. Analysis of data structure and specific use cases of elements in a corpus of XML TEI documents helps in defining further specializations of main concepts in iterative and concentric development.

3.1   TEI Schema Ontological Generalization

Transforming an XML Schema into an OWL ontology involves a general rethinking of its element set, its organization and its related hierarchy of concepts/relations – from a flat hierarchical structure into a multi-layers one – where more complex semantic relations among entities can be stated and where relations among strings of text and their abstract containers shall become relations among real entities.

The conversion of XML Schemas into ontologies is an issue discussed in many papers in the last ten years, and for which many theoretical and computational solutions have been proposed. We cannot get into the technical details of these solutions here. Most of them are based on the mapping of W3C Schemas primitives into OWL primitives [e.g. 12].

TEI has made explicit its conceptual model with the notion of element class in the design of its literate schema language ODD:

The TEI scheme distinguishes about five hundred different elements. To aid comprehension, modularity, and modification, the majority of these elements are formally classified in some way. Classes are used to express two distinct kinds of commonality among elements. [...] A class is known as an attribute class if its members share attributes, and as a model class if its members appear in the same locations. In either case, an element is said to inherit proper-tiesfrom any classes of which it is a member [13, 1.3].

And later, specifically about model classes:

In fact, the nature of a given class of elements can be considered along two dimensions: as noted, it defines a set of places where the class members are permitted within the document hierarchy; it also implies a semantic grouping of some kind. For example, the very large class of elements which can appear within a paragraph comprises a number of other classes, all of which have the same structural property, but which differ in their field of application. Some are related to highlighting, while others relate to names or places, and so on. In some cases, the 'set of places where class members are permitted' is very constrained: it may just be within one specific element, or one class of element, for example. In other cases, elements may be permitted to appear in very many places, or in more than one such set of places. [13, 1.3.2].

Guidelines state that the distinction between those two kind of model classes is epitomized by the naming conventions adopted:

if a model class has a name containing part [...] then it is primarily defined in terms of its structural location [...]. If, however, a model class has a name containing like [...] the implication is that its members all have some additional semantic property in common. [13, 1.3.2].

We can try to identify a proper structural constraints set and an informal semantic/taxonomic directives set from such explanations, but a well-formalized model has to reorganize such functional and pragmatic approach into a more balanced one which take in account formal logic constraints and rules for creation of a taxonomy. Drawing from this analysis of the TEI schema architecture, as a first approximation, we can formulate OWL constructs through a conceptual workflow following a few of minimal required steps.

- General analysis and recognition of entities in the Schema, i.e. all TEI elements that can be converted into OWL classes. This compels a wide conceptualization and study of entities involved in the wide domain of text encoding – and that will create the basic taxonomy of the ontology – which encompasses a description of the context of a document of interest (people and events related to the life cycle of a document), the document as an object itself (through FRBR conceptual model) and information that can be extracted from the content of the document (people, relations, events described in the text). We will then have well-known entities such as *Agent*, meaning a Person, an Organization or a Group somehow involved in the life cycle of the object of interest or simply cited in text); *Document,* identifying the document of interest and all related similar objects); *Time* and *Place* as entities related to documents, agents and events or simply described in the text; *Event* and *Situation* as broad entities for defining any sort of action, situation and specific issue related to the document life cycle, or also as described in the text; finally, we will have different entities for defining document elements, in order to identify both material – concrete- and conceptual elements related to the text. These entities don't cover the wide range of specific concepts needed in a complete description of the domain, but are minimal required entities in order to define a shared conceptualization, according with some of most known ontologies (see Sect. 4).

- Analysis of TEI Model Classes of type "Like" and "Part". Generally, most of -Like type elements can peacefully be converted into OWL classes: this entails that an "automatic" transformation is allowed here for the formalization of such entities. E. g. elements of TEI Model Class `model.persEventLike` – birth, death, event, listEvent – can be transformed in OWL classes with the same name. However they have to be reanalysed in iterative controls for a correct hierarchical characterization without redundancy, wrong or badly conceptualization, following OntoClean methodology [14] as a correct way for creation of a taxonomy. E.g. considering previous example, *listEvent* have to be deleted as a wrong, unnecessary entity; *birth* and *death* have to be correctly declared in taxonomy as kind of events. Indeed, here "automatic" doesn't mean strictly automated, because a general rule for such transformation is unpredictable. Furthermore, we noted that transformation of elements members of-`Like` type Classes into OWL Classes is not generalizable when these ones are also member of TEI Model Class of type-`Part`. When this situation occurs, in most cases-`Like` type elements, and also-`Part` type elements, can be converted in object and data properties. E.g. `model.nameLike` elements – like *name, orgName, persName* – when members of `model.addrPart`, can better be converted into data properties.
- Generalization on elements of-`Att` type Model Classes: these ones are also converted into OWL classes, restricting in an iterative way the scope of elements to be transformed, but neither here a right generalization is possible.
- Generalization on attributes: these ones can be converted into OWL datatype properties, whose domain is the union of all Classes (derived from TEI Model Classes) they apply to, and whose range is the datatype assigned to each of them in the XML Schema. However, they also have to be revised in order to define which attributes point to "real" entities and then have to be declared as object properties (e.g. `@who` attribute, a pointer to a person reference; `@source` attribute, a pointer to a bibliographical source).

This basic set of rules does not cope with the modeling into OWL of structural XML content models, for which a mix of OWL objectProperties and restrictions can be used as proposed in [15].

This mapping capture the basic semantic of the TEI XML schema as whole. Some more ontological axioms can be added to specify other semantic assumptions. In fact, OWL allows multiple inheritance of classes.

In many respects, the construction of a formal high-level TEI ontology could be a partially automated process starting from the implicit semantics in the schema. However, the most of semantic restrictions, which cannot be expressed by common Schema Languages (and ODD), should be explicitly and manually stated, as the most of issues related to the creation of a correct taxonomy itself.

3.2 Intensional Semantics of the Elements

We adopt the term intensional semantics since at this level we can find the specific structures of meaning that a markup term has for a specific user or community. For example, think of a specialization in the use of abstract container elements such as `<div>`, `<ab>`, `<seg>` or of the `@type` attribute that define an intensional, more specific and restricted semantics compared to that described at general ontology level (e.g. `<div>` could have a value associated to `@type` choosen from a controlled vocabulary suggested by the TEI model [act | scene | chapter | part] but it could be manage also values defined by a local community).

These ontology specializations can be expressed as:

1. Restrictions on properties and classes that extend the general ontology in OWL.
2. A set of inference rules expressed through Rule Language (like SRWL), which extend the general OWL ontology.
3. Semantic definitions through specialized formalisms such as EARMARK (see [16] and [17] with TEI-based samples).

How can a user possibly declare these local semantic extensions? The most obvious method is to adopt `<constraint>` element-or to introduce a dedicated element-in the ODD personalization that allows a user to declare the relevant ontological constraints in OWL. Those formulas could then be added to the general ontology during ODD processing.

Once verified these situations they will have to be provided in the ontology, originally created starting from the TEI schema, in an iterative process (from documents to ontology and vice versa).

3.3 Extensional Semantics of the Markup Content

However, this strategy does not cover the need to define semantically specific instances of a markup element. For example, assume that in a given markup application `<seg>`element is used as "manifestation of a character's feature". You may need to qualify a single instance of the element, for example, to indicate what particular feature you are encoding.

The last semantic level concerns the extensional semantics of the individual XML elements content within a document. We adopt the term 'extensional' because, in general, it is suitable for fixing the referent of a linguistic expression identified by the markup through its reference to resources (information entities) via URI, or the connection to items in Linked Data Set. This is a case already widely addressed in several projects.

The current TEI scheme already handles the case of simple extensional link with one or more external resource through the `@ref` attribute (whose value is one or more xsd: anyURI). More complex relations with external semantic data could require as complex standoff markup structures.

Three samples from a digital editon of a collection of letters by Vespasiano da Bisticci[4] shows three references `@ref` where the string in natural language could be treated as specific identified entity or resource through URI and it's connected with

---

[4] Vespasiano da Bisticci, *Letters*, ed. by Francesca Tomasi, Bologna, 2013, http://vespasianodabisticciletters.unibo.it.

more complex formal description: proposopraphy form the person <persname>; codicology for the manuscript <bibl>; lexicography for the vocabulary <term>.

```
<persname ref="http://vespasianoletters.it/people.xml#PS">
       Piero Strozi
</persname>

<bibl ref="http://vespasianoletters.it/manuscripts.xml#P_SN>
        <author>Prinio</author>
</bibl>

<term type="binding" ref=" http://vespasianoletters.it/lexicon.xml#leg">
        legaranno
</term>
```

4 Ontology Alignment and Linked Open Data

As we said above, a particularly relevant aspect of the conceptual model definition process will be the check of the existing ontologies in order to ensure maximum portability in all contexts, in a hybrid approach to ontology development. The TEI ontologies Special Interest Group has already done some relevant work in this area, especially thanks to the work of Ore and Eide with CIDOC-CRM [18]. However, beside the most common existent ontologies devoted e.g. to cultural heritage (CIDOC-CRM also in FRBRoo version[5]), archives (EAD[6] and EAC-CPF[7]), metadata exposure (DC[8] and DC terms[9]), other ontologies, developed in other different domains, provide new form of conceptualization. For example, ontologies as FABIO and CITO could be an interesting application case [19]. FABIO is based on the FRBR approach to the document as a complex entity. The stratification of the levels of analyis, as we said above, enrich the description of cultural entities. CITO is useful in order to manage all the citation process, towards the definition of multiple relationships and cross-relationships between data.

This means that an early mapping stage between potential relevant ontologies will be necessary to align the TEI ontology to the most popular conceptual models[10]. We can assert that: once a conceptual model for TEI is defined the next step is the identification of all the pertinent existent ontologies.

---

[5] http://www.cidoc-crm.org/frbr_inro.html.

[6] http://www.loc.gov/ead/.

[7] http://eac.staatsbibliothek-berlin.de/.

[8] http://dublincore.org/.

[9] http://dublincore.org/documents/dcmi-terms/.

[10] See e.g. the Europeana effort in the EDM (Europeana Data Model) proposal: http://pro.europeana. eu/edm-documentation .

Then the alignment process[11] will contribute to refine the model: already shared classes and properties could be encapsulated in the TEI conceptual model and specific classes and properties as a result of the TEI semantic extension could contribute to populate the cloud. In addition to possibility of exchange among models and then communities, ontology alignment is yet another step to ensure validity of conceptualization: indeed, as in an iterative workflow, first releases of the ontology for TEI have to be managed as feasibility studies, that can't be immediately opened into Linked Data cloud.

Such approach, already used by other Schema conversions into ontologies like EAC-CPF [20], grants a granularity of description that is able to satisfy different needs at different times – firstly taxonomic consistency and then specific issues related to various approaches in markup semantics.

The project of TEI conversion into a LOD compliant version consists then in a sequence of steps that could be described as:

a. formalization of the TEI model by converting the schema into OWL classes and properties for a first macro-modelization;
b. revision of the resulted ontology by working on different corpora of XML TEI in order to refine specifications;
c. TEI ontological model mapping onto selected ontologies in order to guarantee interchange but also expressivity of the model in a reuse perspective;
d. adding URI to in-line markup, when needed, in order to be LOD-compliant.

To finalize then the model in a LOD perspective the following methods have to be explored:

e. creation of the RDF triple store by converting the refined XML TEI files and then populating the LOD Cloud;
f. discover of links in the cloud by using semi-automatic methods of entity recognition in other datasets (e.g. `Dbpedia.org`).

5   Conclusions and Perspectives

In our opinion, the possibility of providing a TEI-formalized semantics using Semantic Web standard technology constitutes a good opportunity to achieve these objectives:

1. strictly set out the general semantics of the markup language in order to facilitate the management and research in open and multi-standard contexts, such as large-scale general libraries and large institutional repositories;
2. facilitate interoperability with other standards relevant in the Digital Cultural Heritage (CIDOC-CRM, EAD/EAC-CPF, METS, EDM) context and the inclusion of any XML/TEI repository in the Open Linked Data environment. TEI could be redefined as a Linked Open Vocabulary able to dialog with other LOV datasets either at vocabulary or element level (PREFIX `tei:`)

---

[11] A first general discussion and set of tools in: http://www.ontologymatching.org.

3. facilitate the conversion of already existent TEI based digital libraries in open and linked datasets able to share the LOD cloud. In an aggregator dimension, as the Archive Hub Linked Data[12], the TEI triplestore could benefit from the relationships with pertinent datasets at all the level of features' description
4. provide users with advanced formal tools to define their interpretations of the texts they apply the markup to and give, in this way, the possibility of innovative computational processing based on semantics intended as a reasoner and semantic query engines.

However, the cost and the practical complexity of such an extension are notable and several theoretical problems, format choices and implementation details are still to be defined.

A possible candidate for a test-bed of the ideas presented in this paper could be the forthcoming "TEI Simple" (formerly known as "TEI Nudge" [21]) customization of the TEI scheme. We are looking forward for the first results of the project to start a practical experimentation.

References

All web sites were last visited on 4 December 2015

1. Kruk, S.R., McDaniel, B.: Semantic Digital Libraries. Springer, Heidelberg (2009)
2. Cover, R.: XML and semantic transparency. Technology report, CoverPages (1998). http://xml.coverpages.org/xmlAndSemantics.html
3. Burnard, L.: Resolving the Durand Conundrum. J. Text Encoding Initiative (6) (2013). doi:10.4000/jtei.842
4. Renear, A., Sperberg-McQueen C.M., Huitfeldt C.: Towards a semantics for XML markup. In: Furuta, R., Maletic, J.I., Munson, E. (eds.) Proceedings of the 2002 ACM Symposium on Document Engineering, DocEng 2002. ACM Press, McLean (2002)
5. Renear, A., Sperberg-McQueen, C.M., Huitfeldt, C.: Meaning and interpretation of markup. In: Markup Languages: Theory & Practice vol. 2 no. 3. MIT Press, Cambridge (2000)
6. Tummarello G., Morbidoni C., Pierazzo E.: Toward textual encoding based on RDF. In: ELPUB2005. Challenges for the Digital Content Chain: Proceedings of the 9th ICCC International Conference on Electronic Publishing. Peeters Publishing, Leuven (2005)
7. Peroni S., Gangemi A., Vitali F.: Dealing with markup semantics. In: Ghidini C., Ngonga Ngomo, A., Lindstaedt, S., Pellegrini, T. (eds.) Proceedings the 7th International Conference on Semantic Systems. ACM, New York (2011). doi:10.1145/2063518.2063533
8. Sperberg-McQueen, C.M., Huitfeldt, C.: What is transcription? Literary Linguist. Comput. 23(3), 295–310 (2008)
9. Sperberg-McQueen, C.M., Huitfeldt C., Marcoux Y.: What is transcription? Part 2. Talk given at Digital Humanities 2009, College Park, Maryland (2009). Slides on the Web at http://blackmesatech.com/2009/06/dh2009/

---

12 http://datahub.io/it/dataset/archiveshub-linkeddata.

10. Sperberg-McQueen, C.M., Huitfeldt C., Marcoux Y.: Transcriptional implicature. A contribution to markup semantics. Paper given at Digital Humanities 2014, Lausanne, Switzerland (2014)
11. Shadbolt, N., Hall, W., Berners-Lee, T.: The Semantic Web Revisited. IEEE Intell. Syst. J. **21**, 96–101 (2006)
12. Ivezic, N., Marjanovic, Z.: Mapping XML schema to OWL. In: Doumeingts, G., Müller, J., Morel, G., Vallespir, B. (eds.) Enterprise Interoperability, pp. 243–252. Spinger, Heidelberg (2007)
13. TEI Consortium, (eds.) *TEI P5: Guidelines for Electronic Text Encoding and Interchange*, http://www.tei-c.org/Guidelines/P5/
14. Guarino, N., Welty, C.A.: An overview of OntoClean. In: Staab, S., Studer, R. (eds.) Handbook on Ontologies, pp. 201–220. Springer, Heidelberg (2009)
15. Bedini, I, Gardarin G., Nguyen B.: Transforming XML schema to OWL using patterns. In: 5th IEEE International Conference on Semantic Computing (ICSC), Palo Alto (2011)
16. Peroni S., Vitali F.: Annotations with EARMARK for arbitrary, overlapping and out-of order markup. In: Proceedings of the 2009 ACM Symposium on Document Engineering (DocEng 2009), pp. 171–180. ACM, New York (2009). doi:10.1145/1600193.1600232
17. Barabucci G., Di Iorio A., Peroni S., Poggi F., Vitali F.: Annotations with EARMARK in practice: a fairy tale. In: Tomasi F., Vitali F. (eds.) Proceedings of the first Workshop on Collaborative Annotations in Shared Environments: Metadata, Vocabularies and Techniques in the Digital Humanities (DH-CASE 2013). ACM, New York (2013). doi:10.1145/2517978.2517990
18. Eide Ø., Ore C.E.: TEI, CIDOC-CRM and a Possible Interface between the Two. In: First ADHO International Conference Digital Humanities 2006, pp. 62–65 (2006)
19. Peroni, S., Shotton, D.: FaBiO and CiTO: ontologies for describing bibliographic resources and citations. Web Seman. Sci. Serv. Agents World Wide Web **17**, 33–34 (2012). doi:10.1016/j.websem.2012.08.001
20. Mazzini S., Ricci F.: EAC-CPF ontology and linked archival data. In: Proceedings of the 1st International Workshop on Semantic Digital Archives (SDA) (2011). http://ceur-ws.org/Vol-801/
21. Mueller M.: TEI-Nudge or Libraries and the TEI, Center for Scholarly Communication & Digital Curation Blog (2013). http://sites.northwestern.edu/cscdc/?p=872

Structured Descriptions of Roles, Activities, and Procedures in the Roman Constitution

Yoonmi Chu[✉] and Robert B. Allen

Yonsei University, Seoul, Korea
yoonmichu@gmail.com, rba@boballen.info

Abstract. A highly structured description of entities and events in histories can support flexible exploration of those histories by users and, ultimately, support richly-linked full-text digital libraries. Here, we apply the Basic Formal Ontology (BFO) to structure a passage about the Roman Constitution from Gibbon's *Decline and Fall of the Roman Empire*. Specifically, we consider the specification of Roles such as Consul, Activities associated with those Roles, and Procedures for accomplishing those Activities.

Keywords: BFO · Community models · Digital humanities · Ontologies · Procedures · Roles · Roman Constitution

1 Introduction

1.1 Full-Text Digital Libraries and Community Models

Full-text digital libraries could incorporate rich descriptions which allow flexible linking and interaction with the content. [2] showed how a structured passage of Gibbon's well-known Decline and Fall of the Roman Empire could be used in a novel content browser. A formal description of Roman culture and legal systems would be useful because the organization of the government of the Empire and the rights of its citizens are keys for Gibbon's analysis. Not only has no one proposed a systematically structured description for the Roman Constitution; there are many open issues about how such a framework should be constructed. Here we focus on Roles, Activities, and Procedures because they are central to such a description.

This work also contributes to broader efforts to describe cultural and historical information. Our approach goes beyond using metadata to describe historical documents and artifacts; we describe the dynamic and systematic structures of entities appearing in history as reflected in various writings and other materials. Some of our earlier work examined the description of text from digitized historical newspapers. The newspapers provided relatively succinct descriptions of a broad range of activities of communities in small towns. While some of the events in the newspapers were disjoint we believe they could be unified through modeling the communities on which the newspapers report. Potentially, such community models would allow continuity and linking across events as the basis for a full-text digital library and could also link in a wide range of non-textual materials.

© Springer International Publishing Switzerland 2016
D. Calvanese et al. (Eds.): IRCDL 2015, CCIS 612, pp. 61–67, 2016.
DOI: 10.1007/978-3-319-41938-1_6

1.2   Upper Ontologies

We apply ontologies with rich semantic structure to model complex entities in historical content. Upper ontologies, particularly the BFO (Basic Formal Ontology)[1], provide a typology of entities which is domain neutral. The BFO is especially well developed and is widely used in biology but it has not previously been applied to cultural-heritage materials. BFO is considered as "realist" ontology. DOLCE [9, 10] is another widely used upper ontology which focuses on linguistic and cognitive entities. While most work in digital humanities and digital history has used DOLCE (e.g., [7, 13]), we decided to explore the BFO because the entities we wished to model were explicit social structures such as those described in a constitution or used in a fact-based news article. In some cases, social structures can be highly nuanced and subjective; indeed, modeling them can become highly contentious.

BFO distinguishes between continuants (or endudrants) which persist through time and occurrents (or perdurants) that occur in time and unfold across time, e.g., processes, events, activities and changes [6]. The BFO creates separate ontologies for continuants and occurrents called SNAP and SPAN respectively. A SNAP ontology represents a snapshot of the state of reality which is composed of continuants. By comparison, a SPAN ontology applies to the reality constituted by processual entities that unfold across spatiotemporal and temporal regions. In other words, SPAN ontologies are four dimensional (4D) [6]. Additionally, BFO defines SNAP-SPAN trans-ontology relationships to coordinate these sub-ontologies in a coherent framework. Historical information should be well described because the SNAP entities can depict states of continuants and can participate in a SNAP-SPAN trans-ontology as bearers of occurrents.

2   Roles, Activities, Processes, and Procedures

The BFO includes Roles in the "specifically dependent continuant" class. A BFO Role is a realizable entity that an independent continuant can take on but does not reflect the physical structure of that independent continuant [3]. This means that Roles are optional and their manifestation is a reflection of surrounding circumstances [8]. Separating Roles and the bearer of Roles allows for an individual to hold multiple Roles. The performance of a specific Role is determined by conditions and situations of its bearer, thus we should be able to model the context. [8] proposed a Role representation model to deal with OWL axioms and SWRL rules.

Roles in the BFO have usually been applied to biological processes such as the Role of DNA in reproduction. They have not been applied to the humanities[2]. Social roles imply privileges (or rights as a broader sense) and obligations (or norms or responsibilities as a broader sense) depending on how the Role is specified. For example, a person has the right to vote in an election of the committee president as a member of a committee and at the same time he/she is expected to pay taxes as a citizen.

---

[1] http://www.ifomis.org/bfo.

[2] DOLCE [10] defines social objects that are further divided into Agentive and Non-agentive but it does not address the complexity of the social objects and interaction between them.

In BFO Processes are processual entities in a SPAN ontology that are occurrents or happenings located at temporal or spatiotemporal regions [6]. They involve SNAP entities as their participants and are dependent on their participants. Simple processes are continuous ongoing activity such as "running". Processes in SPAN can be both "dissective" (composed of other processes) and "cumulative" [6].

We define Procedures, separating from Processes, as an "inherent" attribute of social objects such as operating rules in an organization. According to [4], Procedures are similar to closed processes that consist of a definite sequence of actions or activities leading to a specific result. We can describe Procedures with semantic structures defined in BFO. We believe that Procedures are continuants, since they are complex attributes inherent in their bearer and are just specifications of some things that could happen. A Procedure which is composed of Activities is defined as a subclass of *realizable entity* in contrast with Processes which are occurrents[3].

3   Application to the Roman Constitution

Gibbon's famous historical analysis considered the changes in Roman society during the Roman Empire [5]. Gibbon's text includes a large number of social concepts as well as their relationships and interaction. To explore the issues for modeling complex entities and processes we chose a sample passage dealing with Roman Constitution[4]:

> The consuls had succeeded to the kings of Rome, and represented the dignity of the state. They superintended the ceremonies of religion, levied and commanded the legions, and presided in the assemblies both of the senate and people. ... but whenever the senate empowered the first magistrate to consult the safety of the commonwealth, he was raised by that decree above the laws, and exercised, in the defence of liberty, a temporary despotism.[5]

In Fig. 1, we show a partial ontology to represent the concepts of Roles, Rights and Activities of the Senate and the Consuls that are the highest magistrate in the Constitution of Roman Empire. A person who is the Senate has *senate role* and a person who is the Consuls has *first magistrate role* belonged to *consul role*. In this representation, each Role has some Rights, which consist of Activities. If a Role has a Right and the Right that the Role owns has an Activity, then the Role is permitted to perform the Activity. This can be expressed as a SWRL rule and permitted activities of the Role can be inferred it:

rule_1: *role(?x) ∧ rights(?y) ∧ activity(?z) ∧ has right(?x, ?y) ∧ has activity(?y, ?z) -> permitted activity(?x, ?z)*[6]

---

[3] In forthcoming work we also define Workflows. Procedures and Workflows may be related to the Information Artifacts ontology (IAO) and the Software Ontology (SWO). The authority to exercise those, as well as other aspects of the Constitution depends on the interpretation of the basis of social authority which goes back to the Smith/Searle debate.

[4] The Roman Constitution was not a single document but a set of laws. In addition, the Constitution evolved over time – especially in the transition from Republic to Empire.

[5] From Gibbon Sect. 3: The Constitution In The Age Of The Antonines.—Part I.

[6] This rule can also be expressed with property chains in OWL2.

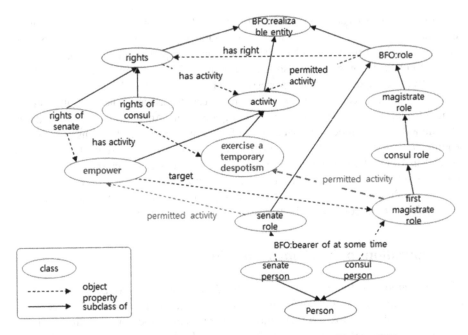

Fig. 1. Representation of the Activities in wartime as specified by Gibbon.

Separating Rights and Activities enables us to dynamically add or delete permitted activities of the Role and also to compose multiple Roles and Rights. Thus, we can describe the variability of Rights that a Role has according to time or context [8].

The final sentence of the sample passage can be regarded as a Procedure which consists of some Activities with sequences to be executed. According to the sentence, the Senate has the right to empower the First Magistrate in wartime. This right could be activated only when the safety of the Roman Commonwealth was threatened.

Figure 2 shows the structure of Processes, Procedures and Activities that compose it. The *wartime* Procedure contains *empower* Activity and *exercise a temporary despotism* Activity, while the former is a prerequisite of *exercise a temporary despotism* Activity. The *prerequisite of* property describes the sequences of these activities. The *wartime* Process, which is a historical event having spatiotemporal regions[7], is associated with the *wartime procedure* with *realized in* property defined in the SNAP-SPAN trans-ontology. This ontological model enables us to describe historical information more semantically and systematically.

---

[7] To focus on the relation of Processes and Procedures having Activities, we simplified the model by excluding spatiotemporal or temporal regions.

4   Discussion and Conclusion

We have examined applying the BFO to the description of Roles, Activities, Procedures and Processes such as required for the description of the Roman Constitution and, more broadly, for governmental structures of communities. With BFO, we can describe complex entities in a 4D perspective. We defined Procedures which consist of activities, distinguishing Procedures from Processes. They are inherent in objects which are its bearers as a complex type of attributes, and can be realized by Processes.

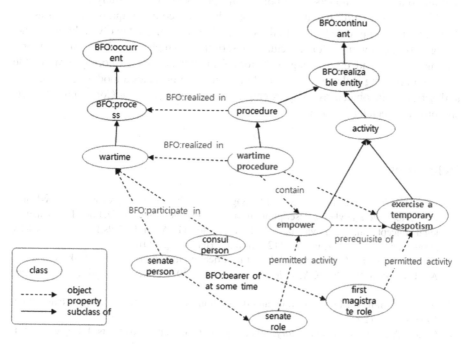

Fig. 2. Example of the relation between Processes and Procedures.

We did not deal with complex workflows in our example; workflows offer several puzzles in terms of ontological modeling. Even the wartime procedure described above has an aspect of workflow since it is granted conditional on whether the Empire is at war. Workflows have same features of programming languages such as conditionals and looping. While ontologies can represent individual states, they do not typically represent full state machines. Rather, state machines are most often associated with programming languages. Some of these issues are covered by a proposed BFO structure known as a Process Profile[8]. However, there is relatively little discussion of it and no formal structures have proposed for it. We suggest that its implementation

---

[8] It describes repeating patterns such as the beating of a heart in BFO2; http://purl.obolibrary.org/obo/bfo/2012-07-20/bfo.owl.

requires concepts such as looping which are integral to programming languages and business process engineering. While importance of programming language features for ontologies is recognized in SPIN[9] and OWL-S,[10] these are for restricted applications and we believe that a broader integration is needed (see [2, 12]).

The AI and Law community has considered ontological models for legal concepts which combine lexical and conceptual meaning [11, 14]. [1] showed the possibility that a legal concept like 'public function' could be modeled in ontologies using FrameNet knowledge. It also showed interconnecting 'LegalRole' and 'Action' through the case study of the 'obligation' concept. We believe there is the opportunity for more work on building ontological models of complex concepts like those we study here.

Although this study has limitations, and there are complex questions such as the difficulty of tracking the changes to the Roman Constitution as it evolved through time, it suggests the potential for structured descriptions which can be useful for representing, linking and discovering of historical knowledge. By exploring some of the issues for applying Roles, Processes and Procedures, it provides a modeling framework to describe social objects as complex entities in the construction of Community Models and broader Societal Models.

References

1. Agnoloni, T., Fernández Barrera, M., Sagri, M.T., Tiscorni, D., Venturi, G.: When a FrameNet-style knowledge description meets an ontological characterization of fundamental legal concepts. In: Casanovas, P., Pagallo, U., Sartor, G., Ajani, G. (eds.) AICOL-II/JURIX 2009. LNCS, vol. 6237, pp. 93–112. Springer, Heidelberg (2010)
2. Allen, R.B., Chu, Y.: Towards a full-text historical digital library. In: Tuamsuk, K., Jatowt, A., Rasmussen, E. (eds.) ICADL 2014. LNCS, vol. 8839, pp. 218–226. Springer, Heidelberg (2014)
3. Arp, R., Smith, B.: Function, role, and disposition in basic formal ontology. Nature Proc. **1941**(1), 1–4 (2008)
4. Galton, A.: Experience and history: processes and their relation to events. J. Logic Comput. **18**, 323–340 (2008)
5. Gibbon, E.: The History of the Decline and Fall of the Roman Empire (1845). http://www.gutenberg.org/files/731/731-h/731-h.htm
6. Grenon, P., Smith, B.: SNAP and SPAN: towards dynamic spatial ontology. Spat. Cogn. Comput. **4**(1), 69–104 (2004)
7. Grossner, K.E.: Representing Historical Knowledge in Geographic Information Systems, Doctoral dissertation, University of California, Santa Barbara (2010)
8. Kozaki, K., Sunagawa, E., Kitamura, Y., Mizoguchi, R.: Role representation model using OWL and SWRL. In: Proceedings of 2nd Workshop on Roles and Relationships in Object Oriented Programming, Multiagent Systems, and Ontologies, pp. 39–46 (2007)
9. Mascardi, V., Cordì, V., Rosso, P.: A comparison of upper ontologies. In: Web-Oriented Architectures, pp. 55–64 (2007)

---

[9] http://www.w3.org/Submission/spin-overview/.

[10] http://www.w3.org/Submission/OWL-S/.

10. Masolo, M., Borgo, S., Gangemini, A., Guarino, N., Oltramari, A.: WonderWeb Deliverable D18 Ontology Library (final). Technical report, ISTC-CNR (2004)
11. Mommers, L.: Ontologies in the legal domain. In: Poli, R., Seibt, J. (eds.) Theory and Applications of Ontology: Philosophical Perspectives, pp. 264–276. Springer, Heidelberg (2010)
12. Puleston, C., Parsia, B., Cunningham, J., Rector, A.: Integrating Object-Oriented and Ontological Representations: A Case Study in Java and OWL, ISWC (2008)
13. Robertson, B: Exploring historical RDF with HEML. Digital Hum. Q. 3(1) (2009). http://www.digitalhumanities.org/dhq/vol/3/1/000026/000026.html
14. Sartor, G., Casanovas, P., Biasiotti, M., Fernández-Barrera, M.: Approaches to Legal Ontologies: Theories, Domains, Methodologies. Springer, New York (2010)

Projects

The AstroBID: Preserving and Sharing the Italian Astronomical Heritage

Mauro Gargano[1]([✉]), Antonella Gasperini[2], Emilia Olostro Cirella[1],
Riccardo Smareglia[3], and Valeria Zanini[4]

[1] INAF-Astronomical Observatory of Capodimonte, Salita Moiariello 16, Naples,
Italy
{gargano,olostro}@oacn.inaf.it
[2] INAF-Astrophysical Observatory of Arcetri, Largo E. Fermi 5, Florence, Italy
gasperi@arcetri.inaf.it
[3] INAF-Astronomical Observatory of Trieste, via Tiepolo 11, Trieste, Italy
smareglia@oats.inaf.it
[4] INAF-Astronomical Observatory of Padua, Vicolo Osservatorio 5, Padua, Italy
valeria.zanini@oapd.inaf.it
http://www.inaf.it

Abstract. The cultural heritage of the National Institute for Astrophysics (INAF), made of rare and modern Books, Instruments and
archival Documents, the AstroBID, marks the milestones in the history
of astronomy in Italy. INAF, in collaboration with the Department of
Physics and Astronomy of the University of Bologna, has developed a
project to preserve, digitize, and valorize its patrimony by creating a
web portal *Polvere di Stelle*. It shows the cultural heritage of 12 libraries
and historical archives, and 13 instrument collections, and allows both
academics and a wider audience to search simultaneously the AstroBID
materials.

Keywords: Astronomical Heritage · Preservation · Digital Infrastructure

1 Italian Astronomical Heritage

The historical and scientific heritage of Italian Astronomy consists of ancient
Books, scientific Instruments, and archival Documents, the AstroBID, which
testify to the important development of astronomy in Italy from pre-Galilean
observations to the present time. Preserved in 12 Astronomical Observatories,
all these objects constitute an interesting and valuable collection, worldwide, in
the field of the history of science. The oldest Italian Observatories hold more than
7000 ancient books (from 1470 to 1830), including 18 Incunabola and 433 Cinquecentine; and they preserve 30 manuscripts also. Some of these books represent
true cultural milestones; the works of Galileo, Copernicus, Ptolemy, Kepler and
Newton (often first editions), considered the banners of the scientific revolution,
have paved the way to modern science.

© Springer International Publishing Switzerland 2016
D. Calvanese et al. (Eds.): IRCDL 2015, CCIS 612, pp. 71–74, 2016.
DOI: 10.1007/978-3-319-41938-1_7

Besides the value due to the content contributing to the history of western culture, these books are also interesting for their fine and precious illustrations. The marvellous star atlases of Hevelius, Doppelmayer, Flamsteed and Bode, the cometographies and selenographies of Northern European astronomers, published in the 16th and 17th centuries, reveal a host of details, illustrated with painstaking care in works of rare beauty that merged art, mythology and science [4]. The oldest document of the National Institute of Astrophysics is a manuscript preserved in the Library of the Copernican Museum in Rome, that dates back to the end of 1300 (Fig. 1). It is a collection of medieval astronomical texts, probably the most popular essays of that period.

The ancient astronomical instruments collection of the Italian Observatories is over 1200 items, from the XI century (Fig. 2) to the first half of the 1900. Exhibited in 13 museums, it consists mainly of quadrants, sextants, telescopes, theodolites, clocks, stopwatches, globes, mathematical instruments, and meteorological instrumentations [2]. Among the most precious instruments, the museum collections preserve some arabic astrolabes, one of the biggest mirror for a telescope made by William Herschel, the telescope used by Schiaparelli to describe the surface of Mars and hypothesize a planet inhabited by Martians, and the instruments manufactured and used by Italian astronomers to realize a "new science", astrophysics.

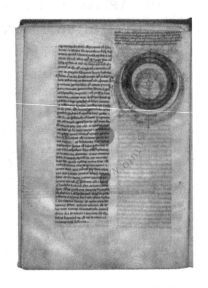

Fig. 1. *Theorica planetarum* by Johannes de Sacrobosco (xiv century). A page from the most ancient manuscript owned by INAF.

Fig. 2. The Arabic astrolabe made by Ibn Sahid el Ibrahim, Valencia, 1096.

The historical archives of the astronomical observatories preserve the documents of some of the oldest scientific institutions in our country: records from countless nights spent at the telescope, beautiful sketches of nebulae, comets and planets, drawn during the observations under an astronomical dome, letters revealing the stream of cognizance to some extraordinary scientific discoveries, journey logbooks, meteorological observations as a continuum line throughout the centuries, settled bills, read books, reports from journeys, maps, sketches.

Over 3 million documents, 122 series containing the fonds of various astronomers are preserved in 12 historical archives [3].

2   *Polvere di Stelle*: the web portal

In order to present and share the AstroBID to the largest number of people, ranging from scientists and historians to amateur astronomers and general public, INAF has realized *Polvere di Stelle* (Stardust)[1] (Fig. 3), the web portal of the Italian astronomical cultural heritage.

Polvere di Stelle presents the modern and ancient library catalogs, the archival inventories, and the museum collections of the Italian Astronomical Observatories and also the astronomical heritage of the Department of Physics and Astronomy of the Bologna University. Besides the historical descriptions for all types of materials, *Polvere di Stelle* allows for simultaneous searches on books, archives, museums, and astronomer's biographies databases, establishing useful interconnections to build particular events and aspects of the history of astronomy.

The AstroBID materials are recorded in different databases following the international standards and the ICCU recommendations for cataloguing modern and ancient books, and manuscripts, for the inventorying of the archive documents, for the description of scientific instruments, artworks, and biographies of astronomers and craftmakers. In addition there are two indexes for authors and bibliographies [5].

The portal permits the performance of interlinking searches among the AstroBID records with simultaneous queries on different databases to build thematic pathways of important astronomical events, discoveries, biographies of astronomers, and the use of astronomical instruments.

Fig. 3. The home page of *Polvere di Stelle* available at www.beniculturali.inaf.it

---

[1] www.beniculturali.inaf.it.

A digital showcase plays a relevant role in *Polvere di Stelle*. Using the know-how for storing and sharing the astronomical data, the Italian data-center for Astronomical Archives, IA2, hosted by the Astronomical Observatory of Trieste, has set up a high availability platform to create a national repository for the digitalized copy of the ancient books. IA2 is a national infrastructure project to implement "a new strategy for preserving and providing access to the astrophysical data heritage". IA2's informatics infrastructure is based on the virtualization and cloud paradigm, hosts data from the main ground based Italian Telescopes and offers proprietary and public data access through user portals and Virtual Observatory (VO) services. All software tools are based on Open Source application and developed in C++, Java and PHP. To best manage all metadata and services information, stored inside, the DMBS plays a main role. Using this infrastructure, and in particular a data cloud storage, we have stored over 100000 pages of about 250 ancient books related to the scientific heritage in the different resolutions: images at 150 DPI are used to publish the books on the web with a watermark on each page, and 300 and 600 DPI images are used to preserve a digital copy of each book and to use them in historical and scientific studies. Hyper resolution images will be also saved as FITS (Flexible Images Transport System). This format is widely used within the astronomical community since 1981. It was developed to ensure long-term preservation of data and documents. In addition to storing images, a FITS file may contain many other additional information inside its keyword header. It is free from legal restrictions and is kept updated by IAU (International Astronomical Union). INAF and Vatican Apostolic Library are working together to extend the FITS keywords dictionary for the needs of cultural heritage data preservation [1].

At present, the digital showcase allows one to consult a little part of the ancient book heritage in a colour digital format and in very good resolution. People can leaf through some terrific volumes like the *Tractatus de Sphaera* by J. Holywood (end of XIV century), and the *De Revolutionibus Orbium Coelestium* by N. Copernicus (1543).

References

1. Allegrezza, S.: Analisi del formato FITS per la conservazione a lungo termine dei manoscritti. Il caso significativo del progetto della Biblioteca Apostolica Vaticana. Digitalia **6**(2), 43–72 (2011)
2. Chinnici, I. (ed.): Astrum 2009: Astronomy and Instruments. Sillabe, Livorno (2009)
3. Gargano, M., Gasperini, A., Mandrino, A.: Polvere di stelle - Stardust: the national historical archive for astronomy on the web. In: LISA VI: 21st Century Astronomy Librarianship. from New Ideas to Action, ASP, San Francisco, vol. 433, pp. 244–247 (2010)
4. Olostro Cirella, E., Caprio, G.: Le Cinquecentine dell'Osservatorio Astronomico di Capodimonte. Giannini, Napoli (2014)
5. Olostro Cirella, E., et al.: The AstroBID: searching through the Italian astronomical heritage. In: LISA VII: Open Science at the Frontiers of Librarianship, ASP, San Francisco, vol. 492, pp. 143–149 (2015)

The EAGLE Europeana Network of Ancient Greek and Latin Epigraphy: A Technical Perspective

Andrea Mannocci, Vittore Casarosa, Paolo Manghi,
and Franco Zoppi$^{(\boxtimes)}$

Consiglio Nazionale delle Ricerche,
Istituto di Scienza e Tecnologie dell'Informazione "A. Faedo",
via Moruzzi 1, 56124 Pisa, Italy
{andrea.mannocci,vittore.casarosa,paolo.manghi,
franco.zoppi}@isti.cnr.it

Abstract. The project EAGLE (Europeana network of Ancient Greek and Latin Epigraphy, a Best Practice Network partially funded by the European Commission) aims at aggregating epigraphic material provided by some 15 different epigraphic archives (about 80 % of the classified epigraphic material from the Mediterranean area) for ingestion to Europeana. The collected material will be made available also to the scholarly community and to the general public, for research and cultural dissemination. This paper briefly presents the main services provided by EAGLE and the challenges encountered for the aggregation of material coming from heterogeneous archives (different data models and metadata schemas, and exchange formats). EAGLE has defined a common data model for epigraphic information, into which data models from different archives can be optimally mapped. The data infrastructure is based on the D-NET software toolkit, capable of dealing with data collection, mapping, cleaning, indexing, and access provisioning through web portals or standard access protocols.

Keywords: Data infrastructure · Aggregation system · Metadata formats · Data interoperability · Data harmonization · Epigraphy · D-NET

1 The EAGLE Project

Ancient inscriptions are a valuable source of information about otherwise undocumented historical events and past laws and customs. However, centuries of unregulated collection by individuals and by different institutions has led to an extremely fractioned situation, where items of the same period or from the same geographical area are presently scattered across several different collections, very often in different cities or countries.

One of the main motivations of the project EAGLE (Europeana network of Ancient Greek and Latin Epigraphy [1], a Best Practice Network partially funded by the European Commission) is to restore some unity of our past by collecting in a single

D. Calvanese et al. (Eds.): IRCDL 2015, CCIS 612, pp. 75–78, 2016.
DOI: 10.1007/978-3-319-41938-1_8

repository information about the thousands of inscriptions now scattered across all Europe.

The collected information (about 1,5 million digital objects at project's end, representing approximately 80 % of the total amount of classified inscriptions in the Mediterranean area) are to be ingested into Europeana, as they represent the origins of the European culture. That information is also made available to the scholarly community and to the general public, for research and cultural dissemination, through a user-friendly portal supporting advanced query and search capabilities.

The EAGLE project comprises 19 partners from 13 European countries. Fifteen partners (called Content Providers) are cultural institutions owning collections of Latin and Greek inscriptions, and are the ones actually providing the data to EAGLE and to Europeana. Four partners (called the Technology Providers) are the ones in charge of setting up the aggregation infrastructure, connecting with Europeana, de-duplicating the received data (the same inscription can appear in the collections of more than one Content Provider) and developing the services available at the EAGLE portal.

In addition to the "normal" query capabilities (full text search a la Google, fielded search, faceted search and filtering), the EAGLE portal supports two applications intended to make the fruition of the epigraphic material easier and more useful. The Mobile Application will enable a (mobile) user to get information about one visible epigraph by taking a picture with a mobile device, and sending it to the EAGLE portal specifying the recognition mode. In Exact Match mode, the EAGLE system will return all the information associated with the recognized image, or a message indicating that the image was not recognized. In Similarity Search mode, the EAGLE system will return a list of the most visually similar epigraphs, ranked in order of similarity.

The Story Telling application will provide tools for an expert user (say a teacher) to assemble epigraphy-based narratives providing an introduction to themes and stories linking various inscriptions together (e.g. all the public works done by an emperor). The stories are then made available at the EAGLE portal, and are (usually) intended for the fruition of the epigraphic material by less knowledgeable users or young students.

Along the same lines, in order to make the epigraphic material more interesting and usable also by non-epigraphists, EAGLE, in collaboration with the Italian chapter of the Wikimedia Foundation, is leading an effort for the enrichment of the epigraphic images and text with additional information and translations into modern languages. This additional material, residing on Wikimedia, is periodically harvested and included in the information associated with each epigraph.

2   The EAGLE Aggregation Infrastructure

As mentioned before, EAGLE aggregates content provided from 15 different archives from all over Europe. While most of them are providing records based on EpiDoc (an application profile of TEI, today the de-facto standard for describing inscription), some archives are supplying records in "personalized" formats. EAGLE aggregates data also from two other different sources: Mediawiki pages, containing translations of inscriptions, and "Trismegistos records", containing information about inscriptions that appear in more than one collection.

The need for expressing queries against such heterogeneous material has led to the definition of a data model being able of relating separate concepts and objects in a seamless way, thus allowing both the scholarly research and the general public to achieve results which could hardly be obtained with the existing EpiDoc archives.

The EAGLE data model [2] consists of an abstract root entity (the Main Object) from which four sub-entities can be instantiated: (*i*) Artefact (capturing the physical nature of an epigraphy); (*ii*) Inscription (capturing the textual and semantic nature of a text region possibly present on an artefact); (*iii*) Visual representation (capturing the information related to the "visual nature" of a generic artefact); (*iv*) Documental manifestation (capturing the description of an inscription's text in its original language and its possible translations in modern languages). All the information to be aggregated in EAGLE will find its place into one or multiple instances of such sub-entities.

The EAGLE Aggregation Infrastructure is built on top of the D-NET software [3], developed by ISTI-CNR in the course of its participation in a number of European projects. D-NET is an open source solution specifically devised for the construction and operation of customized infrastructures for data aggregation, which provides a service-oriented framework where data infrastructures can be built in a LEGO-like approach, by selecting and properly combining the required services [4]. For EAGLE, D-NET has been extended with image processing services to support the Mobile Application(see bottom of Fig. 1). The aggregation process consists of four main phases (see top of Fig. 1):

1. *Metadata mapping.* The definition of the metadata mapping covers two key aspects: (*i*) a *structural mapping* from the archives' local schema to the EAGLE common schema and (*ii*) a *semantic mapping* from the local vocabularies to the EAGLE ones. In cooperation with domain experts from the archives providing records, the structural and semantic rules to map the incoming records into the EAGLE common metadata schema are encoded in the form of XSLT scripts.
2. *Metadata transformation and cleaning.* Metadata records are collected (via FTP, OAI-PMH or other protocols) and processed (using the transformations defined in phase 1) to generate the "EAGLE objects", thus creating the Pre-production Information Space.
3. *Metadata quality control.* The EAGLE records are inspected and validated to identify mapping errors and possible mistakes (e.g., typos). This quality control process may lead to the redefinition of the mapping rules (in Phase 1) and the repetition of Phase 2.
4. *Metadata provisioning.* The EAGLE records that pass Phase 3 are indexed and become available for querying and browsing through the EAGLE portal, or for ingestion to Europeana (after a further transformation to make them compliant with EDM, the Europeana Data Model) or for harvesting through standard APIs by other (external) applications.

In D-NET, data processing is specified by defining *workflows* (i.e. a graph of elementary steps, with optional fork and join nodes) and *meta-workflows* (i.e. a sequence of *workflows*). A (meta)workflow can be easily configured, scheduled and started through a D-NET tool with a graphical user interface, while the implementation of the elementary steps is done by writing programs actually executing the needed

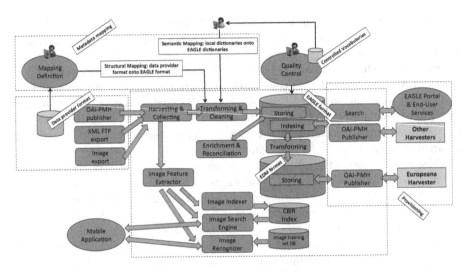

Fig. 1. The EAGLE aggregation infrastructure

processing. For example, the metaworkflow for processing EpiDoc documents consists of the sequence of the following workflows (where each workflow consists in a set of more elementary steps):

- collect (records from an archive);
- transform (the collected records into the EAGLE metadata format);
- clean (metadata quality control);
- index (build the index of the final records for querying and browsing);
- provision (put the final records in the format required by an OAI-PMH harvester).

References

1. The EAGLE project. http://www.eagle-network.eu/
2. Casarosa, V., Manghi, P., Mannocci, A., Ruiz, E.R., Zoppi, F.: A conceptual model for inscriptions: harmonizing digital epigraphy data sources. In: EAGLE International Conference on Information Technologies for Epigraphy and Digital Cultural Heritage in the Ancient World, Paris, 29–30 September and 1 October 2014
3. D-NET Software Toolkit. http://www.d-net.research-infrastructures.eu
4. Manghi, P., Artini, M., Atzori, C., Bardi, A., Mannocci, A., La Bruzzo, S., Candela, L., Castelli, D., Pagano, P.: The D-NET software toolkit: a framework for the realization, maintenance, and operation of aggregative infrastructures. EmeraldInsight Program **48**, 322–354 (2014). doi:10.1108/PROG-08-2013-0045

The TRAME Project – Text and Manuscript Transmission of the Middle Ages in Europe

Emiliano Degl'Innocenti[1]([✉]), Alfredo Cosco[2,3], Fabrizio Butini[1],
Roberta Giacomi[2], and Vinicio Serafini[2]

[1] Fondazione Ezio Franceschini, Florence, Italy
emiliano@fefonlus.it
[2] SISMEL, Florence, Italy
alfredo.cosco@gmail.com
[3] ZKS Foundation, Geneva, Switzerland

Abstract. TRAME is a research infrastructure for medieval manuscripts. The TRAME engine scans a set of sources for searched terms and retrieves links to a wide range of possible information, from simple reference, to detailed manuscript record, to full text transcriptions. Currently, it is possible to perform queries by: free-text, shelfmark, author, title, date, copyst or incipit, on more than 80 selected scholarly digital resources across EU and USA. Since 2014 September 1st, TRAME has entered a new phase and the current work is focused on: extending the meta-search approach to other web resources, leveraging the users interaction to define an ontology for medieval manuscripts, re-designing the front-end towards a new UX approach.

Keywords: Crawler · Meta-crawler · Search engine · Medieval manuscripts · Illuminated manuscripts · Digital humanities · User experience · Design · Responsive · Usability

1 Introduction

TRAME[1] was born in 2011,[2] the main aim is to build a "research infrastructure project focused on promoting interoperability among different digital resources available in the medieval digital ecosystem",[3] by connecting repositories of digitized images of medieval manuscripts, their codicological descriptions, their textual and philological interest, their cultural significance in the context of the european history. Currently it implements a number of features (including simple, shelfmark, advanced search mode etc.) on more than 80 selected scholarly digital resources around western medieval

---

[1] Home page: http://git-trame.fefonlus.it/.

[2] E. Degl'Innocenti, *Trame: Building a Meta Search Tool for the Study of Medieval Literary Traditions* in EVA 2011, Proceedings. Vito Cappellini, James Hemsley (eds.), Bologna, Pitagora, 2011.

[3] TRAME. *Text and Manuscript Transmission of the Middle Ages in Europe. Evolving the System Towards Horizon2020 and VCMS Challenges.* http://www.sismelfirenze.it/index.php?option=com_k2&view=item&task=download&id=68_69e648d4f36e436d0ec96c334a0180a4&Itemid=266&lang=it.

© Springer International Publishing Switzerland 2016
D. Calvanese et al. (Eds.): IRCDL 2015, CCIS 612, pp. 79–85, 2016.
DOI: 10.1007/978-3-319-41938-1_9

manuscripts, authors, and texts across EU and USA, including digital libraries, research databases and other projects from leading institutions.

TRAME is more than just a piece of software: it is a research tool deeply rooted in the international medieval scholarly community, whose development is in line with the Memorandum of Understanding of the COST Action IS1005 "Medieval Europe Medieval Cultures and Technological Resources", representing 260 researchers coming from 39 leading institutions (archives, libraries, universities and research centers) in 24 countries across the EU.

It has been selected for inclusion by the CENDARI e-infrastructure and is part of the DARIAH-IT landscape.

2   How TRAME Engine Works

The crawler engine is written in OO-PHP, the design follows the HMVC Pattern,[4] the RDBMS is MySql and the front-end combines Xhtml and Javascript.

Currently user can choose between more than 80 sources and perform 3 kinds of search: free-text, by shelfmark (city, library, mark) or advanced (title, author, date, incipit, copyst).

... *estendi*...

In function of the "search type", searched terms are pushed to the sources using five methods:

- **GET or POST classes**

The standard *http* method to pass variables by *query string* or a *form*, TRAME uses CURL[5] to build the request. Few sites use a minimal protocol for interoperability of medieval manuscripts.[6] Based on TEI, it provides the base set of information useful for TRAME: a shelfmark and a URL.

- **CACHED class**

Some sites are not directly searchable, others have a limited records number, some have both of these features. For those sources TRAME uses MySQL tables where it imports any possible relevant content. Tables are not public and are only used to perform a better and faster search, the result links point to the original source.

---

[4] "The HMVC pattern decomposes the client tier into a hierarchy of parent-child MVC layers", cf. http://www.javaworld.com/article/2076128/design-patterns/hmvc–the-layered-pattern-for-developing-strong-client-tiers.html.

[5] CURL is a library for transferring data with URL syntax, cf. http://curl.haxx.se/ and http://php.net/manual/it/book.curl.php.

[6] http://git-trame.fefonlus.it/TRAME_protocol_v1.pdf and http://www.tei-c.org/index.xml.

- **SPIRIT class**

Some sites perform searches by a javascript UI, using AJAX[7] calls to show the results. The way to query those sources is a *headless browser*[8] and TRAME uses *casperjs* and *phantomjs*[9] to do this.

Each class, customized for every source, parses the response using *reg-ex* and/or *PHP Simple Html Dom.*[10]

In closing, another class renders and composes the result as a list of shelfmarks and titles linked to the original sources.

3 Extending the Meta-Search Approach

Since September the 1st, the aim is to extend the meta-search approach to other web resources (libraries, portals, individual research projects), using various tools and technologies.

Moreover, the TRAME team is extending the engine in two other ways:

- make TRAME a tool to build a knowledge base for medieval manuscripts;
- ensure a better user experience,

3.1 New Resources

Adding new resources in TRAME implies a deep analysis on sources query methods and of the response code, until 2013 of December 12 new sources were added (Table 1).

To achieve the above we added:

1. a new library to simplify the process to identify and extract pieces of code from results along *reg-ex*:

- **Simple HTML DOM** (http://simplehtmldom.sourceforge.net/);

1. three new tools to perform searches *via* javascript and AJAX interfaces:

- **phantomjs** (http://phantomjs.org/) → An open source headless web-browser, *i.e.* the toolkit to scrape sites;

---

[7] http://www.adaptivepath.com/ideas/ajax-new-approach-web-applications/.

[8] A headless browser may be defined as "a piece of software, that accesses web pages but doesn't show them to any human being" (http://durandaljs.com/documentation/Making-Durandal-Apps-SEO-Crawlable.html).

[9] *phantomjs* (http://phantomjs.org/) is an open source headless browser, *casperjs* (http://casperjs.org/) is a framework built on top of it.

[10] A open source HTML DOM library, written in PHP5, that makes easy to manipulate HTML http://simplehtmldom.sourceforge.net/.

Table 1. New sites added

SITE	Class name	Type	Sources
Schoenberg Database of Manuscripts at UPENN Libraries http://dla.library.upenn.edu/dla/schoenberg	SHON	GET	220889
Manuscripts in the Library of St John's College, Cambridge http://www.joh.cam.ac.uk/library/special_collections/manuscripts/medieval_manuscripts/	SJCAM	CACHE	277
KUL List of microfilmed manuscripts http://hiw.kuleuven.be/apps/microfilm/microfilm.php	KULEUVEN	POST	4807
The MacKinney Collection of Medieval Medical Illustrations http://dc.lib.unc.edu/cdm/search/collection/mackinney/	MACKINNEY	GET	1041
Early Manuscripts at Oxford University http://image.ox.ac.uk/	OXFORDMS	CACHE	90
Beinecke Digital Collections http://brbl-dl.library.yale.edu/	BDC	GET	127641
University of Glasgow http://special.lib.gla.ac.uk/manuscripts/search/	GLASUL	POST	N/d
München http://daten.digitale-sammlungen.de	MDZ	CACHE	1300
LUND University library http://laurentius.ub.lu.se	LUND	CACHE	71
Biblioteca Municipale di Lione http://florus.bm-lyon.fr	BMLYON	CACHE	55
Univeristy Libaries in South Carolina http://digital.tcl.sc.edu/	ULSC	CACHE	264
Medieval Manuscript in Dutch Collections http://www.mmdc.nl/static/site/search/	MMDC	SPIRIT	N/d

- **casperjs** (http://casperjs.org/) → An open source navigation scripting & testing utility for PhantomJS;
- **php-casperjs** (https://github.com/alwex/php-casperjs) → An open source php wrapper for *casperjs*.

A new class, called **SpiritSite.class.php**, has been written to manage the process.

We introduced these new libraries because *CRUL* and *Simple HTML Dom* can only parse synchronous HTML and cannot interact with the page, we introduced the *headless browser* to manage asynchronous calls (AJAX) as in **Medieval Manuscript in Dutch Collections** (http://www.mmdc.nl/static/site/search/).

3.2   Building a Knowledge Base on Medieval Manuscripts

Among others, managing TRAME showed difficulty to know what users do with the site.

During the development process of the engine the issue concerning the interaction between users and the TRAME application raised, to manage that we added an *analytics* back-end, that is made by a set of php functions:

- Tracking users visiting TRAME without performing any search;
- Tracking users performing searches recording:
  - Target resources;
  - Searched terms;
- Recording the user interaction with the result sets.

During this process the team realized that those data were also useful to populate an ontology using a **bottom → up/user driven** pattern.

So we decided to start from those data to design the part of TRAME that will be connected with CENDARI[11] infrastructure following this design:

1. A user performs a search;
2. TRAME logs information about the search and builds a list with relevant resources;
3. Leveraging on above information (i.e. the log) TRAME performs the same search using a *headless browser* approach to import selected pieces of information from web pages:

   - the couple *phantomjs* + *casperjs* works fine also to build a data scraper, through which you can use CSS, Xpath or DOM selectors. Moreover the script follows relevant links to connected pages and imports again data from them;

1. The *scraper* produces a set of XML files with info about authors, manuscript, places etc. to be used by other internal or external knowledge extraction services.

The ontology is parsed by a *Name Entity Recognition* (NER), this process generates an *untrusted* ontology, it is then submitted to a validation, using specific tools, by domain experts.

The validation leads to a *trusted* ontology that can be queried by ad hoc instruments including the TRAME tool OntoQuery[12] and a SPARQL-endpoint.

Both the trusted than the untrusted ontology are hosted in a 'triple-store', at this time our choose was for OpenRDF SESAME[13] as front-end of Openlink Virtuoso[14].

---

[11] "CENDARI (Collaborative European Digital Archive Infrastructure) is a research collaboration aimed at integrating digital archives and resources for research on medieval and modern European history." cf. http://www.cendari.eu/about-cendari/.

[12] Right now OntoQuery is developing and populated by an ontology test.

[13] "Sesame is a de-facto standard framework for processing RDF data. This includes parsing, storing, inferencing and querying over such data. It offers an easy-to-use API that can be connected to all leading RDF storage solutions."cf. http://rdf4j.org/.

[14] cf. http://virtuoso.openlinksw.com/.

3.3   Improving the TRAME User Experience

Between 2013 and 2014 there have been some major changes in the Web, just to say two: the mobile internet exceeded the pc browsing,[15] HTML5 became an official W3C standard.[16]

So the TRAME team thought to re-design the tool, whose first step is to include the engine in a php *fast development framework*.

Why?

- Code maintenance and reuse
- Faster further code development
- Complete separation of engine core from user interfaces
- DB agnostic interfaces
- Implementation of caching mechanisms for a faster response
- Form validation
- Session handling.

Our choice was for CODEIGNITER,[17] it is an open source framework, has a small footprint, is fast and complete; moreover, there is a CMF[18] script built on top of it with some essential features. It's named NotOnlyCMS[19] and provides:

- Access Control List (ACL)
- Scaffolder
- Admin area
- HTML5 Templating with **Bootstrap**.[20]

The introduction of an ACL makes possible to add services to registered users like:

- User shelf for sets of sources
- Pre-built sources sets
- Sort results
- Export results (XML, RDF, FIRB, TEI, RSS)
- Share results on different channels (email, blog, social networks)
- Evaluate results (rating or Like).

---

[15] Cf. http://searchenginewatch.com/sew/opinion/2353616/mobile-now-exceeds-pc-the-biggest-shift-since-the-internet-began.

[16] To read the specs from W3c: http://www.w3.org/TR/html5/ , for an overview on creation of the HTML5 standards see Paul Ford, *The Group That Rules the Web*, The New Yorker, Nov 20, 2014, http://www.newyorker.com/tech/elements/group-rules-web.

[17] CODEIGNITER (http://www.codeigniter.com/) is maintained by the British Columbia Technology Institute (http://www.bcit.ca/cas/computing/).

[18] CONTENT MANAGEMENT FRAMEWORK, a Framework with common pre-built CMS-like features.

[19] The code is on Github: https://github.com/goFrendiAsgard/No-CMS.

[20] Bootstrap is a HTML5 framework built by *twitter* and released free, cf. http://getbootstrap.com/.

The Bootstrap integration means that the next UI will be **prototyped** and **responsive;** furthermore, to get a better **usability** the implementation of a Bootstrap extension called **Assets Framework** is on the ground:

> *"Assets gives you Sect. 508 compliant, cross-browser compatible UI components that you can use in your accessible web site or web application. Assets is an accessible, responsive, and modern framework."*[21]

3.4   TRAME Goes Social

Renewing the project we decided to pay attention to the Internet and Social Networks, a blog has been activated, that will start on January/February 2015:

http://trameproject.blogspot.it/.

We release news in two SN channels too:

Twitter: https://twitter.com/trameproject

Facebook: https://www.facebook.com/trameproject

---

[21] *cf.* http://assets.cms.gov/resources/framework/3.0/Pages/, *for further information on Sect. 508 see:* http://www.hhs.gov/web/508

The PREFORMA Project: Federating Memory Institutions for Better Compliance of Preservation Formats

Linda Cappellato[1], Nicola Ferro[1(✉)], Antonella Fresa[2], Magnus Geber[3], Börje Justrell[3], Bert Lemmens[4], Claudio Prandoni[2], and Gianmaria Silvello[1]

[1] Department of Information Engineering, University of Padua, Padua, Italy
{cappellato,ferro,silvello}@dei.unipd.it
[2] Promoter, Peccioli, Italy
{fresa,prandoni}@promoter.it
[3] National Archives of Sweden, Stockholm, Sweden
{borje.justrell,magnus.geber}@riksarkivet.se
[4] PACKED, Centre of Expertise in Digital Heritage, Brussels, Belgium
bert@packed.be

Abstract. In this paper, we describe the motivations, objectives and organization of the *PREservation FORMAts for culture information/ e-archives (PREFORMA)* project, a *Pre-Commercial Procurement (PCP)* project focused on conformity check of ingested files for the long-term preservation.

1 Introduction

Memory institutions, in Europe and elsewhere, are facing a situation when transfers of electronic documents or other electronic media content for long term preservation are continuously increasing. Data are normally stored in specific file formats for documents, images, sound, video etc. that are produced by software from different providers. This software is controlled neither by the institution that produces the files, nor by the institution that holds the archive. There is a risk that data objects meant for preservation, passing through an uncontrolled generative process, can jeopardise the whole preservation exercise.

PREservation FORMAts for culture information/e-archives (PREFORMA)[1] is a *Pre-Commercial Procurement (PCP)* project (2014-2017), co-funded by the European Commission under its FP7-ICT Programme. Its main objective is to give memory institutions full control of the process for testing the conformity of files to be ingested into their archives. This shall be obtained by developing a set of tools which will enable the testing process to happen within an iteration that is under full control of the institutions.

The paper is organized as follows: Sect. 2 provides an overview of the PCP instrument; Sect. 3 describes the overall approach adopted by the PREFORMA project for facing the problem of conformance check of file formats for long-term preservation; finally, Sect. 4 briefly reports on the current status of the project.

---

[1] http://www.preforma-project.eu/.

D. Calvanese et al. (Eds.): IRCDL 2015, CCIS 612, pp. 86–91, 2016.
DOI: 10.1007/978-3-319-41938-1_10

2   Pre-Commercial Procurement

PCP[2] is an instrument which has been pioneered by the European Commission in the FP7 and is now fully part of Horizon 2020. PCP is appropriate when the required improvements are so technologically demanding that there are no near-to-the-market solutions yet and new R&D is needed. PCP can then be used to compare the pros and cons of alternative competing approaches and to de-risk the most promising innovations step-by-step via solution design, prototyping, development and first product testing.

PCP is a competition-like procurement method which enables public sector bodies to engage with innovative businesses and other interested organisations in development projects, to arrive at innovative solutions that address specific public sector challenges and needs. The new innovative solutions are created through a phased procurement of development contracts to reduce risk.

PCP operates by clustering together stakeholders in a given domain – memory institutions in the case of PREFORMA – which group together in order to face a common technological challenge. The stakeholders consortium is in charge of describing the expected technological solution, specifying its needed features and characteristics, and defining how alternative approaches will be compared and assessed in order to understand their pros and cons. The consortium manages an open call for tenders where technological suppliers can apply and the selected suppliers will go ahead with the design and implementation of the requested technological solution. The consortium is responsible for monitoring the progress of the suppliers work towards the first product testing and for evaluating the final solution developed by the suppliers in order to understand which one best fits with their actual needs.

Several areas are now experimenting the PCP instrument with a range of successful projects: health care and elderly care, transportation, energy, education, safety and public administration [2].

The PCP instrumente has several benefits, among which, to help:

- driving innovation in the public sector;
- reducing fragmentation in the demand of the public sector;
- stimulating the ICT developers to offer more challenging solutions;
- reducing the time-to-market of high-tech solutions.

Moreover, in some areas where there is less abundance of funding, as it is often the case of cultural heritage, grouping together stakeholders may help in promoting the development of required technologies whose costs would not be affordable by the single stakeholder alone.

3   The PREFORMA Approach

PREFORMA aims to establish a set of tools and procedures for gaining full control over the technical properties of digital content intended for long-term preservation by memory institutions [11].

---

[2] http://ec.europa.eu/digital-agenda/en/pre-commercial-procurement.

The procurement, following the rules for tenders in public sector, will match the memory institutions professional knowledge and the supplier's skills in development and promotion of products, creating a win-win situation. Joint procurement enables PREFORMA to build a sustainable network of common interest, where the public procurers can remain in contact and cooperate beyond the EC funding period.

The main objective of the project is the development and deployment of an open source software licensed reference implementation for file format standards aimed for any memory institution (or other organisation with a preservation task) wishing to check conformance with a specific standard. This reference implementation, called the *conformance checker* will consist of a set of modular tools, which will be validated against specific implementations of specifications of standards relevant to the PREFORMA project and used by the European memory institutions for preserving their different kind of data objects.

In order to demonstrate effectiveness (and refine) these conformance checkers, they will be developed in an iterative process with multiple releases and with a number of experiments with "real" data sets (files) from memory institutions during each iteration.

A conformance checker:

- verifies whether a file has been produced according to the specifications of a standard file format, and hence,
- verifies whether a file matches the acceptance criteria for long-term preservation by the memory institution,
- reports in human and machine readable format which properties deviate from the standard specification and acceptance criteria, and
- performs automated fixes for simple deviations in the metadata of the preservation file.

The conformance checker software developed by PREFORMA is intended for use within the *Open Archival Information System (OAIS)* Reference Framework [6] and development is guided by the user requirements provided by the memory institutions that are part of the PREFORMA consortium. The conformance checker facilitates memory institutions in obtaining sufficient control of the information in an OAIS Archive, provided to the level needed to ensure Long Term Preservation [12]. In particular, the conformance check enables implementation of the following OAIS functions [12]: (i) *Quality assurance* at ingestion, validating the successful transfer of the *Submission Information Package (SIP)* to the temporary storage area; (ii) *Generate AIP* at ingestion, transforming one or more SIPs into one or more *Archival Information Packages (AIPs)* that conform to the Archives data formatting standards and documentation standards; and, (iii) *Archival Information Update* at ingestion, providing a mechanism for updating (repackaging, transformation) the contents of the Archive.

The media types addressed by PREFORMA are: (i) *text* for establishing a reference implementation for PDF/A [7–9]; (ii) *images* for establishing a reference implementation for uncompressed TIFF [4,5]; and, (iii) *audio-video* for establishing a reference implementation for an audiovisual preservation file, using

FFV1[3], Dirac[4] or JPEG2000 [10] for encoding video or moving image, uncompressed LPCM [3] for encoding sound and MKV[5] or OGG[6] for wrapping audio- and video-streams in one file.

The experience of applying the reference implementation to the format standards and other observations from the development will be used by PREFORMA to give feedback to relevant standardization organizations and other relevant stakeholder groups (e.g. legislators and other suppliers). Such feedbacks can be used to detail the precise interpretation of the specification during the creation of new versions of the standards.

4   Status of PREFORMA

PREFORMA has been launched in January 2014 and, on April 4th, 2014, it organised an Information Day[7] event in Brussels to present the call for tender, which has been launched as part of the PCP.

The call for tender opened on June 12th, 2014 and closed on August 12th, 2014 with a budget of 2,805,000 euros. 16 high-quality proposals have been submitted to the call out of which 6 have been selected[8] for continuing with the subsequent first design phase, which started in November 2014.

The first design phase will terminated in late February 2015 and the 6 suppliers which won the tender have been evaluated again according to well-defined criteria [1] in order to select those worth continuing with the subsequent development phase. The outcomes of the first evaluation phase have been reported on early March 2015 during a workshop which will be organized in Brussels[9].

After having analyzed the technical and functional specifications submitted by the six groups that completed the design phase, PREFORMA chose the three consortia awarded with contracts for the prototyping phase, which will last until December 2016.

The three awardees are the veraPDF Consortium (led by the Open Preservation Foundation and the PDF Association), who is working on the compliance checker for the PDF/A standard for documents; Easy Innova, who is working on the TIFF standard for digital still images; and MediaArea, who is working on a set of open source standards for moving images, namely: the Matroska wrapper, the FFv1 video codec and LPCM for audio streams.

Connected to their work in PREFORMA Easy Innova and their partner University of Basel are leading an initiative to create an ISO Standard to optimize the TIFF format definition for archival purposes, the so called TI/A Standard Initiative[10].

---

[3] http://www.ffmpeg.org/~michael/ffv1.html.

[4] http://diracvideo.org/.

[5] http://www.matroska.org/.

[6] https://xiph.org/ogg/.

[7] http://www.digitalmeetsculture.net/article/follow-up-of-the-preforma-information-day/.

[8] http://www.preforma-project.eu/successful-proposals.html.

[9] http://www.preforma-project.eu/design-phase-1-final-workshop.html.

[10] http://www.ti-a.org/.

The first releases of the conformance checkers, developed by the three suppliers during the first part of the prototyping phase, are now available for download on the Open Source Portal section of the PREFORMA website[11]. This section provides an overview and references to each open source project, acting as an entry point for all interested suppliers and memory institutions and allowing easy navigation to all externally hosted resources.

The preliminary result of the prototyping phase will be presented and demonstrated during the "Open Source Preservation Workshop Serving the Cultural Heritage", the first in a series of international events planned by PREFORMA. The workshop will take place in Stockholm on April 7, 2016, and will be hosted at the National Library of Sweden[12].

The event will feature keynote presentations by representatives from the PREFORMA project and the open source community, live demonstrations of the three conformance checkers for electronic documents, images and AV files by the suppliers working in the project (veraPDF, Easy Innova, MediaArea) and an informal networking event where all the attendees can share experiences, meet the PREFORMA developers and learn about the tools.

This event is aimed at anyone interested in digital preservation and cultural heritage: developers who want to contribute code to the PREFORMA tools; memory institutions or other cultural heritage organisations involved in (or planning) digital preservation initiatives; standardisation bodies maintaining the technical specifications of preservation file formats; any other person interested in cooperating with us in defining open digital preservation standards.

In addition to the public events, PREFORMA is very much committed to communicate online with its community. To this aim, the project developed two instruments that are constantly updated and monitored to exchange ideas and get feedbacks from all the interested people: the project website[13] and the project blog[14].

Furthermore, fruitful cooperation has been established with many other institutions, organisations and projects that expressed their interest to cooperate with PREFORMA to test the software prototypes and to improve the conformance checkers. In this light, it is worth citing BenchmarkDP[15], an interdisciplinary multi-year research project funded by the Vienna Science and Technology Fund, and Europeana Space[16], an EU-funded CIP Best Practice Network. In the first case, methodologies and approaches of BenchmarkDP could be useful in PREFORMA in establishing an objective frame of reference for the evaluation of the conformance checkers, while in the second case the aim is to test the integration of the open source conformance checkers in the Technical Space developed by Europeana Space.

---

[11] http://www.preforma-project.eu/open-source-portal.html.
[12] http://opensourceworkshop.preforma-project.eu/.
[13] http://www.preforma-project.eu/.
[14] http://www.digitalmeetsculture.net/projects/preforma/.
[15] http://benchmark-dp.org/.
[16] http://www.europeana-space.eu/.

Overall, the experience of PREFORMA is demonstrating that putting in place a joint PCP is very challenging, but it is also offering an opportunity of growth and learning, not only for the procurers (namely the memory institutions) but also for the technical partner who are supporting the implementation of the call.

References

1. Agosti, M., Ferro, N., Lemmens, B., Silvello, G.: Deliverable D8.1 - Competitive Evaluation Strategy. PREFORMA PCP Project, EU 7FP, Contract N. 619568, December 2014. http://www.digitalmeetsculture.net/wp-content/uploads/2014/12/PREFORMA_D8.1_Competitive-evaluation-strategy_v1.0_no-appendix.pdf
2. European Commission: Innovation Procurement - The power of the public purse, May 2014. http://ec.europa.eu/information_society/newsroom/cf/dae/document.cfm?doc_id=5443
3. IEC 60958: Digital audio interface - Part 1: General. Standard IEC 60958-1 Ed. 3.1 b:2014 (2014)
4. ISO 12234-2: Electronic still-picture imaging – Removable memory – Part 2: TIFF/EP image data format. Recommendation ISO 12234-2:2001 (2001)
5. ISO 12639: Graphic technology – Prepress digital data exchange – Tag image file format for image technology (TIFF/IT). Recommendation ISO 12639:2004 (2004)
6. ISO 14721: Space data and information transfer systems – Open archival information system (OAIS) – Reference model. Recommendation ISO 14721:2012 (2012)
7. ISO 19005-1: Document management – Electronic document file format for long-term preservation – Part 1: Use of PDF 1.4 (PDF/A-1). Recommendation ISO 19005-1:2005 (2005)
8. ISO 19005-2: Document management – Electronic document file format for long-term preservation – Part 2: Use of ISO 32000-1 (PDF/A-2). Recommendation ISO 19005-2:2011 (2011)
9. ISO 19005-3: Document management – Electronic document file format for long-term preservation – Part 3: Use of ISO 32000-1 with support for embedded files (PDF/A-3). Recommendation ISO 19005-3:2012 (2012)
10. ISO/IEC 15444: Information technology – JPEG 2000 image coding system: Core coding system. Recommendation ISO/IEC 15444-1:2004 (2004)
11. Lemmens, B., Elfner, P., Lundell, B., Prandoni, C., Fresa, A.: Deliverable D2.2 - Tender Specifications. PREFORMA PCP Project, EU 7FP, Contract N. 619568, June 2014. http://www.digitalmeetsculture.net/wp-content/uploads/2014/05/PREFORMA_D2.2_Tender-Specifications_v2.1.pdf
12. The Consultative Committee for Space Data Systems (CCSDS): Reference Model for an Open Archival Information System (OAIS). Magenta Book, Issue 2. Recommended Practice CCSDS 650.0-M-2, June 2012. http://public.ccsds.org/publications/archive/650x0m2.pdf

Models and Applications

Keep, Change or Delete? Setting up a Low Resource OCR Post-correction Framework for a Digitized Old Finnish Newspaper Collection

Kimmo Kettunen[✉]

Center for Preservation and Digitisation,
National Library of Finland, Mikkeli, Finland
kimmo.kettunen@helsinki.fi

Abstract. There has been a huge interest in digitization of both hand-written and printed historical material in the last 10–15 years and most probably this interest will only increase in the ongoing Digital Humanities era. As a result of the interest we have lots of digital historical document collections available and will have more of them in the future.

The National Library of Finland has digitized a large proportion of the historical newspapers published in Finland between 1771 and 1910 [1–3]; the collection, Digi, can be reached at http://digi.kansalliskirjasto.fi/. This collection contains approximately 1.95 million pages in Finnish and Swedish, the Finnish part being about 2.385 billion words. In the output of the Optical Character Recognition (OCR) process, errors are common especially when the texts are printed in the Gothic (Fraktur, blackletter) typeface. The errors lower the usability of the corpus both from the point of view of human users as well as considering possible elaborated text mining applications. Automatic spell checking and correction of the data is also difficult due to the historical spelling variants and low OCR quality level of the material.

This paper discusses the overall situation of the intended post-correction of the Digi content and evaluation of the correction. We shall present results of our post-correction trials, and discuss some aspects of methodology of evaluation. These are the first reported evaluation results of post-correction of the data and the experiences will be used in planning of the post-correction of the whole material.

Keywords: Historical newspaper collections · OCR post-correction · Evaluation

1 Introduction

Newspapers of the 19th and early 20th century were many times printed in the Gothic (Fraktur, blackletter) typeface in Europe. It is well known that the typeface is difficult to recognize for OCR software [5, 6]. Other aspects that affect the quality of the OCR recognition are the following, among others [6, 7]: quality of the original source and microfilm, scanning resolution and file format, layout of the page, OCR engine training, etc.

D. Calvanese et al. (Eds.): IRCDL 2015, CCIS 612, pp. 95–103, 2016.
DOI: 10.1007/978-3-319-41938-1_11

As a result of these difficulties scanned and OCRed document collections have a varying number of errors in their content. The number of errors depends heavily on the period and printing form of the original data. Older newspapers and magazines are more difficult for OCR; newspapers from the 20th century are easier (cf. for example data of [8] that consists of a 200 year period of The Times of London from 1785 to 1985). There is no clear measure of the number of errors that makes the material useful or less useful for some purpose, and the use purposes of the digitized material vary hugely. A linguist who is interested in the forms of the words needs as error free data as possible; a historian who interprets the texts on a more general level may be satisfied with text data that has more errors.

OCR errors in digitized text collections may have several harmful effects, one of the most important being possibly worse searchability of the documents in the collections. Ranking of the documents in search result list is usually clearly harmed. With high-enough word level accuracy of the OCRed collections searchability is not harmed significantly according to Taghva et al. [9]. Tanner et al. [10] suggest that word accuracy rates less than 80 % are harmful for search, but when the word accuracy is over 80 %, fuzzy search capabilities of search engines should manage the problems caused by word errors.

Other effects of poor OCR quality will show in the more detailed processing of the documents, such as sentence boundary detection, tokenization and part-of-speech-tagging, which are important in higher-level natural language processing tasks [11]. Part of the problems may be local, but part will cumulate in the whole pipeline of NLP processing causing errors. Thus the quality of the OCRed texts is the cornerstone for any kind of further usage of the material.

2   Framework of Post-correction

Correction of the OCR output can be done interactively during the OCR process and interactively or non-interactively after the OCR process has finished. Then it can be based on crowdsourcing or automatic correction. Crowdsourcing with the Digi data has been tried with small amount of data [12], but as the amount of data is ca. 2.385 G words, this approach is clearly not feasible. It is obvious that partial or total re-OCRing and automatic post-correction are the only realistic ways of improving the quality of the data. We shall concentrate on the automatic post-correction in our discussion.

In [4] we evaluated the quality of the Finnish Digi data with seven smallish samples which have about 212 000 words altogether. The results of the evaluation show that the quality varies from about 60 % word accuracy at worst to about 90 % accuracy at best. The evaluation samples, however, are small, and it is hard to estimate what the overall quality of the data is. We expect it to be somewhere in the range of 50–80 % accuracy, but there may be a lot of variation. As the spelling error examples of [4] show, there are lots of really hard misspellings in the data, up to Levenshtein distance of 8 and even further from that. A detailed analysis with a modern Finnish morphological analyser

Omorfi[1] [13], has shown, that about 69 % of the tokens in the collection can be recognized. If *v/w* variation and estimation of out-of-vocabulary words is taken into account, the estimated recognition rate is about 74–75 %. The detailed analysis showed that about 625 M of the words in the collection are unrecognized, and most of them are OCR errors, and probably at least half of them hard errors.

2.1 Post-correction

Our discussion of OCR post-correction in this paper concerns non-word error detection and isolated word error correction as defined in Kukich [14]. Non-word detection detects words that do not occur in the used dictionary or wordlist. Isolated word correction tries to correct single words out of their context. There are several techniques for doing this, and Kukich [14], for example, lists six different approaches. In our result examples we will show results of one particular technique, minimum edit distance aka Levenshtein distance. In this phase we do not aim to do real-world spelling-correction, i.e. context sensitive word correction, as this would clearly be out of the scope of our means and resources.

OCR result evaluation and post-correction evaluation are based on character level match between the characters of the output of the OCR results and the original "error free" data. The originals used as the comparison – many times known as ground truth - are usually hand-edited material or good quality parallel digital versions of the material. Due to lack of availability of high quality comparison material, evaluations of the digitation process and its post-correction are mainly based on quite small samples, which is inevitable.

2.2 Evaluation Data

As evaluation data we use six of the seven parallel samples used in [4]. One of the samples is too large to be used with the OCR Frontiers toolkit and was omitted. Number of words in these six corpuses is about 63 000. Besides that we have two different compiled wordlists. The wordlists are 3850_L (word count 3855), and 3850L_8000 M (word count 11 971). 3850_L has been compiled in Department of Modern Languages at the University of Helsinki. 3850L_8000 M is a mixture of the data of Crohns and Sundell [12] with 8116 words from the crowd-sourced data combined with the 3850_L wordlist. Both of these lists have word pairs where one is the misspelled word and the other the correct version. The accuracy of the lists has not been intellectually checked, they are used on as is basis.

Some comments on the nature of the evaluation data are in order. Newspaper data is realistic in its error counts, and the six different corpuses have different number of errors, as shown in Table 1. Word pair lists are more artificial in their distributions. 3850_L word list has an error percentage of about 17 % (3195 correct word pairs and

---

[1] https://github.com/flammie/omorfi.

660 erroneous ones), which seems low compared to our real data. 3850L_8000 M contains 3393 correct word pairs (72 % errors).

2.3 Evaluation Measures

There are various possible measures to use in OCR post-correction evaluation. In our quality assessment of the Digi data [4] we used word accuracy, word error rate, precision, recall and Fmean for measuring the number of errors the evaluation samples have. We used four different readymade software for the analysis. Two of them were dedicated OCR evaluation software, two MT quality evaluation software. One of them, OCR Frontiers Toolkit 1.0[2], which measures word accuracy, is also used in this paper because the software is able to evaluate the parallel newspaper data comparing the original data to output of the spelling correction with one word per line. Word level accuracy is not a very good measure while it is only sensitive to the number of errors in comparison and does not show details of correction [15: 269]. With this material, however, it is the most suitable available measure, as the data is not in one-to-one correspondence on word level.

For the wordlist data we have compiled later we use recall, precision and F-score [15: 268–269]. Given that we have tuples of error, original and correction, <$1, $2, $3> , we can define true positives, false positives, false negatives and true negatives as follows using Gnu-AWK's notation of *is equal to* (==), *is not equal to* (! =) and *conjunction* (&&):

- (($1 ! = $2) && ($2 == $3)) **TP**, true positive: a wrongly spelled word is corrected
- (($1 == $2) && ($2 ! = $3)) **FP**, false positive: a correct word is changed to a misspelling
- (($1 ! = $2) && ($2 ! = $3)) **FN,** false negative: a wrongly spelled word is wrong after correction
- (($1 == $2) && ($2 == $3)) **TN**, true negative: a correct word is correct after correction

Recall, R, is TP /(TP + FN), Precision, P, is TP /(TP + FP) and F-score, F, is 2*R*P /(R + P).

2.4 Correction Algorithm

After initial trials with different correction approaches in [4] we have been working with a Levenshtein distance (LD) correction algorithm introduced in [16]. The original version is a Python program that uses only LD 2, so it is able to correct two errors per word at maximum. This is a reasonable limit, while many of the OCR errors are in this range. We use the Gnu-AWK (GAWK) version of the algorithm which was

---

[2] https://code.google.com/p/isri-ocr-evaluation-tools/.

implemented by Gregory Greffenstette[3] with some modifications of our own. Levenshtein distance, also known as minimum edit distance, is the minimum number of editing operations necessary to transform one word into another. An editing operation is a character insertion, deletion, substitution or transposition.

The original algorithm uses a frequency dictionary as a language model (LM) and makes corrections according to the model. We added another, much larger dictionary to the algorithm to verify first, that the word being processed is not already included in the lexicon and thus possibly a correct spelling. If it is not, the word will be sent to correction. We'll call this dictionary the verification dictionary (VD). We also added one simple rule, change of c to e ($c \rightarrow e$) between non-vowels, as this is one of the most common OCR errors in the data. Some trash deletion was also added, but the core algorithm is the original GAWK implementation. The algorithm returns only the correction, not a list of correction candidates. If the length of the processed word is less or equal to three characters, correction will not be tried in our version. The dictionaries we use with the algorithm have been compiled from different sources using for example frequency list of Early modern Finnish from Kotus[4] with about 530 000 words, four dictionaries from the 19th century[5] and other available material, also from the Digi collection. We have been experimenting with different lexicons and different LD levels with the algorithm, and will report the results in the following.

3   Results

Results of the newspaper data and wordlists are shown and discussed separately as they use different evaluation measures. Table 1 shows results of the newspaper material. We have tried different Levenshtein distance levels from the basic 2 up to 5, but report only the basic results and the results with LD 5, as there is no real difference in most of the cases between the different LD levels.

Results of the newspaper material correction show that with lower quality data the correction algorithm works reasonably well, it is able to improve word accuracy with 6–10 % units in all three evaluation data sets. With better quality data the results are not that good: correction is able to keep the quality of the data at the same level in two cases, but in one case the quality deteriorates quite a lot, 5.3 % units. Overall the results are fair, but it seems that there is not much possibility for improvement with the used algorithm. Selection of dictionaries used with the algorithm has a modest impact on the results, but it seems that the best results are achieved when the LM dictionary is quite small, about 1.35 M words. Much larger LM dictionaries do not seem to give any gain in performance. Effect of the VD dictionary will be discussed with word list results.

---

[3] http://awk.info/?doc/tools/spellcheck.html.

[4] http://kaino.kotus.fi/sanat/taajuuslista/vns_frek.zip.

[5] http://kaino.kotus.fi/korpus/1800/meta/1800_coll_rdf.xml.

Table 1. Correction results of the newspaper material

Collection	Original word accuracy results from [4]	Correction results with LD 2	Correction results with LD 5	Best correction result vs. original +/−, per cent units
Suometar 1847	71.0 %	79.2 %	79 %	+8.2
Keski-Suomi 1871	60.5 %	70.7 %	70.1 %	+10.2
Sanan Saattaja Wiipurista 1841	73.8 %	80 %	79.6 %	+6.2
Turun Wiikko-Sanomat 1831	80.4 %	80.5 %	80.6 %	+0.2
Oulun Viikko-Sanomia 1841	83 %	83.2 %	82.9 %	+0.2
Kirjallinen Kuukauslehti 1870	82.1 %	76.8 %	76.6 %	−5.3

Results of the word list correction are shown in Tables 2 and 3. Table 2 shows results of the 3850_L wordlist, Table 3 shows results of the 3850L_8000 M list.

There are some clear and mainly expected trends in the results. Usage of the VD, verification dictionary, improves precision and hurts recall to some extent. This can also be seen in the number of false positives, which doubles or almost triples if no lexical check is done before sending the word to correction. Size of the VD is 4.96 M words.

Recall in the 3850_L sample varies from about 0.44 to 0.49. Precision varies from 0.66 to 0.90, and F-score is round 0.55–0.59. In the 3850_8000 M sample recall varies from 0.27–0.34 and precision from 0.89–0.97, F-score being from 0.42 to 0.50. Language model dictionary that has both v and w versions of words containing either letter improves recall with about 1.0 % unit and precision with 2–3 % units. Punctuation and numbers do not occur much in the 3850_L sample and their inclusion or exclusion in the evaluation does not change results. In the 3850_8000 M sample results without punctuation and numbers are about 6–8 % units better than with punctuation and numbers.

We can see that usage of LD 5 does not improve results much. Recall can be slightly better when using LD 5, but precision is worse with 3850_L and at the same level with 3850_8000 M. Usage of the VD is not clearly beneficial with the wordlists, although it gave the best results with the newspaper material. This may be due to different measures: word accuracy hides details of performance, and the improvement VD brings with the newspaper material is shown to be more ambiguous when precision and recall are used as measures.

Table 2. Correction results of the 3850_L word list

3850_L	Basic LM LD 2	LM W/V LD 2	Basic LM LD 5	LM W/V LD 5
With VD	R = 0.43 P = 0.86 F = 0.57 FP = 46	R = 0.44 P = 0.90 F = 0.59 FP = 31	R = 0.44 P = 0.85 F = 0.58 FP = 52	R = 0.49 P = 0.77 F = 0.60 FP = 97
Results without punctuation and numbers	R = 0.42 P = 0.78 F = 0.55 FP = 64	R = 0.44 P = 0.82 F = 0.57 FP = 51	R = 0.44 P = 0.77 F = 0.56 FP = 70	R = 0.49 P = 0.69 F = 0.58 FP = 116
Without VD	R = 0.47 P = 0.74 F = 0.58 FP = 109	R = 0.49 P = 0.77 F = 0.60 FP = 97	Same as in column 2	Same as in column 3
Results without punctuation and numbers	R = 0.48 P = 0.66 F = 0.56 FP = 127	R = 0.49 P = 0.69 F = 0.58 FP = 116	Same as in column 2	Same as in column 3

Table legend: R = recall, P = precision, F = F-score, FP = number of false positives, LD2 and LD 5 = Levenshtein edit distances of 2 and 5, LM W/V = language model dictionary contains both v and w versions of words that have either. v/w variation is one of the basic features of 19th century Finnish orthography.

Table 3. Correction results of the 3850L_8000 M word list

3850L_8000 M	Basic LM, LD 2	LM W/V, LD 2	Basic LM, LD 5	LM W/V, LD 5
With VD	R = 0.28 P = 0.95 F = 0.43 FP = 118	R = 0.28 P = 0.96 F = 0.43 FP = 108	R = 0.27 P = 0.97 F = 0.42 FP = 77	R = 0.27 P = 0.97 F = 0.43 FP = 67
Results without punctuation and numbers	R = 0.34 P = 0.92 F = 0.50 FP = 243	R = 0.35 P = 0.92 F = 0.50 FP = 239	R = 0.34 P = 0.93 F = 0.49 FP = 205	R = 0.34 P = 0.93 F = 0.50 FP = 201
Without VD	R = 0.28 P = 0.93 F = 0.42 FP = 173	Same as in column 2	Same as in column 2	Same as in column 2
Results without punctuation and numbers	R = 0.34 P = 0.89 F = 0.49 FP = 331	Same as in column 2	Same as in column 2	Same as in column 2

4 Discussion and Conclusion

We have reported in this paper first results of post-correction of OCRed data from a Finnish digitized newspaper and magazine collection, that contains 1.95 M pages of data and about 2.385 G words of Finnish from the period between 1771 and 1910. Our sample evaluation data are mainly from years between 1830 and 1870 and year 1882, which is the period of so called Early modern Finnish. Evaluations of the post-correction were partly based on parallel text material gathered earlier [4] and partly on compiled word pair lists of the digitized material. The chosen post-correction method was a straightforward Levenshtein distance based algorithm with some additions.

The results we have shown are fair, but not good enough for realistic post-correction as the only correction method. However, they show that the quality of even quite poor OCR output can be improved with a quite simple approach. If the data were not so bad, we could perhaps be able to improve the quality of the Digi collection even with the current quite simple approach enough for our purposes. Our material contains lots of hard errors, and as it was seen in the results section, only the simplest ones seem to get corrected and usage of deeper LD levels does not help. Usage of the VD dictionary helps in correction, but increasing its size substantially does not bring much improvement. Without VD look-up the correction algorithm creates quite a lot of false positives that decrease precision. Size of the LM dictionary (1.35 M tokens) seems quite optimal. Including the v/w variation in the LM dictionary seems to be beneficial, too.

Many of the OCR post-correction evaluations use data that has already a quite high correctness percentage [6] and thus they can also set high expectations for the results achieved. Examples of our data, the British Library data [10] and The Times of London [8] show that the quality level of a large OCRed 19th century newspaper collection is not very high and thus it is only reasonable to set the aims in correction not too ambitious. If we can improve the quality of the data with usage of re-OCRing and isolated word post-correction cycle to the level of some 80–90 % word correctness overall, that would improve usability of the material a lot, and would also meet our current needs quite well. After that context sensitive real world spelling correction might also be possible, if that would be needed.

The main value of our work so far has been the set-up of the whole correction and evaluation chain and gaining experience with the correction and the data. We have acquired invaluable experience concerning the quality of our material and gathered both useful tools and word list data to be used in the correction. With the experience we can plan further steps of the post-correction realistically.

Acknowledgments. This research was funded by the EU Commission through its European Regional Development Fund, and the program *Leverage from the EU 2007–2013.*

References

1. Bremer-Laamanen, M.-L.: A Nordic digital newspaper library. Int. Preserv. News **26**, 18–20 (2001)
2. Bremer-Laamanen, M.-L.: Connecting to the past – newspaper digitization in the Nordic countries. World Library and Information Congress. In: 71th IFLA General Conference and Council, "Libraries - A voyage of discovery", 14th - 18th August 2005, Oslo, Norway (2005). http://archive.ifla.org/IV/ifla71/papers/019e-Bremer-Laamanen.pdf
3. Bremer-Laamanen, M.-L.: In the spotlight for crowdsourcing. Scand. Librarian Q. **1**, 18–21 (2014)
4. Kettunen, K., Honkela, T., Lindén, K., Kauppinen, P., Pääkkönen, T., Kervinen, J.: Analyzing and improving the quality of a historical news collection using language technology and statistical machine learning methods. In: Proceeding of IFLA 2014, Lyon (2014). http://www.ifla.org/files/assets/newspapers/Geneva_2014/s6-honkela-en.pdf
5. Holley, R.: How good can it get? Analysing and improving OCR accuracy in large scale historic newspaper digitisation programs. D-Lib Mag. **3** (2009). http://www.dlib.org/dlib/march09/holley/03holley.html
6. Furrer, L., Volk, M.: Reducing OCR errors in Gothic-script documents. In: Proceedings of Language Technologies for Digital Humanities and Cultural Heritage Workshop, Hissar, Bulgaria, pp. 97–103 (2011)
7. Klijn, E.: The current state-of-art in newspaper digitization. a market perspective. D-Lib Mag. **14**, 5 (2008). http://www.dlib.org/dlib/january08/klijn/01klijn.html
8. Niklas, K.: Unsupervised post-correction of OCR errors. Diploma thesis, Leibniz Universität, Hannover (2010). www.l3s.de/~tahmasebi/Diplomarbeit_Niklas.pdf
9. Taghva, K., Borsack, J., Condit, A.: Evaluation of model-based retrieval effectiveness with OCR text. ACM Trans. Inf. Syst. **14**, 64–93 (1996)
10. Tanner, S., Muñoz, T., Ros, P.H.: Measuring mass text digitization quality and usefulness. Lessons learned from assessing the OCR accuracy of the british library's 19th century online newspaper Archive, D-Lib Magazine 15 (2009). http://www.dlib.org/dlib/july09/munoz/07munoz.html
11. Lopresti, D.: Optical character recognition errors and their effects on natural language processing. Int. J. Doc. Anal. Recogn. **12**, 141–151 (2009)
12. Chrons, O., Sundell, S.: Digitalkoot: making old archives accessible using crowdsourcing. In: Human Computation, Papers from the 2011 AAAI Workshop (2011). http://www.aaai.org/ocs/index.php/WS/AAAIW11/paper/view/3813/4246
13. Kettunen, K., Pääkkönen, T.: How to do lexical quality estimation of a large OCRed historical Finnish newspaper collection with scarce resources. In: LREC 2016 (2016). http://www.lrec-conf.org/proceedings/lrec2016/pdf/17_Paper.pdf
14. Kukich, K.: Techniques for automatically correcting words in text. ACM Comput. Surv. **24**, 377–439 (1992)
15. Manning, C.D., Schütze, H.: Foundations of Statistical Language Processing. The MIT Press, Cambridge (1999)
16. Norvig, P.: How to write a spelling corrector (2008). norvig.com/spell-correct.htm

Collaborative Information Seeking with Ant Colony Ranking in Real-Time

Tommaso Turchi[1]([⊠]), Alessio Malizia[1], Paola Castellucci[2], and Kai Olsen[3]

[1] Department of Computer Science, Brunel University London, Uxbridge, UK
{tommaso.turchi,alessio.malizia}@brunel.ac.uk
[2] Department of Arts and Humanities, Sapienza University of Rome, Roma, Italy
paola.castellucci@uniroma1.it
[3] Molde College, Molde, Norway
kai.a.olsen@himolde.no

Abstract. In this paper we propose a new ranking algorithm based on Swarm Intelligence, more specifically on the Ant Colony Optimization technique, to improve search engines' performances and reduce the information overload by exploiting users' collective behavior. We designed an online evaluation involving end users to test our algorithm in a real-world scenario dealing with informational queries. The development of a fully working prototype – based on the Wikipedia search engine – demonstrated promising preliminary results.

1 Introduction

Going back to the bibliographical databases in the seventies, text retrieval was based on a Boolean search query on the keywords of a document; predetermined attributes such as date and file size were used to rank results based on their relevance. With faster computers and more direct access storage it became possible to search the document's full text: relevance was then determined by the number of occurrences of each search term in the document, for example in relation to document size. The first search engines on the Web used this approach.

However, search term occurrences are not a good indicator for relevance: for example, when trying to find information on "VW Golf" search engines directed the user to online advertisements for used cars as these had the keywords, combined with a high occurrence to length ratio. Google's PageRank algorithm saved the day: now the number of links to a site determined relevance, higher if the sites with the links also had a high ranking. Then the "VW Golf" query would direct the user to an official site for Volkswagen, which most users would find more relevant than the car-for-sale advertisements.

While the PageRank algorithm functions well and offers a notion of "relevance" that is shared by many users it has the disadvantage of being static. It may be enhanced by other data and other techniques, but is in principle based on the current structure of the Web. The algorithm will even freeze this picture, as the high ranking will make the important sites more important. New interesting sites may get a low PageRank value and be presented further down on

© Springer International Publishing Switzerland 2016
D. Calvanese et al. (Eds.): IRCDL 2015, CCIS 612, pp. 104–115, 2016.
DOI: 10.1007/978-3-319-41938-1_12

the search engine results page, and may therefore be noticed only by the most persistent users; thus, the algorithm may be self-fulfilling.

To make Web searching more dynamic we could try to exploit the experience of these "persistent" users: this could be done as easy as presenting an other-users-found-this list. For example, we have been looking for a small lightweight camera with GPS to take on hiking trips; our search terms are "compact camera GPS". After some effort, trying a site here, another there, we have found what we have been looking for. To indicate that this site is interesting we could use a feature recently introduced by Google, the +1[1] service. However, it will also be possible to extract the "interesting site" information indirectly, for example by evaluating the time used on each site, how many links on the site that were explored, if the user printed anything from the site or if the "buy" button was clicked. The next user giving the same or similar search terms could then go directly to this site, following the "other users found this" link.

In this paper we shall explore this concept and present a model that describes a trend towards new Web-searching paradigms, which are both social and dynamic. The idea is taken from biology, from the way ants forage for food: the image in itself refers also to the seminal work of Norbert Wiener, the pioneer both of Cybernetics and of the political approach to technology. Particularly in [31], Wiener uses the figurative speech of ants as a dystopian one. Ants are perceived as a meek colony instead of an unpredictable cluster of *single* ants, each with its own identity. Therefore, the most appreciated qualities of ants turn out as dangerous disadvantages: ants can be easily controlled by a totalitarian ideology just because of their well organized and collaborative way of behaving.

Our approach to Web searching and ranking relies on the positive meaning of the metaphor of the ants. But, at the same time, it is important not to undervalue the possible risks in a collaborative approach. Any single "ant" (i.e. any *user*) has his own unique and value-added perspective and knowledge, and should then be helped to enhance his sense of awareness about his "singularity". Seen under contemporary eyes, "ants" can easily be exploited by a single-minded, market-oriented society, or by a too generalist and massive search engine and ranking algorithm. Instead, it is time to break monopolistic ways to access the Web. The information need of any single user must be taken into consideration, interpreted, and fulfilled. To that aim, it is necessary to make use of different methodologies of analysis. A variety of distinctive research communities can cooperate like "virtual ants": interdisciplinary approaches will surely prove helpful to find new paths.

2   Related Work

2.1   Search Engines

Although more than half (59 %) of Internet users in the US use a Web search engine during a typical day[2], in general the users' degree of satisfaction with

---

[1] http://www.google.com/+/learnmore/+1/.

[2] http://www.pewinternet.org/2012/03/09/search-engine-use-2012/.

major search engines is - to the best of our knowledge - largely unsettled, and can only be investigated thanks to rather small studies conducted in experimental environments.

According to Silverstein [27] (1) a maximum of two queries is needed to solve users' information needs (67 %) and, usually, (2) users scan only the first page of results (58 %). However, Hawking et al. [16] state that 50 % of proposed search results are irrelevant, thus there are complex informational needs most likely receiving irrelevant results.

Other studies pointed out the low degree of satisfaction with search engine: Fox et al. [13] devised a machine learning approach which employs users' actions (e.g. the time spent on a page, the scrolling usage, the page visits, etc.) concluding that users consider 28 % of search sessions unsatisfactory and 30 % only partially satisfactory. Xu and Mease [34] have measured the average duration of a search session: typically, users end a session – even without satisfying their informational need – after 3 min.

Summarizing, many users employ search engines to satisfy their informational needs and as a starting point of their Web browsing [5]; nevertheless, the search experience is far from being perfect, in fact a substantial amount of searches end up unsatisfied.

In this paper, we deal with the problem of improving search engines' performance by exploiting the actions performed by the users; the problem that we try to address is the information overload, i.e. the inability to take a decision due to the huge quantity of information obtained by the users. As a matter of fact, search engines are tools designed to help people solving their own informational needs and – as we have discussed before – there is much room for improvements.

Persistent users must be taken in due consideration too. On the average, they are also highly specialized users, often with highly specific information needs [12]. The old and dismissed library catalog, the traditional Online Public Access Catalog (OPAC), or even the generalist search engine are any use for them [8,35]. As it has been appropriately underlined by the LIS research community, a Next Generation Catalog (NGC) is tremendously needed, and can cooperate with web-scale discovery service [17].

2.2   Collaborative Filtering

Large scale searching on the Web can be applied only after a careful qualitative and quantitative analysis of user's satisfaction [6,22]. Here the problem of information overload if faced from a personalization perspective, without exploiting users' collective behavior: they focus on personalizing search engines' results rather than improving their performances. LIS research community shares the same critical approach [29]. Therefore, it must be held in due consideration, looking for a synergistic cooperation [24].

The first system employing a real Collaborative Filtering (CR) was the Tapestry mail system at Xerox PARC, described by Goldberg et al. [15] as "people collaborate to help one another perform filtering by recording their reactions to documents they read", which is thus considered orthogonal to content based filtering used by all the previously summarized systems. Following this study, several systems applied CR to face information overload, like GroupLens [23] or Ringo [26], always asking users' feedback on suggested resources.

Rucker and Polanco [25] devised a different and simpler approach in their Siteseer system: it collects users' bookmarks and use them both to find similar users and recommend bookmarks to other users that are unaware of them. In a similar way, the PHOAKX system [28] inspects Usenet groups in order to find posts containing URLs, ranking them according to the number of posts.

2.3 Information Foraging on the Web

One of the theories trying to explain users' behavior while searching for information in complex systems (e.g. the Web) is the Information Foraging [21]; it is inspired by the optimal foraging theory, and one of its key concepts is the so-called "information scent", i.e. the perception the user has of the cost, value and ease to access of a resource, given some available clues (e.g. link, snippet, tag, comments, etc.). Applying the information foraging theory to Web information seeking seems quite natural and many approaches have been developed to improve this process, which can be traced back to this theory [1,7].

Nevertheless, many studies have chosen to extend the information provided by hyperlinks suggesting to users the most promising paths to follow in order to achieve their goals, usually working within a single website [2,3]. ScentTrails [20] continuously allows users to supply keywords and enriches hyperlinks providing a path that achieves the goal described by them. Finally, Wu and Aberer's method [32] operates within a single website, enriching the information provided by hyperlinks with a technique inspired by the ant foraging behavior (i.e. heavily clicked links are recommended in favor of less visited links).

2.4 Other Approaches

There are many other ranking mechanisms exploiting users' behavior, but with a different goal than personalizing the searching/browsing experience. A significant number of contributions comes from a "critical" analysis of PageRank. This "post-monopolistic" approach is currently pushing users beyond Google's way of evaluation, and towards new kind of "metrics" [9].

Probably the first search engine to take into account users' behavior in its ranking computation was the no-longer available DirectHit, devised by Gary Culliss in 1995 and later bought by Ask Jeeves, which combined it with the Teoma search engine; it employed a ranking formula composed by three main factors: (1) content based ranking, (2) Link Analysis Ranking (LAR), and (3) usage based ranking; the latter takes into account all those clicks issued by users on a result in relation to a specific query, besides their own time of access and the time spent on the page.

Baeza-Yates et al. [4] devised a ranking algorithm in which the relevance of each document is boosted in relation to previous users' preferences; their method includes a preliminary phase of clustering, when similar queries are grouped. Then, the URLs are extracted and ordered by the number of clicks.

Summarizing, it's important to notice how none of the techniques just mentioned can be used to adapt a search engine to users in real time; in fact, all of them need to be periodically retrained to adapt the search engine's responses according to the last recorded usage behavior.

3   Ant Colony Ranking

We summarized some techniques to improve search engines' performance, highlighting a few key concepts: (1) the relationship between users seeking information and the optimal foraging theory; (2) the need of a search engine to adapt itself to users' behavior; and (3) the need to perform such adaptation in real time. Almost none of the aforementioned approaches take all those three aspects into account – especially the latter – and those that do might also benefit from a deeper implementation of some of the Information Foraging's key concepts [10].

As stated by Wu and Aberer [32] and by Olston and Chi [20], a swarm-based approach – thus one employing some Swarm Intelligence (SI) ideas – can beyond a doubt take into account all those three key factors, being nonetheless a much more elegant and simple method than all the others "ad-hoc" ones. Swarm Intelligence (SI) refers to the emergence of "intelligent" behaviors from a group of simple and/or loosely organized agents. Ants are a typical example of SI and their use of stigmergic processes[3] inspired the famous family of Ant Colony Optimization (ACO)[4] algorithms. Thus, we'll now introduce a simple ranking algorithm based on SI that can be used to improve search engine's performance, adapting themselves to users' behavior.

Each day ants leave the colony in search of food and building materials; they will exploit the surroundings in all directions in a somewhat random fashion. If an ant finds anything of interest, it will return to the colony depositing pheromone, a chemical substance that ants are able to detect. Thus they create trails to signal the path between the colony and the food. The quantity of pheromone deposited, which may depend on the quantity and quality of the food, will guide other ants to the food source. That is, other ants in the colony may now use the pheromone as trail markers to reach the food. These markers evaporate over time, so that uninteresting trails disappear. Shorter trails will get a higher level of pheromone, thus shorter trails will endure longer, inserting a notion of optimization. This form of organization may be used to characterize social behavior on the Web.

As we have previously stated, we will adapt the strategies employed in food searching by ant colonies in the building of ranking algorithms employing users' behavior: it's pretty intuitive to find a parallelism between the way ants forage for food and the way users employ search engines to satisfy their informational

---

[3] Introduced in 1950s by P. Grasse during his research on termites, it denotes a method of communication whereby individuals modify their surrounding environment.

[4] The ACO is a bio-inspired (ant colony) probabilistic meta-heuristic for solving computational problems related to searching for an optimal path in a graph.

needs [18]; yet the latter don't leave any trace, so they can't provide any clues to users with their same informational needs, and – as about 30–40 % of queries issued have already been submitted [33] – that's a pretty common scenario.

We propose a simple algorithm that implements the model we just proposed; we called it NaïveRank. We will assume that interactions between users and search engine are available in the form of query-sessions (briefly sessions) that are formed by the query and by the different (possibly none) documents selected by the user among the results related to it; so, a session $s \in S$, where S is the set of all the available sessions, is defined by $s = (q, c)$, where $q \in Q$ is the query and $c = (d_1, \ldots, d_{|c|}) \in D_q^{|c|}$ is the ordered sequence of $|c|$ results selected by the user. Moreover, $D_q \subseteq D$ is the set of relevant documents (selected by the search engine) in relation to the query q, Q being the set of all the known queries and D the one of all the available documents.

Given a query $q \in Q$ and a document $d \in D_q$, the pheromone $w \in \mathbb{R}^+$ associated to the couple (q, d) is denoted by $\phi_W(q, d)$, where the function ϕ is defined by

$$\phi : Q \to D \to \mathbb{R}^+ \times T,$$

while the last time the document was clicked among the results of the query is denoted by $\phi_T(q, d) \in T$.

Every time a result $d \in D_q$ is picked among the results of query $q \in Q$, or – carrying on the similarity with ACO – the path $q \to d$ is covered by one user, a certain quantity of pheromone is deposited on it. The straightforward implementation of ACO's principles, also described by Gayo-Avello and Brenes in their paper [14], is to employ the simplest incrementing function ever, namely the successor. Thus, the upgrade is issued applying the rule

$$\phi_W(q, d) = \phi_W(q, d) + 1.$$

Evaporation is obtained by an exponential decay, using the rule

$$\phi_W(q, d) = \phi_W(q, d) \left(\frac{1}{2} \right)^{\frac{t - \phi_T(q, d)}{\delta}},$$

where $t \in T$ is the current time-stamp and $\delta \in \mathbb{R}^+$ is the time required for the pheromone to half its value.

Pheromone evaporation will be performed periodically for each pair query-document, always before the upgrade; the frequency of upgrading is related to the users' perceived relevancy of considered documents: evaporation is a useful mechanism to forget registered behaviors, thus issuing it frequently causes the increase of new registered behaviors' importance.

Finally, we consider the quantity of pheromone deposited on each pair query-document and rank results based on it; thus

$$R_{\phi(q)} = \{(d_i, d_j) : d_i, d_j \in D_q \land \phi_W(q, d_i) \geqslant \phi_W(q, d_j)\}$$

defines the actual documents' ranking: for all known query $q \in Q$, the results' rank will be the one given by the chain $(D_q, R_{\phi(q)})$.

Summarizing, the ranking algorithm based on ACO proposed in this section employs pheromone's traces for each pair query-document; the pheromone increases every time a user selects a page among the results related to a query and, also, vaporizes itself in time, being a simple mechanism to take into account the gradual loss of interest by users. By doing this, once a user performs a known query the search engine is able to present a new ranking based on the behavior shown by users with the same informational need – i.e. users who previously issued the same (or a *similar*) query – by exploiting the pheromone's traces.

Thus, it's important to establish whether it's really possible to improve search engines' performance by employing this new approach; therefore, we devised an experiment involving online participants. In the following section we will present details about the setup and results.

4 Evaluation

We devised an experiment to test the hypothesis that a search engine employing our new approach based on ACO provides a new ranking based on users' behaviors, and that this new ranking somehow improves the users' degree of satisfaction in performing a search.

In fact, given that a search can be considered satisfactory if it's successful, i.e. if the user can easily (and quickly) identify the content he was looking for, we devised the experiment involving 8 participants (for the most part students of the faculty), asking them to find some contents and describing them only the informational need they have to solve (trying, as much as possible, not to give clues about how to formulate the query).

Although we are aware of the reduced size of the sample, its characteristics result compliant with demographics of search engine users, whom are more likely to employ our system in future. However, as a preliminary evaluation 8 users are enough, in fact, according to Nielsen and Landauer [19] conducting a usability testing with a single user a third of the usability problems will be discovered; with five or more users a little more can be gained. Nevertheless, if the goal is to run a controlled experiment, from which a statistical analysis has to be performed, at least twice this number is necessary [11]. Evaluations of user's satisfaction carried out by other disciplinary communities can also offer a proper methodology [30].

For sake of simplicity, we chose an existing search engine, adjusting the default ranking and using the proposed algorithm to compute the new one; the choice fell on the MediaWiki[5] search engine – made available by Wikimedia Foundation to search contents among the famous online encyclopedia Wikipedia. Consequently, we devised a search engine that works over the Wikipedia's contents and uses MediaWiki to fetch them; besides, it records the users' behavior and exploits it to improve the provided results' ranking by using our algorithm.

Moreover, given the small number of participants available, we chose to ignore the evaporation mechanism, since there's no need to adapt to the shifting of users' interests, which we reasonably assumed static.

---

[5] http://www.mediawiki.org/wiki/MediaWiki.

We proposed six informational needs to be solved (summarized in Table 1) to the 8 participants, providing them with the devised search engine that, even if it doesn't display the same Wikipedia graphic, offers the same information about the proposed results (the page title and a brief snippet); besides, the users were only allowed to use the provided search engine, without any time limitation or being in any way controlled by the examiners.

Table 1. The six tasks submitted to the participants of the experiment; the title of the page satisfying the task and the brief description of the informational need given to the participants are reported.

Japan	Colostrum	John Von Neumann
The country with the highest life expectancy	The first milk a mother produces after giving birth	The first computer virus's theorist.
Californium	Saturn	Beagle
The chemical element which takes its name from one of the United States	The last planet of the Solar System which can be seen by naked eye	The breed of dog which shares its name with the ship on which Darwin did his explorations

The search engine, in addition to recording the users' behavior, shows the content of the fetched pages next to the proposed results; this way one can also record the actions carried out inside each page, allowing us to build the entire click graph. These information were included in the ranking computation too, i.e. considering not only the unit length's paths, but also the longer ones; thus we can operate also among those pages considered less relevant by MediaWiki, but considered relevant by the users, even if they reached them with a higher number of clicks than the ones displayed in the results.

4.1 Results

If the proposed approach somehow improves over the default ranking we should witness some changes in a way that could better satisfy new users facing the same informational needs than their predecessors; moreover – given that our approach closely follows the ACO approach's suggestions - in order for the system to exploit the collective behavior of its users, the queries submitted to the search engine shouldn't be too heterogeneous, thus – even with such a limited number of users' interactions – our algorithm could still be effective. Naturally, given the uncontrolled and limited nature of the experiment, the results will be taken as preliminary and only have informative value, but we can still rely on them to better understand some underlying dynamics driving the users during a search, and to analyze how the algorithm performs in a real confined environment.

Once the experiment ended, we gathered the query-click logs and analyzed them to extract the evolution of the pheromones deposited on the key pages solving each task; the chart depicted in Fig. 1 summarizes the results of our experiment. The figure shows a timeline of the interactions that occurred between participants and our system on the x-axis. On the y-axis all the different queries issued to the system are shown, grouped by the corresponding task. Every interaction corresponds to one point on the graph, whose size represents the quantity of pheromone deposited on the document that solved that particular task, related to the corresponding query issued by the user; the shape represents the ranking status in which the interaction occurred. The circle indicates that the page was not found in the first result for the query issued by the user; thus, it was a disadvantageous situation for users seeking the correct page among the other results. The diamond indicates that the page appeared first among the results, being an advantageous situation for users who could immediately spot the answer to their informational need among the list of results.

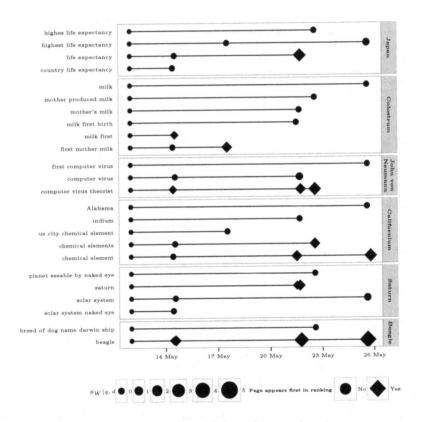

Fig. 1. Results obtained from the experiment.

In general the tasks were solved by the majority of participants, since all of them were solved by at least 6 out of 8 participants, with the "Japan" task solved by 7 and the "Californium" one by everyone; this variation may be caused by several factors, e.g. difficulties encountered by users in performing effective queries to solve specific tasks, such as the "Beagle" one, which was apparently solved indirectly by 5 out of 6 participants, who then searched for the right page.

As we expected, queries performed by a few users – even though they managed to solve the task – don't really affect the ranking in favor of the goal page; indeed users solving tasks through non-specific queries need a higher number of clicks, given that the results aren't enough specific and thus a more accurate inspection is needed. This way, some pheromone has been deposited even onto documents not solving the particular user's informational need, thus voiding the effect of finally reaching the right page among the results.

Furthermore, another beneficial effect noticed through the experiment to be pointed out is the stability yielded by the optimal ranking, since the goal page keeps appearing in the first position of the ranking once earned; this is caused by the algorithm's underlying approach employing user's behaviors, but could also reveal some degree of self-reinforcement in the ranking algorithm: in fact, when a page reaches the first position among the results, it will be prone to be selected by the majority of users, causing the progressive increase of its pheromone and a convergence to a sub-optimal solution. Although in our case the domain makes this effect negligible (it's unlikely that the computed ranking will stop being the optimal one, since an encyclopedia is a rather static collection), in reality here is when the evaporation mechanism takes place, making the ranking more flexible thus preventing the system's convergence to a non-optimal solution.

In conclusion, from our results we could argue that our algorithm could offer a considerable improvement to the online search experience, in the case of informational queries; thus, it could be helpful to consider further relevance measures in our ranking computation, such as Link Analysis Ranking-based ones.

5   Conclusion

Recently, Google introduced their Social Search service declaring: "with these changes, we want to help you finding the most relevant information from the people who matter to you". That is, in a way, our definition of a colony. The mechanism is the Google+1 button, which let users share interesting pages with their contacts - a way of releasing pheromone. This case shows the paradigm shift in Web searching that we are experiencing today, and we hope that our approach can be a first step in modeling and describing this trend, considering even implicit ways of releasing the pheromone.

We designed an algorithm employing an ACO strategy to provide implicit collaborative seeking features in real-time to search engines. It seems particularly adequate for informational queries for retrieving results about relatively static information on the Web, such as looking for products in a catalog or encyclopedia entries. We evaluated the algorithm with a preliminary online experiment with 8 participants employing the MediaWiki search engine augmented with our NaïveRankygorithm. It proved to be effective for the sample set of participants and was relevant to get a first insight about our approach with real users.

In future we plan to extend the online experiment to a more extended sample of participants and test slightly different ACO-based algorithms, in order to validate our approach against different situations (other kinds of queries and search sessions); we are also devising an offline experiment to test our algorithms with publicly available datasets of query-click logs, released by some real-world search engines. We hope to prove that also in an online environment real-time relevant results can be obtained by users employing an implicit collaborative approach for information seeking and selecting the right algorithm depending by the type of query.

References

1. Aggarwal, C.C.: Collaborative crawling: mining user experiences for topical resource discovery. In: IBM Research Report, pp. 423–428. ACM (2002)
2. Ali, K., Ketchpel, S.P.: Golden path analyzer: using divide-and-conquer to cluster web clickstreams. In: Proceedings of the Ninth ACM SIGKDD International Conference on Knowledge Discovery and Data Mining, pp. 349–358. ACM, New York (2003)
3. Armstrong, R., Freitag, D., Joachims, T., Mitchell, T.: WebWatcher: a learning apprentice for the world wide web. In: AAAI Spring Symposium on Information Gathering, pp. 6–12 (1995)
4. Baeza-Yates, R., Hurtado, C.A., Mendoza, M.: Query clustering for boosting web page ranking. In: Favela, J., Menasalvas, E., Chávez, E. (eds.) AWIC 2004. LNCS (LNAI), vol. 3034, pp. 164–175. Springer, Heidelberg (2004)
5. Broder, A.: A taxonomy of web search. ACM Sigir Forum 36(2), 3–10 (2002)
6. Calhoun, K.: The changing nature of the catalog and its integration with other discovery tools (2006)
7. De Roure, D.C., Hall, W., Reich, S., Hill, G.L., Pikrakis, A., Stairmand, M.A.: MEMOIR - an open framework for enhanced navigation of distributed information. Inf. Proces. Manage. 37, 53–74 (2001)
8. Dempsey, L.: Thirteen ways of looking at libraries, discovery and the catalogue: scale, workflow, attention (2013)
9. Devine, J., Egger-Sider, F.: Going beyond Google again (2014)
10. Ding, C., Chi, C.H.: Towards an adaptive and task-specific ranking mechanism in Web searching. In: Proceedings of the 23rd Annual International ACM SIGIR Conference on Research and Development in Information Retrieval, pp. 375–376. ACM, New York (2000)
11. Dix, A.: Human-computer interaction: a stable discipline, a nascent science, and the growth of the long tail. Interact. Comput. 22(1), 13–27 (2010)
12. Exner, N.: Research information literacy: addressing original researchers' needs. J. Acad. Libr. 40(5), 460–466 (2014)
13. Fox, S., Karnawat, K., Mydland, M., Dumais, S., White, T.: Evaluating implicit measures to improve web search. ACM Trans. Inf. Syst. 23(2), 147–168 (2005)
14. Gayo-Avello, D., Brenes, D.J.: Making the road by searching - a search engine based on swarm information foraging, November 2009. arXiv.org
15. Goldberg, D., Nichols, D., Oki, B.M., Terry, D.: Using collaborative filtering to weave an information tapestry. Commun. ACM 35(12), 61–70 (1992)
16. Hawking, D., Craswell, N., Bailey, P., Griffihs, K.: Measuring search engine quality. Inform. Retrieval 4(1), 33–59 (2001)
17. Hull, D., Pettifer, S.R., Kell, D.B.: Defrosting the digital library: bibliographic tools for the next generation web. PLoS Comput. Biol. 4(10), e1000204 (2008)

18. Malizia, A., Olsen, K.: Toward a new search paradigm-can we learn from ants? Computer **45**(5), 89–91 (2012)
19. Nielsen, J., Landauer, T.K.: A mathematical model of the finding of usability problems. In: CHI 1993: Proceedings of the INTERACT 1993 and CHI 1993 Conference on Human Factors in Computing Systems, pp. 206–213. ACM Request Permissions, New York, May 1993
20. Olston, C., Chi, E.H.: ScentTrails: integrating browsing and searching on the Web. Trans. Comput. Hum. Interact. (TOCHI) **10**(3), 177–197 (2003)
21. Pirolli, P., Card, S.: Information foraging in information access environments. In: Proceedings of the SIGCHI Conference on Human Factors in Computing Systems, pp. 51–58. ACM Press/Addison-Wesley Publishing Co., New York (1995)
22. Quint, B.: Attacking our problems. Inf. Today **31**(2), 8 (2014)
23. Resnick, P., Iacovou, N., Suchak, M., Bergstrom, P., Riedl, J.: GroupLens: an open architecture for collaborative filtering of netnews. In: Proceedings of the 1994 ACM Conference on Computer Supported Cooperative Work, pp. 175–186. ACM, New York (1994)
24. Richardson, H.: Revelations from the literature: how web-scale discovery has already changed us. Computers in Libraries (2013)
25. Rucker, J., Polanco, M.J.: Siteseer: personalized navigation for the Web. Commun. ACM **40**(3), 73–76 (1997)
26. Shardanand, U., Maes, P.: Social information filtering: algorithms for automating "Word of Mouth". In: Proceedings of ACM CHI 1995 Conference on Human Factors in Computing Systems, pp. 210–217 (1995)
27. Silverstein, C., Marais, H., Henzinger, M., Moricz, M.: Analysis of a very large web search engine query log. SIGIR Forum **33**(1), 6–12 (1999)
28. Terveen, L., Hill, W., Amento, B., McDonald, D., Creter, J.: PHOAKS: a system for sharing recommendations. Commun. ACM **40**(3), 59–62 (1997)
29. Thomsett-Scott, B., Reese, P.E.: Academic libraries and discovery tools: a survey of the literature. Coll. Undergraduate Libr. **19**(2–4), 123–143 (2012). dx.doi.org
30. Vaughan, J.: Web Scale Discovery Services (2011)
31. Wiener, N.: The Human Use of Human Beings: Cybernetics and Society. A Da Capo paperback (Da Capo Press), New York (1954)
32. Wu, J., Aberer, K.: Swarm intelligent surfing in the Web. In: Cueva Lovelle, J.M., Rodríguez, B.M.G., Gayo, J.E.L., Ruiz, M.P.P., Aguilar, L.J. (eds.) ICWE 2003. LNCS, vol. 2722. Springer, Heidelberg (2003)
33. Xie, Y., O'Hallaron, D.: Locality in search engine queries and its implications for caching. In: INFOCOM 2002. Twenty-First Annual Joint Conference of the IEEE Computer and Communications Societies. Proceedings. IEEE, pp. 1238–1247. IEEE (2002)
34. Xu, Y., Mease, D.: Evaluating web search using task completion time. In: SIGIR 2009: Proceedings of the 32nd International ACM SIGIR Conference on Research and Development in Information Retrieval, pp. 676–677. ACM, New York, July 2009
35. Young, M., Yu, H.: The impact of web search engines on subject searching in OPAC. Inf. Technol. Libr. **23**(4), 168–180 (2004)

Modeling the Concept of Movie in a Software Architecture for Film-Induced Tourism

Giulia Lavarone, Nicola Orio$^{(\boxtimes)}$, Farah Polato, and Sandro Savino$^{(\boxtimes)}$

Department of Cultural Heritage, University of Padua, Padua, Italy
{giulia.lavarone, nicola.orio,
farah.polato, sandro.savino}@unipd.it

Abstract. Film induced tourism is a recent phenomenon, which is rising increasing interest in tourism management and promotion. A research project on this topic is currently investigated at the Department of Cultural Heritage of the University of Padova, with the aim of developing a software architecture for promoting film-induced tourism. One of the challenges in the development of such system was the design of a suitable model to capture the concept of movie and all the related information. This paper presents the design and implementation of this model: how the entity of movie and its related information have been represented, how the design reflects the special needs and purposes of the system, how a database was implemented and populated and the outcomes of the developed software.

Keywords: Film-induced tourism · User requirements · Film annotation

1 Introduction

In a scenario where it is increasingly important to diversify the touristic offer, the development of thematic touristic paths such as the ones of film-induced tourism plays a central role [1]. Film-induced tourism has been defined by Sue Beeton as "visitation to sites where movies and TV programmes have been filmed as well as to tour to production studios, including film-related theme parks" [2]. Film-induced tourism may be very helpful for destination management and destination marketing: it attracts new visitors and also tourists who have already seen the area; it is largely independent from seasonal trends; it conveys tourists from overcrowded sites to new and less explored ones; and eventually can be suitable for a substantial re-branding of a certain area. A number of film-induced tourism related initiatives has been already undertaken at the international level by public and private bodies, which developed movie maps and movie tours or exploited the success of a particular movie as a tool for destination branding [3]. In Italy, increasing attention has been paid to the economic impact generated by the stay and work on-location of film and TV crews, fostering the birth and development of organizations - called film commissions - and funding aimed at the creation of film-friendly areas; nevertheless, excluding some notable exceptions, there is still a lack of coordinated efforts on film-induced tourism [4].

The Department of Cultural Heritage of the University of Padova is currently investigating the topic of film-induced tourism in an ongoing project that brings together

© Springer International Publishing Switzerland 2016
D. Calvanese et al. (Eds.): IRCDL 2015, CCIS 612, pp. 116–125, 2016.
DOI: 10.1007/978-3-319-41938-1_13

the expertise of film scholars and of computer scientists; the goal of the project is to develop an information system that combines the data about a geographical area and the movies produced in it with the purpose of fostering film-induced tourism. At the same time, the project aims at promoting the dissemination of important, yet less-known, movies that have been filmed in the selected area, that is the city of Padova and its province. The system is composed by two main components: a knowledge base storing all the relevant data about the movies shot in a given territory together with touristic information of the film locations, and an advanced interface to query the knowledge base and retrieve the information that could serve not only the tourist, but all the actors involved in film-induced tourism, as film-makers and destination managers.

The system shall store and display detailed description of movies and locations, enriched by geo-referenced movie clips, informative touristic texts about the places, commentaries compiled by cinema experts about the movies, the locations and their relation, provide further information for movie professionals, and be able to filter and aggregate the information and propose it in the form of itineraries or recommendations. A novel characteristic of the system resides in the idea to relate the information not to a movie as a whole (as it is instead commonly done in current systems) but to excerpts of the movie itself, leading to a database that has a very precise and fine-grained description of what appears in the movie. This required us to develop a novel database model to store all the data we need to capture and map the relations among them.

This paper describes the design and implementation of such database and it is organized as follows: the first part illustrates in more details the context, the aim and the requirements of the information system to be developed and, more specifically, those of the database; following in Sect. 3 a review of the existing literature on this topic is given; in Sect. 4 the actual design of the implemented system is described; conclusion and future work are left in the final part of the paper.

2 Analysis of Requirements

The design of the system started with the collection and analysis of requirements.

The requirements for the structure of the system were clear since the beginning: we needed a system capable of storing and retrieving rich and fine-grained data about movies and locations. To define the requirements for the contents of our system we started by identifying our intended users.

As film-induced tourism brings together the two fields of cinema and tourism, there are many actors playing different roles: film and touristic agents, respectively producing movies and creating and managing the touristic offer, and a variety the users, including cinephiles or tourists, with interests of different degree in each of these two fields. In our analysis, we modelled the different users in three main groups, based on their different interests:

- Tourists, interested in information to plan or enrich their visit;
- Agents of the touristic industry, interested in information to exploit and promote locations;
- Representatives of the movie industry, interested in information about locations and film-making related services.

In order for the system to be informative for all the different user groups, the data structure should store information relevant to each of them: using a user-cases analysis, we defined the different interests for each of the user listed above and which data should be represented. The design of the data structure should also reflect the way in which the contents are presented, as different users access the data in a different way (Table 1).

Table 1. Type of data and interests of the different users of the system

User type	Interests	Useful data	Data presentation
Tourist	discover new places, learn new things both on movies and the territory	entertaining, appealing and informative data about movies and territory	maps, itineraries, recommendations, video clips
Tour operator, destination manager	touristic promotion, creation of touristic itinerary	locations used in movies, information on movies produced	textual, video clips
Film maker, location manager	discover locations for new movies, see how the territory was read in previous movies	visual and logistic information on the locations	maps, video clips, data sheets

Some examples can better explain the possible interaction between a user and the system:

- A tourist at home is planning his visit and uses the system to decide the destinations to visit;
- A tourist, who is already visiting an area, uses the system - eventually through a mobile device - to decide his next stop in a tour;
- A travel agent is preparing a touristic route and uses the system to plan a cine-touristic route or to enrich an existing route with cinetouristic related information;
- A travel agent uses the system to gather information (text, images, dialogues, video excerpts) to promote a specific area as a destination or as a location;
- A location manager is looking for new locations and uses the system to find available environments (e.g. a square with palaces of a given historical period) and evaluate their suitability as movie sets, with respect also to the facilities available nearby (parkings, hotels, catering, technicians,....);
- A film maker is looking for existing footage of a specific area and uses the system to find and preview it, and to gather information on the copyright and copyright holders.

The users' profiles can be further refined and expanded. For instance, tourists can be classified whether they are cinephiles or not influencing the type and depth of the information sought out. Moreover, the system could have additional commercial applications, advertising their business in relation to a location or a service for the movie industry.

A fully defined list of the system's users goes beyond the scope of this paper; the classification and the examples above however confirm that, in order to be able to provide punctual and rich information to all the users, we need a deeper granularity in respect to existing data structures for movie representation. In particular, the data structure should store information about the location and its potential interest for tourists besides the mere role as location. Furthermore, the specific context requires the structure to store both geographic and multimedia information. In particular, movie clips play a central role in the interaction with the users. Given that the project aims at promoting both touristic location through movies and unknown movies through touristic paths, the choice of the video excerpts to show needs to be carefully done. This is one of the many contributions that need to be given by film scholars, and motivates the creation of a multidisciplinary team. Finally the structure should be flexible in order to let the system to inter-operate with data coming from different sources, such as existing lists of destinations, tourist attractions and local operators (e.g. hotels, restaurants, shops).

In Sect. 4 we describe how the structure was designed in order to fulfil both the structure and contents requirements defined above.

3   Related Work

Despite being a well studied phenomenon, little or no works can be found in literature approaching the topic of film-induced tourism from the perspective of information systems and digital libraries. Most of the research work on film-induced tourism describe case studies or detail the economic impact of film-induced tourism, but none of them discuss the creation of an information system.

The literature on information systems for tourism, mainly promoted by the International Federation for IT and Travel & Tourism [5] through the ENTER annual conferences [6], is more focussed on business and management. The application of information technologies to tourism allowed the development of a number of software architectures, as Destination Management Systems (DMS) or Travel Recommender Systems (TRS), but do not specifically address the topic of film-induced tourism.

Looking for models and database designs concerning movies, it is possible to find in literature many standards (e.g. MPEG-7, CWS) and many real world examples (e.g. IMDB); despite the wealth of different models available, however, we could not find any model suiting our needs. Most of the models lack the necessary resolution, as they have been designed for the purpose of creating catalogues (e.g. ISBD, ISAN) and as such they index the movie as a whole; on the other hand some are too resolute, indexing single frames (e.g. MPEG-7) and focussing only on some aspects (e.g. music or still images). Furthermore, most models lack completely of spatial attributes for the geo referencing of data or, where present, they refer just to the whole movie and not to excerpts of it as needed for our purposes.

Currently, the only available IT products specifically developed for film-induced tourism are simple databases and apps for smartphones and tablets. These databases are usually just a plain list of movies and a list of related locations, created by local organizations or fan-based [7]; the granularity of the information stored is often quite rough (e.g. one location per movie) and the content is not very rich, with few information both on the locations and the movies and generally lacking any analysis of the relation between these two elements.

The smartphone and tablet apps are usually very basic, consisting of a map with markers, and provide no or little information on the movies and on the territory. They are marketing products, usually specifically developed for a specific area, and albeit they can provide some useful ideas, especially on how to group and present data, they can not be used as a general model.

In general the examples found in literature could provide us only some insights, but none of them addresses the topic of film-induced tourism in a way that is structured and heterogeneous as requested by our needs.

Our attempt to develop a software architecture that brings together both cinematographic and touristic information at a fine grained level, and capable to accommodate the needs of different users seems pretty novel and requires to design an original structure to store all the needed information.

4 Database Design

The design of the database was a long process that required a careful analysis of the requirements and, especially, a close collaboration between the film scholars and the computer scientists to extract and put together their respective knowledge in order to conceive a sound structure able to model all the information we needed.

The structure that we finally designed revolves around five main entities: MOVIE, ESTRATTO (excerpt), MOI (Moment of Interest), POI (Point of Interest) and TAG. MOVIE represents a single film and its relationships with persons and companies involved in its production, and basically overlaps with the data structures normally used in online databases such as IMDB. The two entities ESTRATTO and MOI are entities with a temporal dimension, while POI has a spatial dimension. Finally, TAG has a semantic dimension and is used to add a description to all other entities (Figs. 1 and 2).

To attain the resolution required by our system for the description of a movie and its relation with the territory, the concept of movie has been divided into smaller parts, the MOIs, which we define as consecutive parts of a movie that have been shot in a given location. That is, a MOI corresponds to a sequence of consecutive frames in which a given location can be identified. MOIs are described spatially using the POIs, and semantically using the TAGs that allow for a rich and articulate description of the MOIs and, hence, of the MOVIE; by establishing links between TAGs and POIs, the system is able to expose relations between different MOVIEs and different MOIs, thus letting the user explore both the knowledge base and the territory in a bidirectional way. If the starting and ending points of a MOI can be defined based on what can be seen in the movie, the definition of the boundaries of an ESTRATTO is less precise. We define an ESTRATTO as a movie excerpt that provides the user with a significative portion, from a narrative point of view, of the movie. On the one hand, an ESTRATTO can include a sequence of MOIs when the setting changes place rapidly (e.g. two actors

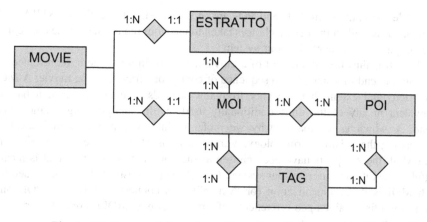

Fig. 1. ER diagram of the main entities and relations of the schema

Fig. 2. Attribute list for the entities and the relations of the ER diagram

are discussing while driving in the city center). On the other hand, an ESTRATTO can be shorter that a single MOI when the setting does not change for a long time (e.g. many facts are happening in the same place, possibly involving different actors).

While the entities MOVIE and POI are of no surprise, the entities ESTRATTO, MOI and TAG reflect the design choices taken to meet our requirements; the concept of MOI in particular is central to our system.

A MOI is thus the atomic part of a movie described in our system, represented by the start and end timestamps of a sequence of contiguous frames of the movie. A MOI has a temporal extent that can vary from few seconds to many minutes; it has no equivalent in any of the units traditionally used in film analysis (e.g. frame, shot, scene...), which is the reason why we prefer to introduce a new term instead of overloading the existing terminology. Various aspects of the movie are described in each MOI: these aspects have been chosen as they provide information that is meaningful to the different users of our system. One of the main aspects being described for each MOI is its geo-localization (or "where"); this connects MOIs with POIs and allows for a fine grained geo-referencing of a movie. A new MOI is created every time that the setting or the location changes.

Together with "where", a MOI also describes the concepts of who, what, when and how; each of these concept is described in one or more attributes of the entity MOI.

The concept of "who" is translated into three attributes, describing people, objects and symbols that are present on screen during the MOI; the first stores the characters, identified both as characters and actors; the second stores specially meaningful or characteristics items; the latter is used for abstract concepts, ideas or even people referenced to during the MOI. The attribute "when" is populated if the scene is set in a particular age; if the field is empty, the temporal setting of the MOI is supposed to be contemporary to the period of the production of the movie itself. This is helpful to find parts of the movies set in the future or in historic ages. Two attributes are used to describe "what" happens on screen during the MOI: a field describes the actions taking place during the MOI, while another is used for the emotions evoked by the events on screen. A MOI has also two attributes to describe "how" the scene was shot: one stores information about how the scene is composed visually and the other about the audio used. Each MOI has also a score that represents how well the MOI contributes to valorise the location and the movie.

A POI (i.e. point of interest) is another key entity in our structure. Each POI has a geographical location and a shape being a point, a line or a polygon. These different geometries are useful to associate the POI with real-world entities as, for instance, a statue (point), a street (line) or a square (polygon). A POI can be related to a MOI in three different ways: it can be the POI where the MOI was shot (its location), the POI where the MOI is set (its setting) or a POI that is visible during the MOI (e.g. a building in the background).

The description of a MOI is done using tags. A TAG is an entity composed by a name, an optional description and an attribute that indicates its "type", i.e. the different attribute of the MOI in which it was used. This allows to avoid homonymy issues between tags describing different aspects of a MOI (e.g. the tag "Saint Anthony" could indicate both the historical character or a church named after him).

The entity MOVIE has all the usual attributes needed to describe a movie (e.g. title, director, genre...) and it is in relation with the entities MOI and ESTRATTO; in our structure, a movie is not directly connected to a POI, but the relation goes through the entity MOI: this choice allows to relate each movie with many POIs, generating an accurate list of the locations used in each movie.

As already described, the entity ESTRATTO is a clip of the movie, i.e. a sequence of contiguous frames. The characteristic of each ESTRATTO is that its length is suitable for viewing on a device and that the clip is sound from the point of view of the plot and of the events on screen (i.e. there are no sudden cuts); this is not always true for the MOIs, whose duration is decided with respect to other parameters. Since the project aims at promoting the movie culture, in our structure the entity ESTRATTO is actually the only way video information is provided to the user. That is, even if the relation with the territory is the main reason why a tourist is interested in a given movie excerpt, the system does not aim to present the use with clips without a significant context.

5 Database Implementation and Population

The first step after the definition of the database structure was its implementation. The need to store georeferenced data required the use of a spatially enabled DBMS: the database was hence implemented on PostgreSQL with the PostGIS extension, one of the most widely used open-source GeoDBMS.

Once the database was ready, the second step was to populate it and an interface was designed and implemented in order to speed up the process of population. It was chosen to develop a web interface, to allow many users to work simultaneously on different movies; the interface has been implemented using PHP and JavaScript on a Apache webserver connected to the PostgreSQL DBMS.

The interface is composed of modules. Each module allows to perform the usual CRUD operations on one specific entity; the most complex and worth noting module is the module to insert and edit a MOI, the key entity in the system (see Fig. 3).

During the development of the interface, and in particular of this module, a lot of care was put in order to make it easy to use and fast: due to the big amount of data to input for each movie and to the fact that the data entry has to be done mostly by expensive resources as film scholars, it is of big importance for the system that the interface was efficient; this was obtained developing an interface that could reduce the number of actions needed to perform a task and the possibility of errors. Among the aids developed, where possible, buttons or visual tools are used to insert data avoiding direct typing of text (e.g. for coordinates or timestamps): in the module to insert and edit a MOI, an auto-complete function helps the user in the insertion of TAGs, reducing the chances of typos whilst allowing the use of free TAGs; the module for the POIs, contains a map tool that allows to define the shape of the POI by directly drawing it on screen; the modules for MOIs and ESTRATTOs have an embedded video player that allows to create and edit these entities while watching the movie.

To make the interface meet the users' needs, it was developed iteratively, with cycles of prototyping and testing.

Finally the interface was fully implemented and tested and it is currently used by five to ten people to populating the database.

Fig. 3. Screen capture of the module to insert and edit a MOI. The module is visually divided in sections (where, who, what, when, how and other) and allows for a quick access to the movie player and a map to define POIs. The description uses both TAGs and free text; TAGs are inserted as free tags, suggested by an auto-completion system.

6   Conclusions and Future Work

In this paper we have described a database structure to be used in a software architecture to promote film-induced tourism. We proposed a novel design to model the concept of movie that goes further than existing known structures: the design that we propose is capable of describing at a very fine resolution a movie, its contents and its relation with locations. This model is to be used in a system to convey different types of rich contents, elaborated by film scholars, to different types of users. The data structure is currently being populated by a number students of film studies, coordinated by a scholar who is part of the research team.

Our next steps regard the design of a personalized search engine, to create tourist paths across the territory according with user's interest on movies and location.

Acknowledgments.   The work reported has been partially funded by the European Commission under the FSE (Fondo Sociale Europeo - European Social Fund) initiative.

References

1. Aci Censis: L'auto e i turismi tematici. Rapporto Turismo (2008). http://www.aci.it/fileadmin/documenti/bassihome/RapportoTurismo2008.pdf
2. Beeton, S.: Film-Induced Tourism, p. 11. Channel View Publications, Clevedon (2005)
3. Di Cesare, F., Rech, G.: Le produzioni cinematografiche, il turismo, il territorio, Carocci, Roma, pp. 45–88 (2007)
4. Provenzano, R.: Al cinema con la valigia. I film di viaggio e il cineturismo, FrancoAngeli, Milano, pp. 256–283 (2007)
5. International Federation for IT and Travel & Tourism. http://www.ifitt.org/
6. Buhalis, D., Law, R.: Progress in information technology and tourism management: 20 years on and 10 years after the internet—the state of eTourism research. Tourism Manage. **29**(4), 609–623 (2008)
7. Il Davinotti - il correggibile. http://www.davinotti.com/

Content Analysis

Unsupervised Author Identification and Characterization

Stefano Ferilli[1,2(✉)], Domenico Redavid[3], and Floriana Esposito[1,2]

[1] Dipartimento di Informatica, Università di Bari, Bari, Italy
{stefano.ferilli,floriana.esposito}@uniba.it
[2] Centro Interdipartimentale per la Logica e sue Applicazioni,
Università di Bari, Bari, Italy
[3] Artificial Brain S.r.l., Bari, Italy
redavid@abrain.it

Abstract. Author identification is a hot topic, especially in the Internet age. Following our previous work in which we proposed a novel approach to this problem, based on relational representations that take into account the structure of sentences, here we present a tool that computes and visualizes a numerical and graphical characterization of the authors/texts based on several linguistic features. This tool, that extends a previous language analysis tool, is the ideal complement to the author identification technique, that is based on a clustering procedure whose outcomes (i.e., the authors' models) are not human-readable. Both approaches are unsupervised, which allows them to tackle problems to which other state-of-the-art systems are not applicable.

1 Introduction

Especially in the last decades, electronic publishing facilities and the spread of the Internet have made the writing activity faster and easier. In this landscape, the huge amount of available documents and writers caused an increase in the number of plagiarism cases, and a much more difficult identification of these cases with traditional (mainly manual) approaches. Although clearly defined, the authorship attribution task is amenable to several variations. We are interested in the following setting: given a small set (no more than 10, possibly just one) of 'known' documents written by a single person, and a 'questioned' document, determine whether the latter was written by the same person who wrote the former. For the sake of clarity, from now on we will refer to the known author (and the corresponding texts) used as a reference as the *base*, and to the unknown author (and the corresponding text) that must be classified as *target*.

Capturing the peculiarities of an author is not trivial, because it requires a deep understanding of many aspects of his behavior. Traditional propositional approaches are not able to seize the whole complex network of relationships between events, objects or a combination thereof that implicitly or explicitly underly a written text. Conversely, relational approaches may provide additional representational power. Adopting this perspective, we express the unstructured

D. Calvanese et al. (Eds.): IRCDL 2015, CCIS 612, pp. 129–141, 2016.
DOI: 10.1007/978-3-319-41938-1_14

texts in natural language by complex patterns on which automatic (relational) techniques can be applied. Exploiting such patterns, the author's style can be modeled, and the model can be in turn used in order to classify a new document and decide whether it was likely written by the same author or not. Since the modeling approach is based on clustering techniques whose outcomes are not human-readable, in this paper we provide a tool that allows to have an insight into the texts under comparison to comfortably check their similarities and differences. This insight may be considered as a kind of (statistical) characterization of the texts themselves.

After describing related works in the next section, the proposed approach to author identification is described and evaluated in Sect. 3. Then, Sect. 4 presents the characterization tool. Lastly, we conclude with some considerations and future works.

2 Related Work

The last decade has witnessed the flourishing of a significant amount of research conducted on Author Identification. Researchers focused on different properties of texts, the so-called *style markers*, to quantify the writing style under different labels and criteria. Generally speaking, the features can be divided into five main groups. Lexical and character features consider a text as a mere sequence of word-tokens (as in [1,12]) or characters (as in [15]), respectively. Syntactic features are based on the idea that authors tend to unconsciously use similar syntactic patterns when writing. Therefore, some approaches (e.g., in [2,13]) exploit information such as PoS-tags, sentence and phrase structures to model the authors. These approaches are affected by two major drawbacks: the former is the need of robust and accurate NLP tools to perform syntactic analysis of texts; the latter is the huge amount of extracted features they require. Semantic approaches, such as the one in [9], rely on semantic dependencies obtained by external resources, such as taxonomies or thesauri. Finally, there are special-purpose approaches, that define application-specific measures to better represent the text style in a given domain. Such measures are based on the use of greetings and farewells in the messages, types of signatures, use of indentation, paragraph length, and so on [7].

All these approaches use a flat (vectorial) representation of the documents. Even syntactic and semantic approaches, such as the one in [14], subsequently create new flat features, losing in this way the relations embedded in the original texts. A different approach that preserves the phrase structure is presented in [10], based on probabilistic context-free grammars (PCFG), but it is practically not applicable in settings in which a small set of documents of only one author is available.

Differently from all of these works, the approach proposed in this paper aims at preserving the informative richness of textual data by extracting and exploiting complex patterns from such complex data.

3   Relational Author Identification

Text documents in Natural Language are a complex kind of data, because they have several (often hidden) connections to the culture, feelings and objectives of the authors, which are partly expressed by their writing style. The approach to Author Identification proposed in [3], that will be briefly summarized in the following, aims at exploiting as much as possible of this rich deal of information. It translates textual data into a structural description that tries to explicitly capture (part of) the complex patterns representing the author's style. These descriptions can be clustered, provided that a similarity measure for relational representations and a stopping criterion for the grouping procedure are available. Applying this procedure to both the base and the target text we build two corresponding models, and obtain a final classification as a result of the comparison between these two models. The underlying idea is that, assuming that each model describes a set of ways in which the author composes the sentences, if the writing habits expressed by the target model can be brought back to the base model, then one can conclude that the author is the same.

We borrowed the following pre-processing techniques, that transform the text into a more standard and machinable form, from ConNeKTion [6,11], a system for conceptual graph learning and exploitation that also provides a structured representation of the processed texts:

Collocation Extraction. Collocations are linguistic expressions consisting of two or more words that denote a compound concept whose meaning results from the specific composition of the constituent words.

Anaphora Resolution. Anaphora are references to concepts already cited in previous portions of a text, usually expressed by pronouns. So, to make a sentence autonomous, it is necessary to identify the referred concept and replace the pronoun by the explicit concept.

Parsing. A significant improvement in text understanding can be obtained by stepping up from the purely lexical level to the syntactic level. The syntactic relationships between subjects, verbs and (direct or indirect) objects in a sentence can be represented in a tree that reproduces its phrase structure.

Dependencies Extraction. Based on the parse tree of a sentence, a set of grammatical (typed) dependencies among the sentence components can be identified. These dependencies can be expressed as binary relations between pairs of words, the former of which represents the governor of the grammatical relation, and the latter its dependent. ConNeKTion can currently deal only with English, although the proposed strategy is general and applicable, in principle, to any language for which such dependencies can be extracted.

Term Normalization. Since word inflection is nearly irrelevant for identifying the underlying concepts expressed by terms, it is useful to select as a reference a normalized version of each word in the text. ConNeKTion uses lemmatization instead of stemming, which may allow to distinguish the grammatical role of the word and is more comfortable to read by humans.

These pre-processing steps allow to translate each sentence into a relational pattern, that is expressed as a Horn clause [8].

After obtaining a relational description for each sentence in the available documents (both base and target ones), the author identification procedure evaluates the similarity between all pairs of sentences using the similarity framework presented in [4]. In the resulting upper triangular matrix of similarities, the top-left part reports the similarity scores between pairs of sentences both belonging to known documents (base); the bottom-right part includes the similarities between pairs of sentences both belonging to the unknown document (target); and the top-right part reports the similarity scores across known and unknown documents.

Then, two separate agglomerative clustering procedures are carried out on the base and on the target sub-matrices, respectively. Initially, each description yields a different singleton cluster. Then, the dendrogram is built according to a *complete link* strategy, by which two clusters are merged if "the similarity of the farthest items of the two clusters under consideration must be greater than a given threshold". Note that more than one pair might satisfy such a requirement, and that the ordering in which the pairs of clusters are merged affects the final model. To deal with these issues, the procedure ranks the pairs of clusters that might be merged according to the average similarity among all pairs of elements (i.e., sentences) taken from each of the two clusters. Then, for each iteration, only the pair of clusters yielding the highest average similarity is merged. In the end, the resulting set of clusters is considered as a *model* of the writing style of the clustered documents. Since the outcome of the clustering procedure is determined by threshold T, and since it is unlikely that a single fixed threshold works for all possible cases, a flexible approach to determining such a threshold for each specific set of input data is proposed in [3].

As soon as the appropriate thresholds are chosen, the base and target models have been defined, each having its own threshold, and the classification phase may take place. This phase considers only clusters that are not singletons. The ratio of such clusters in the target model that can be merged with at least one such cluster in the base model under the complete link assumption is computed, and taken as a *Score* expressing how much the two models overlap. Such merging check exploits the similarities in the top-right submatrix and the maximum threshold obtained in the previous step for the base and target models. If *Score* passes a pre-defined value τ, then the response is that author is the same, otherwise it is not. The lower such value, the less overlapping is required between the models to classify the target as being written by the same author as the base, and hence the less reliable the classification. E.g., using $\tau = 1.0$ encourages accurate classifications: indeed, it denotes a cautious behavior and makes harder a full alignment between the models. The approach also provides for an option by which it may understand, using suitable heuristics, that the available data are too poor to obtain a reliable outcome, and abstains from returning a decision. We call this setting *smoothed evaluation*, in contrast to the normal setting that is called *boolean evaluation*.

Table 1. Author identification outcomes (NC = not classified)

Type	boolean evaluation		smoothed evaluation					
Set	acc	err	acc	err	NC	Δ_{err}	Δ_{acc}	
Training	0.7	0.3	0.7	0.1	0.2	0.2	0	
Test 1	0.7	0.3	0.65	0.15	0.2	0.15	0.05	
Test 2	0.45	0.55	0.41	0.28	0.31	0.27	0.04	
Total	**0.58**	**0.42**	**0.55**	**0.20**	**0.25**	**0.22**	**0.03**	

Type	boolean evaluation			smoothed evaluation					
Set	P	R	F	P	R	F	Δ_P	Δ_R	Δ_F
Training	0.7	0.7	0.7	0.87	0.7	0.77	0.17	0	0.07
Test 1	0.7	0.7	0.7	0.81	0.65	0.72	0.11	-0.05	0.02
Test 2	0.45	0.45	0.45	0.6	0.41	0.49	0.15	-0.04	0.04
Total	**0.58**	**0.58**	**0.58**	**0.73**	**0.55**	**0.62**	**0.15**	**-0.03**	**0.04**

The author identification procedure was evaluated using the English dataset provided in the '9th Evaluation Lab on Uncovering Plagiarism, Authorship, and Social Software Misuse' (PAN), held as part of the CLEF 2013 conference. The dataset is split into 3 sub-datasets: a training set 'Training' (involving 10 problems for the English dataset), an early-bird evaluation dataset 'Test 1' (involving 20 problems for the English dataset) and the complete evaluation dataset 'Test 2' (involving 30 problems for the English dataset), which is a superset of 'Test 1'. Table 1 reports the results of an experiment aimed at investigating how good the approach is in the boolean and smoothed evaluation setting. As regards the difference in error rate (err) and accuracy (acc) between the two settings, a positive difference in the former (Δ_{err}) can be interpreted as a *gain* in performance, while a positive difference in the latter can be interpreted as a *loss*, in using the smoothed evaluation with respect to the boolean one. Table 1 shows that, for each sub-dataset (and hence for the entire dataset as well), the gain is much more than the loss. E.g., in Test 1 the gain (i.e., reduction in error rate) is $0.3 - 0.15 = 0.15$, whereas the loss (in accuracy) is just $0.7 - 0.65 = 0.05$. Concerning to Precision (P), Recall (R) and F1-measure (F). In this case, a positive difference Δ_P between the Precision scores in the smoothed and boolean evaluation settings can be seen as a *gain* (since, reducing the number of cases in which a classification is given, we keep only the most reliable cases, and thus we expect the undecided cases to contain more errors than correct outcomes). Conversely, the difference Δ_R between the Recall scores can be seen as a *loss* (since, reducing the number of cases in which a classification is attempted, we expect that also some correct outcomes having a borderline classification are lost). Unlike Accuracy and Error Rate, here both gain and loss are referred to correct classifications. In particular, the gain represents the decrease in misclassifications with respect to the cases in which the approach gives a response, whereas the loss represents the correct classifications over the entire dataset. As for Accuracy and Error Rate, the gain is always much more than the loss. Such a good performance of the smoothed evaluation setting, and the positive balance between gain and loss, is confirmed by the F-measure.

4   Author Characterization

When people write texts, they (often unconsciously) make choices, based on their preferences or on the type of document under development. These choices involve the selection and composition of terms and other linguistic elements and patterns. Based on this consideration, it might be sensibly assumed that the linguistic features of the text may somehow characterize the author, reflecting his style and acting as a kind of fingerprint for him. For these reasons, we developed a tool for document comparison that can extract and manage statistics on several kinds of document features: frequency of words, letters, part-of-speech tags, punctuation, words bi-grams, part-of-speech tags bi-grams and letters n-grams ($n = 2, \ldots, 5$). Also, we used the linguistic features extracted by the unsupervised methods provided by the tool in [5]: word suffixes, prefixes, stems and stopwords.

Given two documents, the tool allows to compare them according to the normalized frequency of occurrence of items for each of the above features, and to

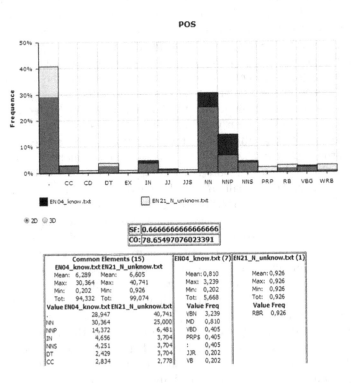

Fig. 1. Document comparison tool (pairwise histogram comparison)

display a graphical and numerical report of the outcome, as shown in Figs. 1 and 2 for the 'PoS' statistic comparison. At the bottom it shows the list of items that are present in both documents, and the lists of the items that occur in either of the two. For the common items, a histogram is plot at the top, that visually summarizes the occurrences of each item in the two documents (see Fig. 1). For each item, the bars representing the percentage of occurrence in the two documents are overlapped. In gray is the overlapping part, in light gray the exceeding percentage when it is due to the former document, and in black the exceeding percentage when it is due to the latter document. Alternatively, the user may display a histogram that shows, for each item, a single bar representing the difference in occurrences between the two documents, i.e., it corresponds to the exceeding part of the overlapping bars for that item in the previous histogram (see Fig. 2). The color (black or light gray) indicates which document this exceeding part comes from. Global statistics are also provided to the user: in addition to the average, minimum and maximum values for the frequencies, two similarity measures are computed. The former (CO) is the sum of the overlapping parts of the bars in the first histogram (i.e., the gray parts in Fig. 1), expressed in percentage of occurrences: the larger this value, the more similar the documents. The latter (SF) is based on the formula in [4], using $\alpha = 0.5$, l as the number of common items in the two documents, and n, m as the number of

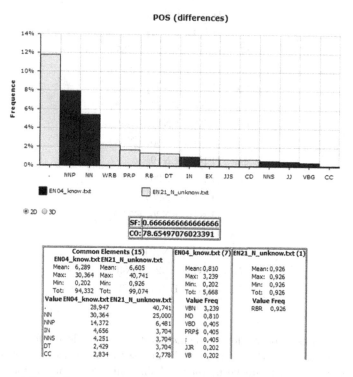

Fig. 2. Document comparison tool (difference histogram)

items that are present in only either of the two, respectively. CO only considers the common information; SF smooths it with the different information, providing a different perspective to the user. While the author identification procedure described in the previous section did not provide any intuitive explanation for its classification, this tools allows the user to have a clear (both numerical and graphical) insight into the documents under comparison, which may be very valuable in order to understand how much the two documents/authors differ, and in what exactly.

As a first test, we used the comparison tool to study the author identification dataset, and specifically the Training subset of its English portion. It allowed us to discover that the 10 problems actually described just 5 cases. More specifically, each set of base documents for a known author was repeated twice, once associated to an unknown document by the same author, and once associated to an unknown document by a different author. This was discovered since the tool reported a substantial similarity in all statistics for those groups of documents. Encouraged by this result, we ran the same analysis on the test sets, and discovered other correspondences, as summarized in Table 2 (where each G_i denotes a group of problems sharing the same base documents).

Table 2. Correspondences in the English portion of the author identification dataset

G_1	{EN01, EN12}
G_2	{EN02, EN08}
G_3	{EN03, EN28, EN37}
G_4	{EN04, EN07, EN36}
G_5	{EN05, EN09}
G_6	{EN06, EN22, EN34}
G_7	{EN10, EN17, EN39}
G_8	{EN11, EN30, EN38}
G_9	{EN13, EN19}
G_{10}	{EN14, EN29}
G_{11}	{EN15, EN25}
G_{12}	{EN16, EN26, EN35}
G_{13}	{EN18, EN24}
G_{14}	{EN20, EN32}
G_{15}	{EN21, EN23, EN40}
G_{16}	{EN27, EN31, EN33}

This allowed us to better focus on single authors, considering for each of them the subset of problems that exploit the same set of known documents against different positive and negative unknown documents. First of all, for each such subset of problems, we built a single document consisting of the concatenation

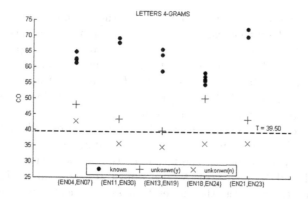

Fig. 3. Similarity of known and unknown documents, and corresponding threshold

of all known documents. Then, we compared it with the corresponding unknown documents and with the single known documents. Finally, we computed all the above statistics for each group of problems and used CO and SF to compare the documents for each feature. A graphic representation of the comparison on the letters 4-grams for the groups of problems in the Training set is shown in Fig. 3, where comparisons with single known documents are represented as filled circles, comparisons with positive test documents are represented as '+', and comparisons with negative test documents are represented as '×'. Interestingly, we observed that not only positive examples usually yield higher similarity values than negative ones, as expected. In fact, there is a clear separation among positive and negative examples throughout the different problems. This suggested the possibility that a similarity threshold could be found that separates positive and negative examples, to be used as an additional criterion for author identification: documents whose similarity value with the compound base document is greater than the threshold are classified as written by the same author. Conversely, document whose similarity value with the compound base document is less than the threshold are classified as written by a different author. To assess such a threshold, for each feature, we considered in turn each example in the training set, partitioned all the remaining examples in two groups (those having similarity above and below the similarity of the selected example, respectively) and counted the number of misplaced examples (i.e., the negative ones above the example under consideration, and the positive ones below it). Then, we fixed the threshold as the similarity value of the example that minimizes the number of misclassifications. E.g., in Fig. 3, the best value is 39.05, because it allows to separate positive and negative examples making a single misclassification.

After determining the thresholds for the different features on the Training set, we applied them on the test set to classify unknown documents, and check whether those thresholds could be used for prediction purposes as well. Indeed, we noted that, overall, a correlation emerges between accuracy on the training and on the test set, which can be used to predict how reliable a learned threshold will be on unknown documents. So, the similarity value between the base and target document can be used as a support or as a complement to the outcome of the relational author identification technique proposed in the previous sections. More precisely, CO reaches higher average accuracy than SF, both in the training ($CO = 80.56\%, SF = 68.89\%$) and in the test set ($CO = 66.85\%, SF = 53.70\%$). For this reason, in the following we will focus on the predictive performance of the former.

Table 3 reports, for each feature, the selected threshold and its performance, both in discriminating the training documents (as regards Accuracy and F1-measure) and in predicting the test ones (for all statistics: Accuracy, Precision, Recall and F1-measure). Values above 70% are highlighted in bold. As regards the training set, the values express how neat were the thresholds, revealing that the most reliable features are single words, word 2-grams and non-stopwords (100% for both Accuracy and F1-measure), followed by letter 4-grams, letter 5-grams, stopwords and word length. Of these, only the non-stopwords feature does not have a corresponding good performance on the test set. Except for this, bold values on the training set always correspond to at least

Table 3. Classification performance of CO similarity for the different statistics: Threshold (T), Accuracy (A), Precision(P), Recall (R) and F-measure (F)

	T	Training		Test			
		A (%)	F (%)	A (%)	P (%)	R (%)	F (%)
words	43.25	**100.00**	**100.00**	**73.33**	66.67	**85.71**	**75.00**
words 2-grams	10.63	**100.00**	**100.00**	**73.33**	**80.00**	57.14	66.67
pos 2-grams	53.93	**80.00**	**75.00**	66.67	**100.00**	28.57	44.44
pos	84.43	**80.00**	**75.00**	66.67	**83.33**	35.71	50.00
punctuation	86.91	**70.00**	66.67	66.67	**83.33**	35.71	50.00
sentence letters	56.28	60.00	33.33	60.00	**100.00**	14.29	25.00
sentence words	70.83	**80.00**	**80.00**	63.33	61.54	57.14	59.26
word length	90.72	**90.00**	**88.89**	**83.33**	**76.47**	**92.86**	**83.87**
prefixes	20.67	60.00	33.33	53.33	50.00	14.29	22.22
suffixes	5.09	**70.00**	**76.92**	50.00	47.83	**78.57**	59.46
stems	20.67	60.00	33.33	53.33	50.00	14.29	22.22
stopwords	50.92	**90.00**	**90.91**	**76.67**	**70.59**	**85.71**	**77.42**
non-stopwords	13.33	**100.00**	**100.00**	66.67	64.29	64.29	64.29
letters	90.14	**70.00**	**76.92**	60.00	53.85	**100.00**	**70.00**
letters 2-grams	76.95	**80.00**	**83.33**	63.33	56.52	**92.86**	**70.27**
letters 3-grams	56.95	**80.00**	**83.33**	66.67	59.09	**92.86**	**72.22**
letters 4-grams	39.05	**90.00**	**90.91**	**80.00**	**72.22**	**92.86**	**81.25**
letters 5-grams	26.90	**90.00**	**90.91**	**80.00**	**78.57**	**78.57**	**78.57**

one bold value on the test set. Concerning the test set, the values express the predictive performance of the thresholds. The highest performance in Accuracy and F1-measure is obtained using words length (83.33 % accuracy), followed by letter 4-grams and 5-grams. The lowest overall performance corresponds to suffixes (50 % accuracy), prefixes and stems (22.22 % F1-measure). Prefixes and stems, together with non-stopwords and sentence words, do not pass the 70 % performance for any parameter. Conversely, word length, stopwords, letter 4-grams and letter 5-grams have predictive performances above 70 % for all parameters. This is somehow surprising, since one would expect more content-based features to be more significant. A possible explanation is that the unknown documents are so short that they do not allow a correct extraction of language resources, which in turn leads to ineffective comparison. Also, the language is likely to affect the results: indeed, English has a much poorer inflection than other languages (e.g., Italian, French), which clearly penalizes suffixes and skews the letter n-grams frequency toward the stems rather than the suffixes. For this reason, in future work, we plan to evaluate the result of these statistics with a multi-language dataset. However, a deeper analysis reveals that content-based features (e.g., PoS, punctuation, word 2-grams) tend to yield better precision, while low-level ones (e.g., letter n-grams with $n \leq 3$) tend to improve recall, which is intuitive. Interestingly, except for word 2-grams, F1-measure is greater than Accuracy in all highlighted cases. Cases in which Accuracy and F1-measure are not both above 70 % are usually associated to very high values in only one between Precision and Recall, and in low values on the other.

5   Conclusions

This work proposed an approach to author identification and characterization based on both relational and statistical representations. The former are exploited for identification purposes, and are motivated by the assumption that the syntactic structure of the sentences written by an author somehow capture his writing style. Experimental results have shown that this technique reaches results that are comparable with the state-of-the-art, while not requiring any training and being effective even for short texts. The technique can be applied to any natural language for which suitable linguistic resources are available. Moreover, it is able to autonomously identify cases in which the classification is less reliable.

The relational approach provides a classification that can be hardly traced back to the original texts, in order to provide the user with a better understanding and insight on what makes the two texts/authors alike or different. For this reason, the author identification mechanism was complemented by a tool that computes statistics on several different linguistic features of a given text. Applying these statistics to the two texts under comparison, it obtains indicators that are shown to the user in the form of lists of similar/different items, frequencies, aggregate similarity values and histograms. In addition to providing the user with an intuitive description of what makes the two texts similar or different, it turned out that these statistics are related to the classification in a way that can be mathematically captured. This provides matter for future work, that, in addition to improving the relational approach, may check whether and how these statistics may be used to improve the author identification performance in the smoothed evaluation setting.

Acknowledgments. The authors would like to thank Fabio Leuzzi, Fulvio Rotella and Domenico Grieco for their work in setting up the system and running the experiments. This work was partially funded by the Italian PON 2007–2013 project PON02_00563_3489339 "Puglia@Service".

References

1. Argamon, S., Whitelaw, C., Chase, P., Hota, S.R., Garg, N., Levitan, S.: Stylistic text classification using functional lexical features: research articles. J. Am. Soc. Inf. Sci. Technol. **58**(6), 802–822 (2007)
2. Feng, V.W., Hirst, G.: Authorship verication with entity coherence and other rich linguistic features notebook for PAN at CLEF 2013. In: CLEF 2013 Labs and Workshops - Online Working Notes, Padua, Italy, PROMISE, September 2013
3. Ferilli, S.: A sentence structure-based approach to unsupervised author identification. J. Intell. Inf. Syst. 1–19. Published on-line: 19 December 2014
4. Ferilli, S., Basile, T.M.A., Biba, M., Di Mauro, N., Esposito, F.: A general similarity framework for horn clause logic. Fundamenta Informaticæ **90**(1–2), 43–46 (2009)
5. Ferilli, S., Esposito, F., Grieco, D.: Automatic learning of linguistic resources for stopword removal and stemming from text. Procedia Comput. Sci. **38**, 116–123 (2014)
6. Leuzzi, F., Ferilli, S., Rotella, F.: ConNeKTion: a tool for handling conceptual graphs automatically extracted from text. In: Catarci, T., Ferro, N., Poggi, A. (eds.) IRCDL 2013. CCIS, vol. 385, pp. 93–104. Springer, Heidelberg (2014)
7. Li, J., Zheng, R., Chen, H.: From fingerprint to writeprint. Commun. ACM **49**(4), 76–82 (2006)
8. Lloyd, J.W.: Foundations of Logic Programming, 2nd edn. Springer, Heidelberg (1987)
9. Mccarthy, P.M., Lewis, G.A., Dufty, D.F., Mcnamara, D.S.: Analyzing writing styles with coh-metrix. In: Florida Artificial Intelligence Research Society International Conference (FLAIRS), pp. 764–769. AAAI Press (2006)
10. Raghavan, S., Kovashka, A., Mooney, R.: Authorship attribution using probabilistic context-free grammars. In: ACL 2010 Conference Short Papers, ACLShort 2010, pp. 38–42. Association for Computational Linguistics (2010)
11. Rotella, F., Ferilli, S., Leuzzi, F.: A domain based approach to information retrieval in digital libraries. In: Agosti, M., Esposito, F., Ferilli, S., Ferro, N. (eds.) IRCDL 2012. CCIS, vol. 354, pp. 129–140. Springer, Heidelberg (2013)
12. Seidman, S.: Authorship verification using the impostors method - notebook for PAN at CLEF 2013. In: CLEF 2013 Labs and Workshops - Online Working Notes, Padua, Italy, PROMISE, September 2013
13. van Halteren, H.: Linguistic profiling for author recognition and verification. In: 42nd Annual Meeting on Association for Computational Linguistics, ACL 2004. Association for Computational Linguistics (2004)

14. Vilariño, D., Pinto, D., Gómez, H., León, S., Castillo, E.: Lexical-syntactic and graph-based features for authorship verification - notebook for PAN at CLEF 2013. In: CLEF 2013 Labs and Workshops - Online Working Notes, Padua, Italy, PROMISE, September 2013

15. Zheng, R., Li, J., Chen, H., Huang, Z.: A framework for authorship identification of online messages: writing-style features and classification techniques. J. Am. Soc. Inf. Sci. Technol. **57**(3), 378–393 (2006)

A Content-Based Approach to Social Network Analysis: A Case Study on Research Communities

Dario De Nart[1], Dante Degl'Innocenti[1(✉)], Marco Basaldella[1],
Maristella Agosti[2], and Carlo Tasso[1]

[1] Artificial Intelligence Lab, Department of Mathematics and Computer Science,
University of Udine, Udine, Italy
{dario.denart,carlo.tasso}@uniud.it,
{deglinnocenti.dante,basaldella.marco.1}@spes.uniud.it
[2] University of Padua, Padua, Italy
agosti@dei.unipd.it

Abstract. Several works in literature investigated the activities of research communities using big data analysis, but the large majority of them focuses on papers and co-authorship relations, ignoring that most of the scientific literature available is already clustered into journals and conferences with a well defined domain of interest. We are interested in bringing out underlying implicit relationships among such containers and more specifically we are focusing on conferences and workshop proceedings available in open access and we exploit a semantic/conceptual analysis of the full free text content of each paper. We claim that such content-based analysis may lead us to a better understanding of the research communities' activities and their emerging trends. In this work we present a novel method for research communities activity analysis, based on the combination of the results of a Social Network Analysis phase and a Content-Based one. The major innovative contribution of this work is the usage of knowledge-based techniques to meaningfully extract from each of the considered papers the main topics discussed by its authors.

Keywords: Content-based · Social network analysis · Social semantic · Research communities · Text processing · Clustering · Scientific publishing

1 Introduction

Finding a suitable venue for presenting a research project is a critical task in the research activity, especially in a research community such as Computer Science, where there are several established conferences with very low acceptance rates. Conference venues typically aggregate researchers from a specific community (e.g.: Semantic Web, Digital Libraries, User Modelling, etc.) interested in

© Springer International Publishing Switzerland 2016
D. Calvanese et al. (Eds.): IRCDL 2015, CCIS 612, pp. 142–154, 2016.
DOI: 10.1007/978-3-319-41938-1_15

discussing their results, however it is hard for young researchers to identify the right venue to introduce their work, as well for experienced researcher to find new venues and communities that might be interested in their projects/results.

Social Network Analysis [20] (herein SNA) based on co-authorship can produce interesting insights on the activities of a research community, even if it does not take into account the actual content produced by the community. In the next section we illustrate how only few research works have explored the real contents of research papers in order to analyse trends emerging inside a scientific community, mostly because of the difficulties in gaining access to the full text of papers and to the complexity of Natural Language Processing (herein NLP) techniques required to extract meaningful concepts from unstructured text.

In this paper we propose a new approach to analyse the semantic and social relationship among scientific conferences, in order to discover shared topics, competences, trends, and other implicit relationships. More specifically we have experimented the proposed approach on two data sets: CEUR conference and workshop proceedings published from January 1st 2014 to December 1st of the same year and the proceedings of ten editions of the Italian Research Conference on Digital Libraries (herein IRCDL) from 2005 to 2014. CEUR[1] is a website that provides open access to a large number of Workshop and conference proceedings of events held all over the world, but mostly in Europe. Such resource is extremely valuable in order to gain a global view of the current interactions among different research communities. CEUR offers information about the conferences, the co-located events, and the contributing authors; such data can be used to perform analysis based upon author contribution and to group conferences according to their location and participating authors. On the other hand, ten editions of IRCDL proceedings represent a considerable amount of peer reviewed literature generated by a cohesive community over a relatively long span of time, allowing the identification of research trends over time.

The work presented in this paper presents two case studies of social and content-based analysis over a research community: the grouping of CEUR volumes according to contributing authors and topics covered and the analysis of topics dealt by the IRCDL community over ten years. We claim that both social and semantic analysis [3] can provide meaningful insights on the activity of scientific communities such as the ones publishing their proceedings on CEUR. On the social side, we are employing established techniques to group events according to the authors involved, while on the semantic side, we take advantage of advanced NLP techniques and tools that we have developed over the years ([5,16]) for analyzing the textual content of each article in each volume and to group events according to their shared topics.

The rest of the paper is organized as follows: in Sect. 2 we briefly introduce some related work, in Sect. 3 we present our original approach, in Sect. 4 the results of our analysis are discussed, and Sect. 5 concludes the paper and presents some planned future work.

---

[1] http://ceur-ws.org/.

2   Related Work

The study of the connections between people and groups has a long research tradition of at least 50 years [2,18,20,21]. Moreover, SNA is an highly interdisciplinary field involving sociology, psychology, mathematics, computer science, epidemiology, etc. [15] Traditional social networks studies have been performed in many fields. The traditional approach towards SNA consists in selecting a small sample of the community and to interview the members of such sample. This approach has proved to work well in self contained communities such as business communities, academic communities, ethnic and religious communities and so forth [12]. However the increasing digital availability of big data allows to use all the community data and the relations among them. A notable example is the network of movie actors [1,22], that contains nearly half a million professionals and their co-working relationship [14].

Academic communities are a particularly interesting case due to the presence of *co-authorship* relations between their members. Several authors in literature have analysed the connections between scholars by means of co-authorship: in [12–14] a collection of papers coming from Physics, Biomedical Research, and Computer Science communities are taken into account in order to investigate cooperation among authors; in [2] a data set consisting of papers published on relevant journals in Mathematics and Neuroscience in an eight-year period are considered to identify the dynamic and the structural mechanisms underlying the evolution of those communities. Finally, the authors of [15] consider in their analysis the specific case of the SNA research community.

VIVO [9] is a project of Cornell University that exploits a Semantic Web-based network of institutional databases to enable cooperation between researchers and their activities. The system however is quite "ad-hoc", since it relies on a specific ontology and there is no automatic way to annotate the products of research with semantic information, requiring in such a way a huge preliminary effort to prepare the data. Another SNA tool that is used in the academic field is *Flink* [11]. The system performs the extraction, aggregation, and visualization of on-line social networks and it has been exploited to generate a Web-based representation of the Semantic Web community. In [8] the problem of content-based social network discovery among people who appear in *Google News* is studied: probabilistic Latent Semantic Analysis [7] and clustering techniques have been exploited to obtain a topic-based representation. Another system that exploits the full text of email messages between scholars is presented in [10]. The authors claim that the relevant topic discussed by the community can be discovered as well as the roles and the authorities within the community. The authors of [17] perform deep text analysis over the Usenet corpus. However their tool is an exploratory system that serves for visualization purposes only. Finally the authors of [19] introduce a complex system for content-based social analysis involving NLP techniques which bears strong similarities with our work. The deep linguistic analysis is performed in three steps: (i) concept extraction (ii) topic detection using semantic similarity between concepts, and (iii) SNA to detect the evolution of cooperation content over time.

However the approach relies on a domain ontology and therefore cannot be applied to other cases without extensive knowledge engineering work, whereas the work presented in this paper relies for content-based analysis on a knowledge-based domain-independent approach. Moreover our experiment has been performed on a much larger scale considering over 2100 research papers.

3   Proposed Methodology

In order to support our analysis a testbed system was developed to access documents, integrate the keyphrase extraction system presented in [5], and aggregate and visualize data with purposes of inspection and analysis. Our approach is twofold: we take into account social connections between events, considering the authors who contributed, and the semantic connections, analysing the topics discussed. These two different perspectives are then used to get a better overall picture of the considered research community.

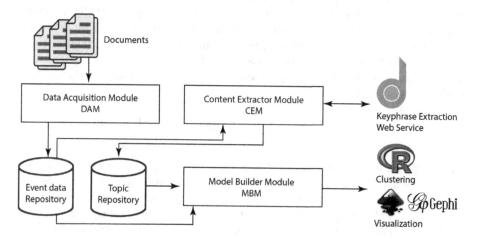

Fig. 1. System architecture overview.

The testbed system is constituted by three modules: the Data Acquisition (DA) module, the Content Extraction (CE) module, and the Graph Builder (GB) module, as shown in Fig. 1. The DA module reads the considered documents and populates the Event Data repository, that contains the list of considered events and their related data including contributing authors, venue, date, and links to full text papers. The CE module retrieves the full text of each considered paper and acts as interface for a Keyphrase Extraction system. Such system extracts a set of meaningful keyphrases (KPs) from each article's full text using the algorithm described in [5]. Keyphrases identify relevant concepts in the document and each of them is associated with an estimated relevance score called *keyphraseness*. Keyphraseness is evaluated using a knowledge-based approach that exploits different kinds of knowledge: Statistical Knowledge, Linguistic Knowledge, Meta/Structural Knowledge, and Semantic/Social Knowledge [4]. Keyphraseness therefore can be considered a fine estimation of the real relevance of a phrase inside a long text such as a scholarly paper. Associations between KPs and papers are then stored in the Keyphrase Repository.

The GB module, finally, handles the creation of the network models: the SNA-based one and the Content-based one. Clustering and Visualization are handled by external tools such as R and Gephi.

The SNA part of our study is performed by exploiting established and well known methods: an *Author Graph* (AG) is built where events are nodes and the fact that two events share some authors is represented by an undirected link between the corresponding nodes. Nodes are weighted according to the number of authors involved in the corresponding event, links are weighted proportionally to the number of authors shared. Communities of similar events in the graph are then identified applying the Girvan-Newman clustering algorithm [6] which allows to cluster events corresponding to well connected communities.

The Content-based part of the study, instead, is performed in a novel way: the usage of automatic KP extraction allows us to model the topics actually discussed in a conference and to group events according to semantic similarities. For each considered event, all the accepted papers are processed creating a pool of *event keyphrases*, where each keyphrase is associated to the *Cumulative Keyphraseness* (*CK*) i.e. sum of the related keyphraseness values in the considered documents, as shown in Formula (1).

$$CK(k, event) = \sum_{paper \in event} Keyphraseness(k, paper) \qquad (1)$$

By doing so a topic mentioned in few papers, but with an high estimated relevance, may achieve an higher CK than another one mentioned many times but with a low average estimated relevance. For each keyphrase an *Inverse Document Frequency* (*IDF*) index is then computed on event basis, namely we compute the logarithm of the number of events considered divided by the events in which the considered keyphrase appears, as shown in Formula (2).

$$IDF(k) = \log \frac{|AllEvents|}{|EventsContainingKPk|} \qquad (2)$$

Intuitively, the larger the IDF, the least events are charcterized by the considered keyphrase. When a keyphrase is relevant in all the considered events, its IDF is zero. Such value is then combined with the CK, as shown in Formula (3) to create, for each KP in each event a $CK - IDF$ score.

$$CK - IDF(k) = CK(k) * IDF(k) \qquad (3)$$

The $CK - IDF$ score promotes keyphrases that are relevant within an event and, at the same time, not widely used throughout the whole set of considered events. This measure behaves in a manner that closely resembles the well known

$TF - IDF$ measure; however there is a substantial difference: the CK part of the formula takes into account features more complex than mere term frequency. Subsequently, a *Topic Graph* (*TG*) is built, where events are represented by nodes and the fact that two events share some keyphrases is represented by an undirected link between such nodes. Nodes are weighted according to the number of different keyphrases extracted from their papers, and links according to the sum of $CK - IDF$ values of the keyphrases shared between two events. Communities of similar events in the graph are then identified, as in the previous scenario, with the Girvan-Newman clustering algorithm.

Both the social-based and the content-based graphs are then exported in different formats to allow visual inspection of the obtained graphs and clusters.

4   Results

In this section we present two case studies on research community analysis. In the first part of the section we present the analysis performed on the CEUR events published in 2014. The goal of such an analysis is to detect clusters of events that represent the meeting points of a specific research community (e.g. the Semantic Web community, the Recommender System one, the Digital Libraries one, and so on) and to identify groups of events dealing with similar or complementary topics. Once research communities are identified it is possible to further investigate their activities by analysing the evolution of the topics dealt with in the published papers. In the second part of this section we outline the methodology used to detect trending topics and provide examples built upon the second considered data set which includes the proceedings of ten IRCDL editions.

4.1   CEUR Proceedings Analysis

The first case study is based upon 2014 CEUR volumes, upon which both social and semantic analysis are performed, thus generating both an AG and a TG. The considered data set contains all CEUR volumes published before December the 1st 2014 that are proceedings of events held during 2014; it consists in 135 events with over 8400 contributing authors and over 2000 accepted papers.

To get an overview of both the AG and the TG, we are considering five features: the number of edges, the average degree, that is the average number of outgoing edges for each node, the network diameter, that is the longest path in the graph, the graph density, that is a measure of how well connected the graph is, spanning between 0 (all isolated nodes) and 1 (perfectly connected graph), and the average path length, that is the average length of a path connecting two distinct nodes. The number of nodes is omitted because we are assuming that each event is represented by a node and therefore their count is 135 in both cases.

At first glance the AG presents a sparse network structure, with a very low density as shown in Table 1, with a few isolated nodes, meaning that relatively

Table 1. Author Graph global statistics

# of edges	Average degree	Network diameter	Graph density	Average Path length
405	6	8	0.045	3.078

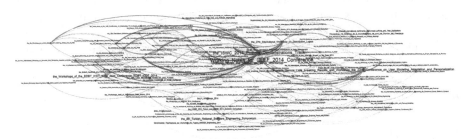

Fig. 2. Overview of the Author Graph.

few authors contribute to more than one conference and some events do not share authors with the others.

Figure 2 shows a visualization of the AG in which the size of the nodes is proportional to the number of authors who contributed to the event, and the colour depends on the *betweenness centrality* of the node (namely the number of shortest paths containing that node); edge size is proportional to the number of authors who contributed to both the events connected by the edge and edge color depends on the betweenness centrality. Nodes and edges with a high centrality are red, while low centrality ones are blue. The centrality value allows to identify the events that serve as hubs for different communities: events with a high centrality, in fact, might be interdisciplinary meetings where members of otherwise distinct communities get together. On the other hand, events with a low centrality might be more focused and therefore interested only for the members of a single community.

It can be noticed how the largest event in term of contributing authors (CLEF 2014) is not the most central one from a network perspective (which is the ISWC 2014 Poster and Demo Session), few events have an high centrality and some of them are relatively small in terms of number of contributing authors (such as the Workshops, Poster, and Demo Session of UMAP 2014), and, finally some large events in terms of contributing authors have an extremely low centrality (such as the Turkish Software Engineering Symposium or the International Workshop on Description Logics), meaning that they serve as the meeting point of a relatively closed community rather than a point of aggregation for diverse research areas.

In order to identify groups of events representing meeting points of wide research communities, a clustering step is performed, removing edges with an high betweenness centrality value. By doing so only groups of strongly interconnected events remain connected. The result of the clustering step is shown in Fig. 3, where all the isolated nodes are omitted.

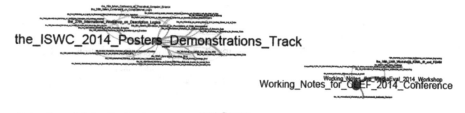

Fig. 3. The three main clusters in the Author Graph.

Three clusters can be observed: the first and largest one groups, with little surprise, the ISWC 2014 Poster and Demo Session which is clearly a massively aggregating event, with all its co-located events and other Semantic Web related events as well; the other two clusters are much smaller and revolve around CLEF 2014 and the Workshops, Poster, and Demo Session of UMAP 2014. However, due to the sparsity of the graph, most of the events cannot be clearly clustered and therefore other kinds of correlations between events should be considered to get a better picture.

The TG, on the other hand is, as shown in Table 2 much more dense with a graph density of 0.94 and a diameter of 2. These data highlight how the papers presented at the considered events share a common lexicon, which is an expected result, since CEUR publishes only computer science proceedings.

Table 2. Topic Graph global statistics

# of edges	Average degree	Network diameter	Graph density	Average Path length
8543	126.56	2	0.94	1.041

The generated TG is therefore extremely well connected and, considered as-is, it does not provide useful insights.

After pruning low-weight edges, representing the sharing of low $CK - IDF$ terms between two events, and application of the Girvan-Newman clustering technique we obtain the clusters shown in Fig. 4 which are significantly different from the ones obtained by analyzing the AG. There is an higher number of clusters and, even though many events remain isolated, more events are grouped in a cluster. The largest cluster includes two of the most central events, namely CLEF and UMAP, meaning that, although merging different communities, they deal with similar or tightly related topics. ISWC, the most central event in the AG, however, in the TG is included in a relatively small cluster in which only few of its co-located events appear. The majority of the events that are included in the ISWC cluster in the AG are, indeed, in the TG included in the UMAP/CLEF cluster or form a cluster on their own, like the ISWC Developers' Workshop and

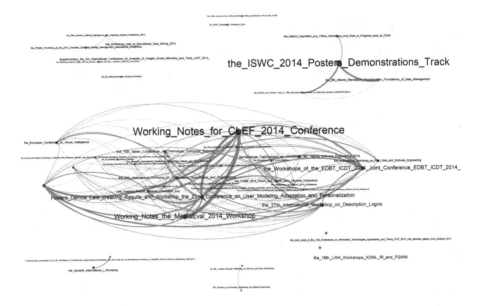

Fig. 4. Clusters obtained from the Topic Graph.

the LinkedUp Challenge. Several other small clusters are present, representing topics discussed only by a handful of events.

One final interesting insight about what research communities actually debate can be obtained by looking at the extracted concepts with the lowest IDF, which means the most widely used in the considered data set. They are listed in Table 3. Since we used the logarithm to the base 2, an IDF of 1 means that the considered concept is relevant in half of the considered conferences, and with an IDF of 0.5 in about 2/3. Even though all these concepts are relevant in most of the analyzed papers, their extremely broad adoption makes them nearly irrelevant when considered for differentiating and grouping events according to the discussed topics.

Most of these concepts are, as expected, very generic (such as "System" or "Model") in the field of Computer Science and Information Technology (to which all the considered events belong), however some of them are very specific and usually associated with a precise research community, such as Semantic Web, Machine Learning, and Natural Language Processing. Semantic Web, in particular, appears in almost half of the considered events, even if the Semantic Web research community identified by cluster analysis is far from including half of the considered events.

4.2 IRCDL Proceedings Analysis

The second case study is focused on the evolution over time of the academic debate within a single community. Since our interest is focused on topics, only the TG of these events is generated.

Table 3. Most commonly extracted keyphrases ranked by their IDF

Topic	IDF
system	0.427
model	0.474
data	0.601
information	0.671
computer science	0.700
semantic web	1.076
language	1.144
web	1.144
semantics	1.191
software engineering	1.241
natural language processing	1.267
machine learning	1.267

To achieve temporal modelling, papers are grouped by year, then using the approach described in Sect. 3 to model the TG, every group of papers is represented as a node in a network. The first relevant insight about how the scientific debate evolved over time is given by the mere distribution of extracted topics among the considered years: buzzwords come and go and their presence inside the full text of published papers reflects the trends in the research community. The fraction of papers including a specific term is a significant measure of how much widespread such term is at a specific time. In Fig. 5 we show the result of this kind of analysis over the 10-years-wise most relevant buzzwords found in the IRCDL proceeedings. It can be noticed how "Digital Libraries", which is the focus of the conference, is by far the most widespread term and consistently appeared in accepted papers over the ten years. On the other hand, some growing and diminishing trends can be easily spotted: "Information Retrieval" was a widespread topic in the first editions, however in the more recent ones its presence diminished significantly; "Cultural Heritage", instead has encountered a growing popularity in recent editions while is was somehow less relevant in first ones.

This analysis, however, does not provides actual insights on the topics that actually characterized a specific year or a given time frame in research. In other words it does not answers the question "what was that year about?". To achieve this goal we must evaluate a time-wise IDF that allows us to set apart buzzwords consistently present in the domain and concepts that surfaced only in a certain time frame. Again, creating a Topic Graph where papers are grouped by year to form nodes allows this kind of analysis.

Figure 6 shows the Topic Graph built upon IRCDL accepted papers grouped by year annotated with the most significant topics for each node (i.e. the ones with the highest $CK - IDF$). In this graph nodes represent editions of the conference, the larger the node is drawn, the more distinct topics were extracted from its associated

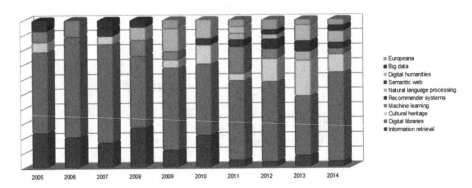

Fig. 5. Most frequent topics over ten editions of the IRCDL conference. (Color figure online)

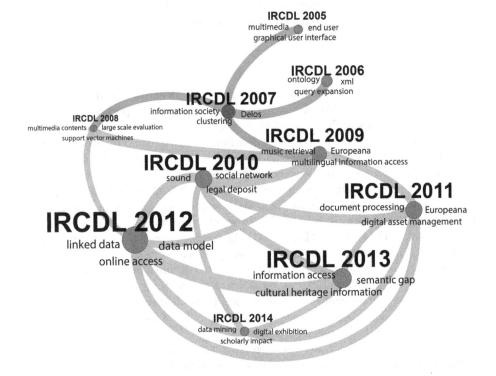

Fig. 6. Characterizing topics of each IRCDL edition.

papers; the presence of an arc between two nodes implies a significant overlap in the associated topics. Nodes in the figure are coloured according to their centrality with a "hot" color (tending to red) meaning a high centrality in the network. Highly central nodes, such as the 2007 edition are to be considered turning points in the history of the conference, since they represent a bridge between distinct groups of topic-wise similar editions. It is interesting to note how, in this example, the part of the graph representing the first editions of the conference is relatively sparse indicating little overlap aside from buzzwords, while more recent editions are much more connected, indicating a great deal of shared topics which implies that the conference has found a consistent core of topics.

5 Conclusions and Future Works

In this paper we presented a new approach to discover the semantic and social relations among scientific conferences with the aim of discovering shared interests, spotting research communities and, hopefully, help scientist addressing the problem of finding the right venue for their work. Moreover we have also shown how our approach can be applied to track the evolution of the academic debate over time as well.

The dual analysis on author participation and topics dealt by a conference is, in our opinion, the most notable feature of our approach: traditional social network based analysis can detect existing communities, but is unlikely to identify complementary communities that discuss the same topics and therefore should talk each other, meet or join. On the other hand, our approach exploits state of the art knowledge extraction techniques to investigate the topics actually dealt by a community and, by comparing the topology of the SNA based model and the content-based model one can identify communities that deal with the same topics, but have little or no social connections at all. Identifying such communities, in our opinion, might help scholars to find relevant literature and, hopefully, to foster knowledge transfer from one community to another, improving the quality of research. Editors and organizers as well might obtain from temporal analysis meaningful insights over the trends within their community and exploit such information to provide a more attractive venue or tracks for authors.

However, we won't proceed further in these speculation and simply conclude this work remarking that, due to the modularity and domain independent nature of the system and methodology here proposed, the analysis presented could be easily applied to others languages, domains, and communities.

As future work, we are planning to apply our techniques over larger data sets, possibly with the collaboration of scientific journal editors, to model entire domains such as Computer Science, Mathematics, and Environmental Sciences, rather than relatively small subsets like in this introductory work.

References

1. Albert, R., Jeong, H., Barabási, A.L.: Internet: diameter of the world-wide web. Nature **401**(6749), 130–131 (1999)
2. Barabsi, A., Jeong, H., Nda, Z., Ravasz, E., Schubert, A., Vicsek, T.: Evolution of the social network of scientific collaborations. Phys. A Stat. Mech. Appl. **311**(34), 590–614 (2002)

3. Dattolo, A., Ferrara, F., Tasso, C.: On social semantic relations for recommending tags and resources using Folksonomies. In: Hippe, Z.S., Kulikowski, J.L., Mroczek, T. (eds.) Human – Computer Systems Interaction: Backgrounds and Applications 2. AISC, vol. 98, pp. 311–326. Springer, Heidelberg (2012)

4. De Nart, D., Tasso, C.: A domain independent double layered approach to keyphrase generation. In: Proceedings of the 10th International Conference on Web Information Systems and Technologies, WEBIST 2014, pp. 305–312. SciTePress (2014)

5. Degl'Innocenti, D., De Nart, D., Tasso, C.: A new multi-lingual knowledge-base approach to keyphrase extraction for the Italian language. In: Proceedings of the 6th International Conference on Knowledge Discovery and Information Retrieval, pp. 78–85. SciTePress (2014)

6. Girvan, M., Newman, M.E.: Community structure in social and biological networks. Proc. Natl. Acad. Sci. **99**(12), 7821–7826 (2002)

7. Hofmann, T.: Probabilistic latent semantic indexing. In: Proceedings of the 22nd Annual International ACM SIGIR Conference on Research and Development in Information Retrieval, SIGIR 1999, pp. 50–57. ACM, New York (1999)

8. Joshi, D., Gatica-Perez, D.: Discovering groups of people in Google news. In: Proceedings of the 1st ACM International Workshop on Human-Centered Multimedia, pp. 55–64. ACM (2006)

9. Krafft, D.B., Cappadona, N.A., Caruso, B., Corson-Rikert, J., Devare, M., Lowe, B.J., et al.: Vivo: enabling national networking of scientists. In: Proceedings of the Web Science Conference, vol. 2010, pp. 1310–1313 (2010)

10. McCallum, A., Corrada-Emmanuel, A., Wang, X.: Topic and role discovery in social networks. Computer Science Department Faculty Publication Series, p. 3 (2005)

11. Mika, P.: Flink: semantic web technology for the extraction and analysis of social networks. Web Semant. Sci. Serv. Agents World Wide Web **3**(2), 211–223 (2005)

12. Newman, M.: Scientific collaboration networks. I. network construction and fundamental results. Phys. Rev. E **64**, 016131 (2001)

13. Newman, M.: Scientific collaboration networks. II. shortest paths, weighted networks, and centrality. Phys. Rev. E **64**, 016132 (2001)

14. Newman, M.E.J.: The structure of scientific collaboration networks. Proc. Natl. Acad. Sci. **98**(2), 404–409 (2001)

15. Otte, E., Rousseau, R.: Social network analysis: a powerful strategy, also for the information sciences. J. Inf. Sci. **28**(6), 441–453 (2002)

16. Pudota, N., Dattolo, A., Baruzzo, A., Tasso, C.: A new domain independent keyphrase extraction system. In: Agosti, M., Esposito, F., Thanos, C. (eds.) IRCDL 2010. CCIS, vol. 91, pp. 67–78. Springer, Heidelberg (2010)

17. Sack, W.: Conversation map: a content-based usenet newsgroup browser. In: Leug, C., Fisher, D. (eds.) From Usenet to CoWebs, pp. 92–109. Springer, New York (2003)

18. Scott, J.: Social Network Analysis: A Handbook. SAGE Publications, London (2000)

19. Velardi, P., Navigli, R., Cucchiarelli, A., D'Antonio, F.: A new content-based model for social network analysis. In: ICSC, pp. 18–25. IEEE Computer Society (2008)

20. Wasserman, S., Faust, K.: Social Network Analysis: Methods and Applications, vol. 8. Cambridge University Press, Cambridge (1994)

21. Watts, D.: Small Worlds: The Dynamics of Networks Between Order and Randomness. Princeton University Press, Princeton (1999)

22. Watts, D.J., Strogatz, S.H.: Collective dynamics of small-world networks. Nature **393**(6684), 440–442 (1998)

Analysis and Re-Use of Videos in Educational Digital Libraries with Automatic Scene Detection

Lorenzo Baraldi[✉], Costantino Grana, and Rita Cucchiara

Dipartimento di Ingegneria "Enzo Ferrari", Università Degli Studi di Modena e
Reggio Emilia, Via Vivarelli 10, 41125 Modena, MO, Italy
{lorenzo.baraldi,costantino.grana,rita.cucchiara}@unimore.it

Abstract. The advent of modern approaches to education, like Massive
Open Online Courses (MOOC), made video the basic media for educating and transmitting knowledge. However, IT tools are still not adequate to allow video content re-use, tagging, annotation and personalization. In this paper we analyze the problem of identifying coherent
sequences, called scenes, in order to provide the users with a more man-
ageable editing unit. A simple spectral clustering technique is proposed
and compared with state-of-the-art results. We also discuss correct ways
to evaluate the performance of automatic scene detection algorithms.

Keywords: Scene detection · Performance evaluation · Spectral
clustering

1 Introduction

In recent years, the research efforts in video access and video re-use have
expanded their interest boundaries beyond traditional fields like news, web
entertainment, and sport broadcasting to explore new areas, given the perva-
sive availability of huge amounts of digital footage. One of such emerging field
is surely education that is a key-topic of many international research programs,
like the European programs on Smart Communities and the 2020 European Digital Agenda, and that can benefit considerably in accessing the available digital
material.

Indeed, many modern approaches to education try to engage the students
with technological novelties, such as touch screens [3], hand and body pose
recognition [2,10] or multimedia contents. In particular, Massive Open Online
Courses (MOOC) already make use of video as the basic media for educating
and transmitting knowledge. Moreover, recent educational projects rethink the
concepts of the classical transmission model of the education, towards a socio-
cultural-constructivist model where the massive use of video and multimedia
content becomes the principal actor in the process of construction of new knowledge centered on the student in strict collaboration between broadcasting bodies,

© Springer International Publishing Switzerland 2016
D. Calvanese et al. (Eds.): IRCDL 2015, CCIS 612, pp. 155–164, 2016.
DOI: 10.1007/978-3-319-41938-1_16

content owners, teachers and the whole society [8]. For this aim, new instruments should be provided to each level of school for accessing and re-using media contents in different topics, allowing a personalized creation of knowledge, a sharing of multi-cultural practices and the assessment of new social experiences.

In the "Citt Educante" research project, in which we are involved, we are developing new solutions for the re-use of educational video production. The goal is to provide efficient tools for students to access the video content, creating their personalized educational experience on specific topics (e.g. geography or art) and across-topics, to share experiences by enriching the footage with user-generated content and data coming from web and social media. In this scenario, even if a huge amount of video from national broadcasting agencies is available and pedagogy researchers are trying to leverage this new possibility in education, the IT tools are still not adequate to allow video content re-use, tagging, annotation and personalization [4].

Nowadays, people can access video through web or specific apps, but it is difficult to find which section is really the one they want (e.g. a two minute scene withing a two hour program). Even if we know what is the part of interest, extracting and integrating it in our own presentation and re-using it in a suitable manner is still challenging. One basic necessary tool should allow an "access by scene" that improves the level of abstraction from single frame or shot to the scene, i.e. a conceptually meaningful and homogeneous element, composed by more than one shot. Unfortunately, most of the reusable content, owned by broadcast agencies, has not pre-defined sub-units and is not annotated. Therefore, we need accurate scene detection to identify coherent sequences (i.e. scenes) in videos, without asking manual segmentation to editors or publishers. The problem has been approached in the past in the literature with some promising, but not conclusive, results.

We present a novel proposal for scene segmentation, based on spectral clustering, which shows competitive results when compared to state-of-the-art methods. As well, also the broad concept of accuracy should be better defined for scene detection, especially when the goal is not only an algorithm comparison but a concrete result, which should be useful in many applications where a successive human interaction is expected, e.g. for browsing, tagging, selecting etc. In this case, for instance, the precise position of the cut is not important while skipping a scene and integrating it in another longer, preventing people (in our case students) to find a useful part of the video without seeing all the material, is more important. Thus we compare classical precision/recall measures with a better suited definition of coverage/overflow, which solves frequently observed cases in which the numeric interpretation would be quite different from the expected results by users.

The rest of this paper is organized as follows: Sect. 2 presents a summary of the existing approaches to scene detection and temporal clutering. In Sect. 3 we describe our algorithm; in Sect. 4 we discuss performance evaluation and in Sect. 5 experimentally evaluate them and show a sample use case.

2   Related Work

Video decomposition techniques aim to partition a video into sequences, like shots or scenes. Shots are elementary structural segments that are defined as sequences of images taken without interruption by a single camera. Scenes, on the contrary, are often defined as series of temporally contiguous shots characterized by overlapping links that connect shots with similar content [6]. Therefore, the fundamental goal of scene detection algorithms is to identify semantically coherent shots that are temporally close to each other. Most of the existing works can be roughly categorized into three categories: *rule-based methods*, that consider the way a scene is structured in professional movie production, *graph-based methods*, where shots are arranged in a graph representation, and *clustering-based methods*. They can rely on visual, audio, and textual features.

Rule-based approaches consider the way a scene is structured in professional movie production. Of course, the drawback of this kind of methods is that they tend to fail in videos where film-editing rules are not followed, or when two adjacent scenes are similar and follow the same rules. Liu *et al.* [7], for example, propose a visual based probabilistic framework that imitates the authoring process and detects scenes by incorporating contextual dynamics and learning a scene model. In [5], shots are represented by means of key-frames, thus, the first step of this method is to extract several key-frames from each shot: frames from a shot are clustered using the spectral clustering algorithm, color histograms as features, and the euclidean distance to compute the similarity matrix. The number of clusters is selected by applying a threshold Th on the eigenvalues of the Normalized Laplacian. The distance between a pair of shots is defined as the maximum similarity between key-frames belonging to the two shots, computed using histogram intersection. Shots are clustered using again spectral clustering and the aforesaid distance measure, and then labeled according to the clusters they belong to. Scene boundaries are then detected from the alignment score of the symbolic sequences.

In graph-based methods, instead, shots are arranged in a graph representation and then clustered by partitioning the graph. The Shot Transition Graph (STG), proposed in [13], is one of the most used models in this category: here each node represents a shot and the edges between the shots are weighted by shot similarity. In [9], color and motion features are used to represent shot similarity, and the STG is then split into subgraphs by applying the normalized cuts for graph partitioning. More recently, Sidiropoulos *et al.* [11] introduced a new STG approximation that exploits features automatically extracted from the visual and the auditory channel. This method extends the Shot Transition Graph using multimodal low-level and high-level features. To this aim, multiple STGs are constructed, one for each kind of feature, and then a probabilistic merging process is used to combine their results. The used features include visual features, such as HSV histograms, outputs of visual concept detectors trained using the Bag of Words approach, and audio features, like background conditions classification results, speaker histogram, and model vectors constructed from the responses of a number of audio event detectors.

We propose a simpler solution based on the spectral clustering approach, where we modify the standard spectral clustering algorithm in order to produce temporally consistent clusters.

3   A Spectral Clustering Approach

Our scene detection method generates scenes by grouping adjacent shots. Shots are described by means of color histograms, hence relying on visual features only: given a video, we compute a three-dimensional histogram of each frame, by quantizing each RGB channel in eight bins, for a total of 512 bins. Then, we sum histograms from frames belonging to the same shot, thus obtaining a single L_1-normalized histogram for each shot.

In contrast to other approaches that used spectral clustering for scene detection, we build a similarity matrix that jointly describes appearance similarity and temporal proximity. Its generic element κ_{ij}, defines the similarity between shots $\mathbf{x}_i$ and $\mathbf{x}_j$ as

$$\kappa_{ij} = \exp\left(-\frac{d_1^2(\psi(\mathbf{x}_i), \psi(\mathbf{x}_j)) + \alpha \cdot d_2^2(\mathbf{x}_i, \mathbf{x}_j)}{2\sigma^2}\right) \tag{1}$$

where $\psi(\mathbf{x}_i)$ is the normalized histogram of shot $\mathbf{x}_i$, d_1^2 is the Bhattacharyya distance and $d_2^2(\mathbf{x}_i, \mathbf{x}_j)$ is the normalized temporal distance between shot $\mathbf{x}_i$ and shot $\mathbf{x}_j$, while the parameter α tunes the relative importance of color similarity and temporal distance. To describe temporal distance between frames, $d_2^2(\mathbf{x}_i, \mathbf{x}_j)$ is defined as

$$d_2^2(\mathbf{x}_i, \mathbf{x}_j) = \frac{|m_i - m_j|}{l} \tag{2}$$

where m_i is the index of the central frame of shot $\mathbf{x}_i$, and l is the total number of frames in the video. The spectral clustering algorithm is then applied to the similarity matrix, using the Normalized Laplacian and the maximum eigen-gap criterion to select k:

$$k = \arg\max\left(\lambda_{i+1} - \lambda_i\right) + 1 \tag{3}$$

where λ_i is the i-th eigenvalue of the Normalized Laplacian.

As shown in Fig. 1, the effect of applying increasing values of α to the similarity matrix is to raise the similarities of adjacent shots, therefore boosting the temporal consistency of the resulting groups. Of course, this does not guarantee a completely temporal consistent clustering (i.e. some clusters may still contain non-adjacent shots); at the same time, too high values of α would lead to a segmentation that ignores color dissimilarity. The final scene boundaries are created between adjacent shots that do not belong to the same cluster.

4   Evaluating Scene Segmentation

The first possibility to evaluate the results of a scene detection algorithm is to count correctly and wrongly detected boundaries, without considering the

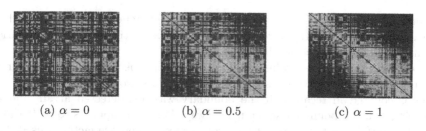

(a) $\alpha = 0$ (b) $\alpha = 0.5$ (c) $\alpha = 1$

Fig. 1. Effect of α on similarity matrix κ_{ij}. Higher values of α enforce connections between near shots and increase the quality of the detected scenes (best viewed in color). (Color figure online)

Fig. 2. Two consecutive scenes from the RAI dataset.

temporal distance between a ground truth cut and the nearest detected cut. The most used measures in this context are precision and recall, together with the F-Score measure, that summarizes both. Precision is the ratio of the number of correctly identified scenes boundaries to the total number of scenes detected by the algorithm. Recall is the ratio of the number of correctly identified boundaries to the total number of scenes in the ground truth.

Of course this kind of evaluation does not discern the seriousness of an error: if a boundary is detected one shot before or after its ground truth position, an error is counted in recall as if the boundary was not detected at all, and in precision as if the boundary was put far away. This issue appears to be felt also by other authors, with the result that sometimes a tolerance factor is used. For example, [9] uses a *best match* method with a sliding window of 30 s, so that a detected boundary is considered correct if it matches a ground truth boundary in the sliding window.

To deal with these problems, Vendrig *et al.* [12] proposed the Coverage and Overflow measures. Coverage $\mathcal{C}$ measures the quantity of shots belonging to the same scene correctly grouped together, while Overflow $\mathcal{O}$ evaluates to what extent shots not belonging to the same scene are erroneously grouped together. Formally, given the set of automatically detected scenes $\mathbf{s} = [\mathbf{s}_1, \mathbf{s}_2, ..., \mathbf{s}_m]$, and the ground truth $\tilde{\mathbf{s}} = [\tilde{\mathbf{s}}_1, \tilde{\mathbf{s}}_2, ..., \tilde{\mathbf{s}}_n]$, where each element of $\mathbf{s}$ and $\tilde{\mathbf{s}}$ is a set of shot indexes, the coverage $\mathcal{C}_t$ of scene $\tilde{\mathbf{s}}_t$ is proportional to the longest overlap between $\mathbf{s}_i$ and $\tilde{\mathbf{s}}_t$:

$$C_t = \frac{\max_{i=1...m} \#(\mathbf{s}_i \cap \tilde{\mathbf{s}}_t)}{\#(\tilde{\mathbf{s}}_t)} \tag{4}$$

where $\#(\mathbf{s}_i)$ is the number of shots in scene $\mathbf{s}_i$. The overflow of a scene $\tilde{\mathbf{s}}_t$, $\mathcal{O}_t$, is the amount of overlap of every $\mathbf{s}_i$ corresponding to $\tilde{\mathbf{s}}_t$ with the two surrounding scenes $\tilde{\mathbf{s}}_{t-1}$ and $\tilde{\mathbf{s}}_{t+1}$:

$$\mathcal{O}_t = \frac{\sum_{i=1}^{m} \#(\mathbf{s}_i \setminus \tilde{\mathbf{s}}_t) \cdot \min(1, \#(\mathbf{s}_i \cap \tilde{\mathbf{s}}_t))}{\#(\tilde{\mathbf{s}}_{t-1}) + \#(\tilde{\mathbf{s}}_{t+1})} \tag{5}$$

The computed per-scene measures can then be aggregated into values for an entire video as follows:

$$C = \sum_{t=1}^{n} C_t \cdot \frac{\#(\tilde{\mathbf{s}}_t)}{\sum \#(\tilde{\mathbf{s}}_i)}, \quad \mathcal{O} = \sum_{t=1}^{n} \mathcal{O}_t \cdot \frac{\#(\tilde{\mathbf{s}}_t)}{\sum \#(\tilde{\mathbf{s}}_i)}. \tag{6}$$

Finally, an F-Score measure can be defined to combine Coverage and Overflow in a single measure, by taking the harmonic mean of $\mathcal{C}$ and $1 - \mathcal{O}$.

5   Evaluation

We evaluate the aforesaid measures and algorithms on a collection of ten challenging broadcasting videos from the Rai Scuola video archive[1], mainly documentaries and talk shows. Shots have been obtained running the state of the art shot detector of [1] and manually grouped into scenes by a set of

---

[1] http://www.scuola.rai.it.

human experts to define the ground truth. Our dataset and the corresponding annotations are available for download at http://imagelab.ing.unimore.it/files/RaiSceneDetection.zip.

We reimplemented the approach in [5] and used the executable of [11] provided by the authors[2]. The threshold Th of [5] was selected to maximize the performance on our dataset, and α was set to 0.05 in all our experiments.

Figure 3 shows the results of the compared methods on a frame sequence from our dataset.

Fig. 3. Samples results on our dataset. Row (a) shows the ground-truth segmentation, (b) the individual shots boundaries, row (c) shows the results of our method, (d) those of [11] and (e) those of [5] (best viewed in color). (Color figure online)

Table 1. Performance comparison on the RAI dataset using the boundary level measures (Precision, Recall, F-Score)

Video	Spectral Clustering			Chasanis et al. [5]			Sidiropoulos et al. [11]		
	F-Score	Precision	Recall	F-Score	Precision	Recall	F-Score	Precision	Recall
V_1	0.12	0.09	0.17	0.25	0.20	0.33	**0.29**	0.25	0.33
V_2	**0.36**	0.27	0.55	0.00	0.00	0.00	0.30	0.33	0.27
V_3	**0.37**	0.29	0.53	0.13	0.13	0.13	0.31	0.36	0.27
V_4	**0.30**	0.23	0.43	0.10	0.10	0.10	0.22	0.50	0.14
V_5	**0.44**	0.31	0.75	0.00	0.00	0.00	0.36	0.31	0.42
V_6	0.18	0.10	0.75	0.00	0.00	0.00	**0.36**	0.29	0.50
V_7	**0.18**	0.33	0.13	0.00	0.00	0.00	0.13	0.13	0.13
V_8	0.10	0.06	0.27	0.13	0.10	0.18	**0.21**	0.25	0.18
V_9	**0.25**	0.16	0.62	0.00	0.00	0.00	0.21	0.33	0.15
V_{10}	0.23	0.15	0.60	**0.26**	0.38	0.20	0.19	0.33	0.13
Average	0.25	0.20	0.48	0.09	0.09	0.09	**0.26**	0.31	0.25

---

[2] http://mklab.iti.gr/project/video-shot-segm.

Table 2. Performance comparison on the RAI dataset using the Shot level measures (Coverage, Overflow and F-Score)

Video	Spectral Clustering			Chasanis *et al.* [5]			Sidiropoulos *et al.* [11]		
	F-Score	$\mathcal{C}$	$\mathcal{O}$	F-Score	$\mathcal{C}$	$\mathcal{O}$	F-Score	$\mathcal{C}$	$\mathcal{O}$
V_1	0.64	0.81	0.48	0.70	0.64	0.24	**0.72**	0.84	0.37
V_2	**0.68**	0.61	0.22	0.36	0.80	0.77	0.59	0.85	0.55
V_3	**0.65**	0.68	0.38	0.58	0.73	0.52	0.58	0.90	0.57
V_4	**0.74**	0.69	0.22	0.50	0.65	0.60	0.33	0.94	0.80
V_5	**0.77**	0.68	0.11	0.25	0.93	0.86	0.66	0.76	0.41
V_6	0.51	0.37	0.17	0.18	0.89	0.90	**0.71**	0.77	0.34
V_7	0.30	0.97	0.82	0.37	0.70	0.75	**0.51**	0.78	0.62
V_8	0.59	0.53	0.33	**0.62**	0.57	0.32	0.45	0.88	0.70
V_9	**0.67**	0.55	0.15	0.27	0.87	0.84	0.43	0.92	0.72
V_{10}	**0.57**	0.42	0.12	0.54	0.91	0.62	0.44	0.94	0.71
Average	**0.61**	0.63	0.30	0.44	0.77	0.64	0.54	0.86	0.58

Tables 1 and 2 compare the two different approaches using Boundary level and Shot level performance measures. As show in Table 1, detected boundaries rarely correspond to ground truth boundaries exactly, therefore leading to poor results in terms of precision and recall, even when considering a recent and state-of-the-art approach like [11].

As expected, the two measures behave differently and there is not a complete agreement among them: [5] performs worse than the other two methods according to both measures, while [11] performs equal to the spectral clustering approach with boundary level measures, but slightly worse than the spectral clustering approach according to shot level measures.

Nautilus - Crisis of the book

Last trip of our journey through the crisis. We address a particular kind of crisis, that of book and reading, with our guests Andrea Bajani, writer, Filippo Nicosia, bookseller, and Gino Roncaglia, publishing specialist.

Tags: Nautilus, crisis, reading
Categories: Moneys, Life stories, Culture

episode, crisis, journey   public, Fahreneit, books   book, writer, society, periodicals

Fig. 4. Effective video browsing using our algorithm. Users can visualize a summary of the content by means of the extracted scenes.

Detected scenes, finally, can be used as an input for video browsing or re-using software. As an example, we built a web-based browsing interface for broadcasting videos (see Fig. 4) where users can visualize a summary of the content by means of the extracted scenes. Scenes are represented with key-frames in a timeline fashion, and when a particular scene is selected, all its shots are unfolded. To ease the browsing even more, most frequent words, obtained from the transcript of the audio, are reported under each scene. Users can jump from one part of the video to another by clicking on the corresponding scene or shot.

6   Conclusions

We investigated the problem of evaluating scene detection algorithms with tests conducted on two different performance measures and on three different and recent approaches to scene segmentation. Results show that the problem of scene detection is still far from being solved, and that simple approaches like the suggested spectral clustering technique can sometimes achieve equivalent or better results than more complex methods.

Acknowledgments. This work was carried out within the project "Città educante" (ctn01_00034_393801) of the National Technological Cluster on Smart Communities cofunded by the Italian Ministry of Education, University and Research - MIUR.

References

1. Apostolidis, E., Mezaris, V.: Fast shot segmentation combining global and local visual descriptors. In: IEEE International Conference on Acoustics, Speech and Signal Processing, pp. 6583–6587 (2014)
2. Baraldi, L., Paci, F., Serra, G., Benini, L., Cucchiara, R.: Gesture recognition in ego-centric videos using dense trajectories and hand segmentation. In: Proceedings of 10th IEEE Embedded Vision Workshop (EVW). Columbus, Ohio, June 2014
3. Battenberg, J.K., Merbler, J.B.: Touch screen versus keyboard: a comparison of task performance of young children. J. Spec. Educ. Technol. **10**(2), 24–28 (1989)
4. Bertini, M., Del Bimbo, A., Serra, G., Torniai, C., Cucchiara, R., Grana, C., Vezzani, R.: Dynamic pictorially enriched ontologies for video digital libraries. IEEE MultiMedia Mag. **16**(2), 41–51 (2009)
5. Chasanis, V.T., Likas, C., Galatsanos, N.P.: Scene detection in videos using shot clustering and sequence alignment. IEEE Trans. Multimedia **11**(1), 89–100 (2009)
6. Hanjalic, A., Lagendijk, R.L., Biemond, J.: Automated high-level movie segmentation for advanced video-retrieval systems. IEEE Trans. Circ. Syst. Vid. Technol. **9**(4), 580–588 (1999)
7. Liu, C., Wang, D., Zhu, J., Zhang, B.: Learning a contextual multi-thread model for movie/tv scene segmentation. IEEE Trans. Multimedia **15**(4), 884–897 (2013)
8. Mascolo, M.F.: Beyond student-centered and teacher-centered pedagogy: teaching and learning as guided participation. Pedagogy Hum. Sci. **1**(1), 3–27 (2009)
9. Rasheed, Z., Shah, M.: Detection and representation of scenes in videos. IEEE Trans. Multimedia **7**(6), 1097–1105 (2005)

10. Serra, G., Camurri, M., Baraldi, L., Benedetti, M., Cucchiara, R.: Hand segmentation for gesture recognition in ego-vision. In: Proceedings of ACM Multimedia International Workshop on Interactive Multimedia on Mobile and Portable Devices (IMMPD), Barcelona, Spain, October 2013
11. Sidiropoulos, P., Mezaris, V., Kompatsiaris, I., Meinedo, H., Bugalho, M., Trancoso, I.: Temporal video segmentation to scenes using high-level audiovisual features. IEEE Trans. Circ. Syst. Vid. Technol. **21**(8), 1163–1177 (2011)
12. Vendrig, J., Worring, M.: Systematic evaluation of logical story unit segmentation. IEEE Trans. Multimedia **4**(4), 492–499 (2002)
13. Yeung, M.M., Yeo, B.L., Wolf, W.H., Liu, B.: Video browsing using clustering and scene transitions on compressed sequences. In: IS&T/SPIE's Symposium on Electronic Imaging: Science & Technology, pp. 399–413 (1995)

Digital Library Infrastructures

An Interoperability Infrastructure for Digital Identifiers in e-Science

Barbara Bazzanella[1(✉)] and Paolo Bouquet[2]

[1] University of Trento, Trento, Italy
barbara.bazzanella@unitn.it
[2] OKKAM Srl, Trento, Italy
bouquet@okkam.it

Abstract. The rapid increase of scientific digital assets in the last years has made clear that digital identifiers are crucial for effectively publishing, accessing and managing digital information in e-science contexts. From persistent keys for access to digital objects in network environments, the concept of persistent identifiers has been more recently extended to identify also physical objects like people, institutions and any type of relevant entity in the e-Science domain, opening the way to the creation of an integrated information space where a network of resources can be resolved, linked, navigated and analyzed, as the Linked Open Data approach envisions for the Web. However, the creation and full exploitation of this valuable network of connections is currently hindered by the fragmentation and lack of coordination of the digital identifier ecosystem. The aim of this paper is to propose an open, distributed and scalable infrastructure for interoperating existing Persistent Identifiers and other digital identifier systems (like Cool URIs) in e-science, overcoming geographical, disciplinary and organizational boundaries. The Digital Identifier interoperability infrastructure is presented as a cross-cutting solution of core services enabling interoperability at three different levels: identifier, co-reference and semantic.

1 Introduction

In the last 20 years, Internet and the application of computer technology to the scientific production and dissemination have contributed to change the nature of the scientific research, promoting the transition from science to e-science and posing new challenges in terms of preservation, management and sharing of digital scientific content. Digital Identifiers are at the core of this transformation and they have been largely invoked as fundamental elements for realizing the potential of e-science by providing global keys for information access, reuse and exchange and creating a complex network of connections among the relevant entities in the research data landscape (e.g. linking publications to authors and datasets, authors to institutions and projects, projects to research products and fundings). The creation and full exploitation of this valuable network of connections is currently hindered by the fragmentation and lack of coordination of the digital identifier ecosystem.

© Springer International Publishing Switzerland 2016
D. Calvanese et al. (Eds.): IRCDL 2015, CCIS 612, pp. 167–178, 2016.
DOI: 10.1007/978-3-319-41938-1_17

On the one hand, the community of librarians, publishers and public administrations have developed and implemented models and systems for assigning Persistent Identifiers (PIs) to digital and non-digital resources, like electronic documents and authors. However, the lack of interoperability between PIs and related vocabularies, together with the creation of multiple identifiers from different systems for the same objects[1], represents an obstacle for the creation of services that manage and integrate data over multiple systems and is the first major hurdle for the development of a globally connected e-science landscape.

In parallel, the WWW has increasingly evolved into a platform for publishing data (including user-generated data and Semantic Web data) becoming a virtually infinite publication space where each resource is uniquely identified by a web name (URI) and made retrievable through standard protocols. In this context, the Linked Data community, with its concept of Cool URI, is emerging as a potential different approach to manage identifiers for digital objects, authors and other e-science entities (using the Web as a platform). Despite some criticisms concerning persistence, authority and trust issues, an increasing awareness[2] is emerging in part of the PI community that the Linked Data practices and tools may offer a way for extending the value of data (in particular, through cross-linking) and cover use cases which traditional solutions were not designed to address. However, currently an integrating solution for harmonizing and coordinating the two approaches is far to be realized and this lack of integration represents a second crucial interoperability issue for the realization of a navigable digital identity space within the e-science landscape.

The aim of this paper is to propose an open, distributed and scalable infrastructure which both enables the interoperability among current PI systems, minimizing the drawback of the co-existence of multiple PI systems for the same objects and at the same time creates a bridge between PIs and other digital identifiers, like Cool URIs to address the challenge of managing persistent identifiers on a vast scale in open distributed environments and across systems boundaries. The Digital Identifier interoperability infrastructure is presented as a thin layer of core services enabling interoperability at three different levels: identifier, co-reference and semantic. These core services are conceived as essential building blocks for developing value-added e-infrastructure services such as services for (1) data and information discovery and navigation, (2) data sharing and linkage, (3) reputation assessment and citation.

---

[1] An author for example may have multiple identifiers from different systems, like discovery services (e.g. Google scholar profile, AuthorClaim, ORCID), libraries (VIAF, ISNI), disciplinary systems (arXiv, PubMed Author ID), publishers (Scopus ID, Researcher ID) or social networks (LinkedIn, Research Gate), and this redundancy makes difficult to link the author to his/her research activities and scholarly work, having strong consequences in terms of discovery, reputation and impact tracking.

[2] Several initiatives like the Persistent Object Identifiers seminar at The Hague in June 2011 and the Links That Last workshop in Cambridge in July 2012 have highlighted the need of developing a co-ordinated solution to identifier issues across the PI and the Linked Data community, as stated for example in the Den Haag Manifesto available at http://www.knowledge-exchange.info/Default.aspx?ID=462.

1.1   Research and Initiatives on Identifier Interoperability

In the last few years a number of initiatives and projects have started to address the problem of (persistent) identifier interoperability as one of the big issues for the realization of global information infrastructures for science and cultural heritage. One of the first studies on this topic, named DIGOIDUNA [5], was conducted on behalf of the EC in 2011. The study has investigated the fundamental role of digital identifiers as enablers of value in e-science infrastructures and has performed a detailed analysis of strengths, weaknesses, opportunities and threats of the current digital identifier landscape in order to identify the main challenges and propose a set of recommendations which policy makers and relevant stakeholders should address to develop an open and sustainable persistent identifier infrastructure supporting information access and preservation. One of the main conclusions of the study is that to transform digital identifiers from simple means to manage data to keys for delivering value to the stakeholders within the research production, it is necessary to foster the development of an interoperable, cross-domain infrastructure for persistent identifiers supporting data access and sharing across national, organizational, disciplinary and technological boundaries. The implementation of this infrastructure poses not only technical challenges but raises a multidimensional spectrum of organizational, social and economical issues which should be addressed to ensure a coordinated ecosystem. A recent effort in investigating this multifaceted set of issues with the purpose of harmonizing the current identifiers solutions has been made within two working groups of the Research Data Alliance (RDA), an international forum focused on solutions for enabling open sharing of data. The RDA PID Interest Group[3] aims to bring together relevant stakeholders and practitioners to define emerging PID use cases in the domain of data and coordinate the use of persistent identifiers for supporting referencing and citation of research products and authors, and manage the lifecycle of research data production. The PID Information Types Working Group[4], is focused on the definition of a common framework of information types to be associated with PIs for a proper data management and access.

In line with the DIGOIDUNA idea that identifier interoperability should be built on the social and organizational complexities of the current solutions, some initiatives have started to define cooperation agreements and complementary architectures to ensure interoperability between independent systems or organizations. ORCID and ISNI for example have agreed to render ORCID compatible with the ISNI ISO standard and assigning a block of numbers for identifying ORCID entities which can not be reassigned by ISNI to different people[5]. In addition, ORCID has entered into an agreement with Ringgold to use it as Registration Agency for ISNI Institutional Identifiers to support the persistent identification of researcher institutional affiliations in the ORCID registry. The integration between Researcher ID and ORCID is another example of

---

[3] https://rd-alliance.org/internal-groups/pid-interest-group.html.

[4] https://rd-alliance.org/groups/pid-information-types-wg.html.

[5] http://orcid.org/blog/2013/04/22/orcid-and-isni-issue-joint-statement-interoperation-april-2013.

a bi-directional integrating initiative aimed at making information on the two systems interoperable and complementing. Similarly, the ODIN project[6] aims to define a roadmap for the integration and scalability of the DataCite and ORCID identifiers solutions to create a layer of interoperability between persistent identifiers for researchers, research works and their outputs (publications and data). The proposed solution is based on a conceptual model of interoperability [3] for linking research data and their contributors (embedding the corresponding PIs into metadata) through the coordination and alignment of the information flow across data centers, DataCite, and ORCID.

These solutions have made a concrete step forward in the coordination process within the identifier landscape but they have the limit to define interoperability in a point-to-point way. A more broad and integrated approach can be found in the APARSEN project. Within APARSEN, the research on persistent identifiers has focused mainly on the definition of an interoperability framework for persistent identifier systems [1] which defines some key assumptions and requirements to identify the trustable candidate systems which can take part to the framework, an ontology which specifies the structure of data and the core set of relationships linking the identified entities within the framework and finally a small set of services which can be implemented on top of the framework. A demonstrator[7] has also been developed to provide evidence of the potential applicability of the model and the value of related basic services [2].

Finally, other initiatives have been started within specific communities. In the library domain, the BIBFRAME initiative[8] has defined a lightweight framework (metamodel) for bibliographic description based on linked data principles to improve the integration, discoverability and reuse of library resources and their descriptions in a networked distributed environment. At the core of the model, there is the concept of BIBFRAME authority which is a resource representing a person, organization, place, topic, temporal expression and other entities associated with a BIBFRAME Work, Instance, or Annotation. BIBFRAME authorities are used non only to identify (via URIs) the above mentioned entities within the description, but also to link to external resources (for example traditional authorities) referring to the same entities by including their corresponding IDs. In this way, the mechanism of BIBFRAME authorities should provide a common lightweight interoperability layer over different Web based authority resources connecting a BIBFRAME resource to one or more authorities for related entities, such as a person, organization, or place, identified by other identifiers systems like a ID.LOC.GOV, ISNI, VIAF and others.

All these initiatives have the merit to have increased the awareness and consensus among the relevant stakeholders and communities about the crucial role of a coordinated ecosystem of persistent identifiers at the heart of a global infrastructure for e-science. However, a solid technological solution for interoperating identifiers for digital objects, contributors, authors and other

---

relevant entities is still a lacking aspect in the effort of developing a sustainable infrastructure providing an invisible layer of interoperability on which cross-cutting advanced services for science and education can be implemented. This is pointed out in the recent EU Framework Programme for Research and Innovation (Horizon 2020)[9] which includes the implementation of a Digital-identifier e-infrastructure for digital objects, contributors and authors, among the key actions for implementing an open, interoperable e-infrastructure for scientific data. Based on the valuable results of the above initiatives, but also exploiting the experience on global identifiers for the Semantic Web gained in the course of the OKKAM FP7 project[10], this paper proposes a technical solution to address this challenge by implementing an interoperability cross-cutting system for Persistent Identifiers and other identifiers used in e-science.

2 Implementing an Interoperability Infrastructure for Digital Identifiers

The infrastructure that we propose is an open, distributed, decentralized and scalable service for managing unique identification of digital and non-digital resources over digital networks and implementing interoperability services for existing identifier systems, including PIs and Cool URIs. The implementation of the infrastructure has been driven by the following requirements:

– IDENTITY MANAGEMENT: the infrastructure is aimed at managing the unique identification of digital, physical or abstract entities of any type (e.g. person, organization, event, artifact, location), where there is a need to distinguish them from other objects in digital content and interoperate all the external identifiers used to identify the same entities. It is important to keep separate the ID management from the management of the information identified by the ID. While the interoperability infrastructure should perform ID management, in our approach content management should be handled outside the infrastructure by data managers and content providers. However, since different identifiers use different identifier schemes to identify the same objects, the ID management should ensure not only interoperability at the level of identifier (e.g. connecting equivalent identifiers from different sources) but also interoperability at the level of the identifier metadata which includes the defining attributes that are considered sufficient to establish the unique reference between communicating parties. ID management should also be kept separated from the implementation of value-added community services. The interoperability infrastructure is conceived as a thin layer of core ID management services on top of which advanced services can be built to address specific needs and requirements of specific users. These value-added services are not part of the infrastructure but are enabled by the infrastructure and can be developed by third parties and driven by targeted business models.

---

[9] http://ec.europa.eu/research/participants/data/ref/h2020/wp/2014_2015/main/ h2020-wp1415-infrastructures_en.pdf.

[10] http://project.okkam.org/.

- PERSISTENT COOL IDs: the identifier solution implemented by the system should be compatible both with persistence and authority requirements of the PI users and with openness and decentralization principles of the Web community.
- OPENNESS: the infrastructure should not present entrance barriers for existing identifier providers and users which are encouraged to build their applications and services on the infrastructure.
- DISTRIBUTION and DECENTRALIZATION: the infrastructure operations and data can be distributed and replicated over any number of different machines both geographically and logically in a seamless way. Moreover, the infrastructure must have no single point of failure and it must be able to survive any damage in any node of its architecture. This redundancy is crucial for ensuring the PERSISTENCE and RELIABILITY of the service. The distributed and decentralized architecture contributes also to the SUSTAINABILITY of the system whose costs can be shared and distributed among multiple organizations hosting the nodes of the infrastructure.
- SCALABILITY: the infrastructure should be able to cope with billions of digital identifiers from any number of providers and serve hundreds of interoperability requests per second.
- TRUST: The infrastructure is conceived as a trusted infrastructure where an operating organization is committed to the long term (i.e. Trustee) under the surveillance of an international board of protectors representing its main stakeholders.

The proposed infrastructure is the result of the evolution of the Entity Name System (ENS),[11] a scalable Web service, developed in the context of the EU-funded OKKAM project[12] for assigning and managing unique identifiers for Web entities and foster their global reuse. The first prototype of this system has emerged as a solution for the entity identification problem in the Semantic Web [6], that is the problem of integrating information about entities which are assigned multiple identifiers (i.e. URIs) in different systems or by different users [7]. Recently, the scope of the system has been extended to address the problem of the proliferation of identifiers (i.e. PIs) in other distributed management information contexts like libraries, archives, publisher systems and e-science infrastructures, evolving into a bridge infrastructure for Web identifiers and PIs.

The first aim of the ENS is to provide a service to assign globally unique identifiers to entities named in information sources and reuse these identifiers across systems boundaries regardless of the place or domain where they have been first assigned. To this purpose, the ENS has a scalable repository[13] for storing entity identifiers along with a short set of descriptive metadata, i.e. an entity profile, which is used to disambiguate each entity from the others. When a human user

---

[11] http://api.okkam.org/.

[12] http://project.okkam.org/.

[13] The storage and access components of the infrastructure are based on Apache Hadoop, a scalable software framework for distributed storage and processing of big data.

or an application inquire the system for an identifier (for example by keywords through the Web search interface[14]), the information of the entity profiles is used to establish (through advanced entity matching algorithms) if an identifier has been already assigned and stored for that entity. Otherwise, a new identifier is minted and returned by the system. The systematic reuse of the identifiers created and maintained in the ENS is aimed at reducing the multiplication of identifiers for entities and enabling a straightforward solution for entity-centric integration of information spread across different systems and platforms. However, since the convergence of different users on the use of a unique identification standard is desirable but very hard to be realized at a global level, the coordination and interoperability of different identifier systems has emerged as the second main function implemented in the ENS. Therefore, the ENS implements a service to store (within the entity profiles) and manage equivalent identifiers (i.e. alternative IDs) assigned to the same entities by different systems. This service, called Mapping service, together with the other services described in Table 1 support the core operation of the ENS. Local private nodes (replicas) of the infrastructure can be implemented to include the same core services with the aim of managing entities or sensitive information which need to be maintained physically separated from the rest of the public infrastructure. Today, more than 9 millions of entities are managed by the system and the number is growing every day. In the next section we will discuss how on top of this core infrastructure, the ENS has been evolved into an interoperability infrastructure bridging digital identifiers in use in e-science and other digital contexts. We name this infrastructure "Entity Identifier Bridge".

2.1   From the Entity Name System to the Entity Identifier Bridge

The Entity Identifier Bridge (EIB) provides interoperability services at three different levels:

1. The identifier level: offering an identification solution which is compatible both with the persistence and authority requirements of the PI community and with the openness and decentralization principles of the (Semantic) Web community.
2. The co-reference level: supporting cross-linkage of different PIs and other digital identifiers for the same object (identifier mapping).
3. The semantic level: storing mappings between the different metadata / vocabularies which are associated with each identifier in different systems.

The Identifier Level: As discussed in [4], one of the first actions that contributed to evolution of the ENS into the EIB is the change of the ENS identifier syntax to offer a reconciling identification solution which can be used both by PI communities to implement trusted authority-based services and by the Semantic Web and Linked Data users to publish and distribute structured content

---

[14] Available at http://api.okkam.org/search/.

Table 1. ENS core services

Service	Description	Function
STORAGE	A large-scale ENTITY REPOSITORY which stores identifiers, entity profiles and other information about different types of entity	To ensure the uniqueness and persistence of the binding between an entity identifier and the entity
MATCHING	A set of ALGORITHMS to decide whether an ID already exists, given the information a user or application presents to the system	To make identifiers searchable and easily retrievable by humans and applications
LIFECYCLE MANAGEMENT	to support few BASIC OPERATIONS on entity profiles and ENS IDs (create, edit, merge, split..) and deal with evolving entity	To ensure adequate maintainability and the secure long-term evolution of the system
ALTERNATIVE ID MANAGEMENT	to store known MAPPINGS between the ENS ID and any other available ID for the same entity	To enable identifier interoperability

on the Web. The simple change consists of the separation of the ENS-ID (e.g. ens:eid-a5afe3ae-071f-4ec3-b904-3481aa5a6a05) from the resolver (http://www.okkam.org). This introduces a level of indirection between the identifier and its referent, decoupling persistent identification from resolution and retrieval. When the ENS-ID is combined with the ENS default resolver, its resolution returns a small set of metadata (included in the ENS entity profile) related to the identified entity. The real potential of separating the token ID from the resolver rests on the possibility of associating the same ID to multiple resolvers, enabling a mechanism of multiple resolution and distribution of authority in the management of data. Different actors can create or reuse Persistent ENS-IDs for entities of interest using the ENS and through their local resolvers or domain names enable precise (and possibly long-term) access to information they want to provide. In this way, ID management and default resolution are addressed by the ENS, whereas information management, including persistence of content and reliable resolution, is managed by content providers. The ENS-IDs can be used to create Cool URIs (through the web resolution protocol and the DNS) allowing Linked Data users to create URIs resolvable to any information source they like. At the same time, persistent identifiers users can reuse the same IDs to identify information objects and resources managed by trusted institutions which ensure their persistent access and association to a physical location. This improvement of the ENS may offer a co-ordinated solution to identifier issues across the PI and the Linked Data communities, enabling data creators and curators to combine the technical strengths and opportunities of the (Semantic) Web vision with the organizational, economical and social requirements legitimately raised by PI stakeholders with the result of opening new forms of interactions between open structured data published on the Web and content stored and preserved by more traditional cultural heritage institutions.

The Co-reference Level: At this level the EIB implements a small set of core interoperability services on top of the Mapping Service of the ENS to enable access and reuse of mappings between alternative identifiers for the same entity. Currently three services have been implemented. The first two services support the retrieval of alternative IDs. The third service implements the multiple resolution of entity identifiers.

Alternative ID Retrieval Service (by ID): The first service allows to retrieve an alternative ID of a specific type (which can be a PI or Cool URI) or all the available alternative IDs for a given entity ID (which can be a PI or Cool URI). The user for example can enter the ISNI of a person to get the ORCID ID of the same person (as shown in Fig. 1) or retrieve all the alternative identifiers stored in the system for her.

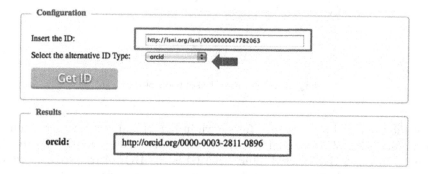

Fig. 1. Alternative ID Retrieval Service (by ID)

Alternative ID Retrieval Service (by Query): The second service supports the same function as the previous one with the only difference that the identified entity is searched by a keyword query. Going back to the previous example, the user can enter a keyword query (e.g. the name of the person) to get an alternative ID of a specific type (e.g. the ISNI) or all the available alternative IDs for that entity.

Alternative Resolution Service: The last service allows to enter an ID and resolve it through the resolver of an alternative ID. For example, the user can

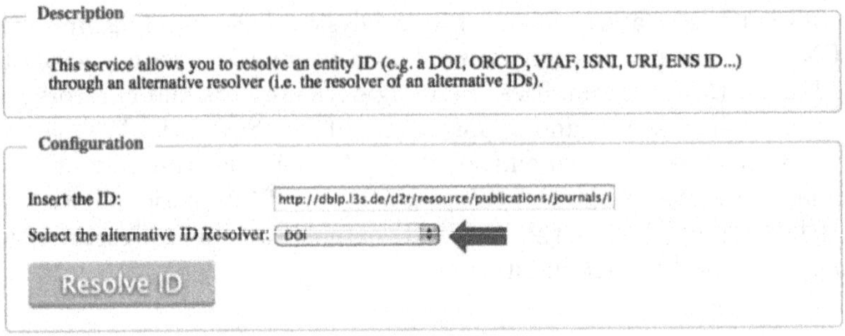

(a) Input

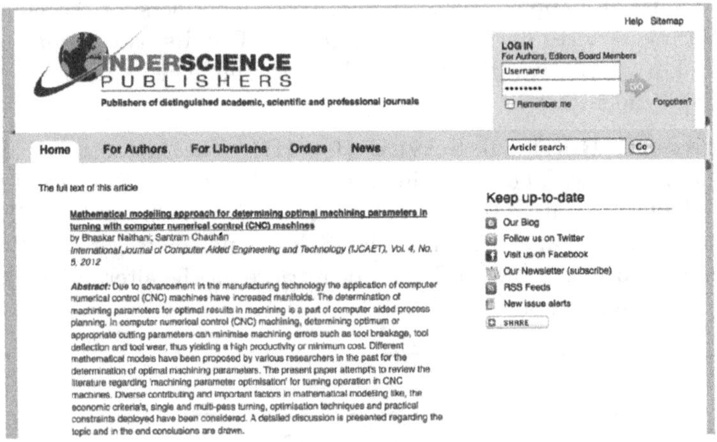

(b) Output

Fig. 2. Alternative Resolution Service

enter the Cool URI of a resource (as shown in Fig. 2) and access to the resource
(or a description of it) through the resolver of a selected alternative ID. In the
example in Fig. 2 the selected alternative ID is the DOI of the resource which
resolves to the InderScience Publishers page for the identified article.

The Semantic Level. At the third level, identifiers are linked across meta-
data/vocabularies. Different persistent IDs are usually associated to different
metadata models. If a mapping among them is available, the information represented according to a data model in one source can be translated into a different
model and re-used to integrate or update the information of another source
adopting that model. Therefore, in order to support semantic interoperability
across services and communities, the ENS should provide an extensive mapping
of vocabularies and schemes adopted in different PID domains. In addition, since
these mappings can be also defined contextually and different users can have their
own mappings for the same vocabularies, a solution for managing these mappings

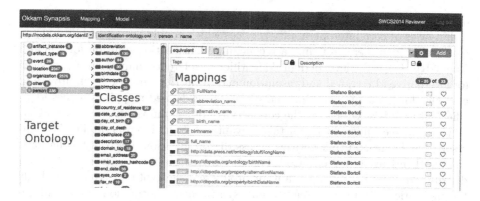

Fig. 3. Synapsis Interface

and making them reusable, should be the result of a large-scale social process where users can create their mappings but also reuse the mappings defined by other users. Following this idea, a Web service, called OKKAM Synapsis[15], has been developed to store and maintain user-defined mappings between terms in controlled vocabularies, models and ontologies. Through the application, a user (human user or API user) can search the available mappings for the classes and properties of the models present in the system, add new mappings, rate (like it) and edit existing mappings (e.g. tagging, adding a description). In addition, the user can upload a new model (i.e. the target ontology) and define his/her own mappings for the model. The mappings are defined by specifying the Resource URI, that is the URI of the resource mapped towards the element of the target ontology and the type of relation between them[16]. The service allows to filter the stored mappings by author, tags, status and type of relation. While in the APARSEN Interoperability Framework semantic interoperability is addressed by proposing a common ontology which should be used by content providers to expose their data in a common way, the ENS approach focuses on the alignment of different vocabularies through ontology mapping. This has the advantage that users can maintain their own vocabularies and ontologies, without the need of restructuring their content according to a new model. The mapping of vocabularies allows to support the building of crosswalks between them and can be extended to include an indefinite number of vocabularies (Fig. 3).

3   Conclusion

In this paper, we propose an open scalable interoperability infrastructure (EIB) for persistent identifiers and other digital identifiers in e-science. The proposed

---

[15] http://api.okkam.org/synapsis/.

[16] The user can select among a number of relations types including OWL meta-relations such as owl:EquivalentProperty, owl:EquivalentClass, owl:SubClass, owl:SubProperty and SKOS meta-relations skos:exact, skos:close, skos:broader, skos:narrower.

infrastructure is based on the OKKAM Entity Name System and is presented as a thin layer of core interoperability services which enable interoperability (1) at the level of identifier, providing a reconciling identification solution for PIs and Cool URIs, (2) at the level of digital identifier co-reference, implementing services for alternative id retrieval and resolution and (3) at the semantic level, providing a service for managing, sharing and reusing user-defined mappings across identifier data models. On top of the core services of the infrastructure value-added services can be built which can take advantage of the interoperability layer to resolve, navigate and link entities across digital curation, discovery, collaboration, authentication and other e-Infrastructures services and extract value from distributed data. For example, author profile management services can be built to automatically import, integrate and synchronize information from multiple sources like authoritative sources (e.g. libraries and publishers), auto-claiming services or Web content and trace the provenance of the information. Empowered information discovery services can provide multiple access to digital resources stored in different systems via alternative IDs or provide integrated views of these resources through the mash-up of metadata from different sources using different schemes. Discovery and navigation tools can be built which allow to go through the chain of links connecting the identified entities in the e-science landscape (e.g. authors-publications-datasets-projects-fundings), discover hidden relationships and generate new valuable knowledge (e.g. who contributed in what ways to the research outputs with the support of which fundings and institutions.).

References

1. APARSEN D22.1: Persistent identifiers interoperability framework (2012). http://www.alliancepermanentaccess.org/wp-content/uploads/downloads/2012/04/APARSEN-REP-D22-1-01-1_9.pdf
2. APARSEN D22.3: Demonstrator set up and definition of added value services (2013). http://www.alliancepermanentaccess.org/wp-content/uploads/downloads/2014/02/APARSEN-REP-D22_3-01-1_0.pdf
3. D4.1: Conceptual model of interoperability (2013). http://files.figshare.com/1239137/D4.1_Conceptual_Model_of_Interoperability.pdf
4. Bazzanella, B., Bortoli, S., Bouquet, P.: Can persistent identifiers be cool? IJDC 8(1), 14–28 (2013)
5. Bouquet, P., Bazzanella, B., Dow, M., Riestra, R.: DIGOIDUNA FINAL REPORT: Digital Object Identifiers and Unique Author Identifiers to enable services for data quality assessment, provenance and access (2011). http://cordis.europa.eu/fp7/ict/e-infrastructure/docs/digoiduna.pdf
6. Bouquet, P., Stoermer, H., Bazzanella, B.: An entity name system (ENS) for the semantic web. In: Bechhofer, S., Hauswirth, M., Hoffmann, J., Koubarakis, M. (eds.) ESWC 2008. LNCS, vol. 5021, pp. 258–272. Springer, Heidelberg (2008)
7. Bouquet, P., Stoermer, H., Niederée, C., Na, A.M., Niederee, C., Mana, A.: Entity name system: the backbone of an open and scalable web of data. In: ICSC, pp. 554–561. IEEE Computer Society (2008). CSS-ICSC 2008-4-28-25

Finding a Needle in a Haystack

The BEIC Digital Library in Search of Its Space on the Web: A Case Study

Chiara Consonni[1(✉)] and Paul Gabriele Weston[2]

[1] Fondazione BEIC, Milan, Italy
chiara.consonni@beic.it
[2] University of Pavia, Pavia, Italy
paul.weston@unipv.it

Abstract. The paper describes the strategies undertaken by BEIC Digital Library in order to find its identity and space on the Web. It will be of interest and value to other digital libraries facing the same challenges or in search of new strategies to promote their collections and to monitor their use.

Keywords: Identity · Statistics · Online exhibition · Navigator · Partnership · Community involvement · Dissemination · BEIC · Digital library · Assessment

1 Setting the Scene

The Biblioteca Europea di Informazione e Cultura (BEIC) was established in Milan "with the purpose of offering the community a state-of-the-art structure which would provide universal access to information and knowledge under any form by sharing online bibliographic and documentary resources from the metropolitan area of Milan and thanks to the extensive use of digital technology[1]". When its mission was defined in such terms, the library project involved two tightly intertwined components: a physical section intended as a public library hosting a vast collection of items covering all fields of knowledge, in both analogue and digital format, and, as its integration, a digital library largely built on a collection of ancient and rare material which the physical library could not have ignored, but far too expensive to be purchased on the antiquarian market.

With this perspective in mind, in designing the collection development plan within the feasibility study, great effort was made to identify the most appropriate bibliography in every area of knowledge – by evaluating factors such as extension, granularity, form of speech, language – in order to offer readers a service of the intended quality.

Over the years, the creation of the physical library was postponed over and over again thus making the decision to count solely on the digital component quite inevitable. This has implied a radical reconsideration of the criteria underlying its design, as well as the need to change course of action in regard to the collection development plan, which has since turned into a digital collection and service plan.

---

[1] www.beic.it.

© Springer International Publishing Switzerland 2016
D. Calvanese et al. (Eds.): IRCDL 2015, CCIS 612, pp. 179–190, 2016.
DOI: 10.1007/978-3-319-41938-1_18

Nowadays the Beic Digital Library (BeicDL) counts more than 26,000 digital items ranging from books and manuscripts to artworks and audio-video and stands out for its selectiveness and the multidisciplinary nature of its collections. Indeed, it makes a variety of works freely accessible, including some of the most important titles in the field of science, the arts and humanities stretching across a timeframe spanning from the ancient world to the modern age.

Before even agreeing on the infrastructure, it was decided that each component should be compliant to international and national standards in order to ensure interoperability and long-term sustainability. Two examples are the format of the images (TIFF, Tagged Image File Format) which, given its specifications, is a *de facto* standard, and the images metadata. The latter, consisting of XML files, are coded according to the METS schema (Metadata Encoding and Transmission Standard), the sections of which contain metadata compliant with other standards: MARC XML (XML schema based on the standard MARC, Machine Readable Cataloguing), MIX (metadata for Images in XML standard) and PREMIS (Preservation metadata: Implementation Strategies). All these standards are supported either by the World Wide Web Consortium or by the Library of Congress, and are used by the major digital libraries in the world. Once principles and standards were defined, the infrastructure, housed in one of the server farms operated by the Politecnico di Milano, was set up. The infrastructure includes six modules: Digital Collections Archive (Secure Image, Imago Libris, IBM System Storage TS3310 Tape Library); Repository (Digitool from Exlibris); Cataloguing (Koha); Structural Maps (the software is still under development); Viewer (the basic Digitool METSViewer was customized to support more advanced features, a specific player was developed and Vimeo PRO was purchased); Discovery tool (Primo from ExLibris).

Two main threats derive to the BeicDL from the loss of its physical component: a weakened identity and the lack of visibility over the Internet. Because the two issues are so tightly bound, they should be considered together in designing a strategy, or even better a set of strategies, aiming at providing a renovated identity to the DL, thus making its contents more appealing and its services more efficient, and contributing to its popularity among Web users [2]. Identity and popularity don't always mix well in DLs [1]. On the one hand, one can hardly deny that Gallica is rich in both factors. Deeply rooted in a prestigious, centuries-old institution such as the BNF, with an incredible amount of bibliographic and multimedia resources, and a crucial role to play in the international arena, Gallica appears to benefit greatly in terms of identity and popularity. Its digital patrimony, which is constantly increased due to the format conversion of the ancient and rare book collections as well as the acquisition of the digital native current publications, bears witness to the strong identity of that Country, deriving from its literary, artistic and scientific production [7]. In comparison, Europeana, notwithstanding its undisputed popularity and heavy usage, appears to have a much weaker identity, as a consequence of its being the result of aggregating metadata deriving from projects quite different in nature, scope, quality and criteria. A massive intake of data and the involvement of a wider number of partners were both considered inevitable, maybe even desirable, initially. However, insufficient project coordination and a flimsy connection among its contents has produced what one would hardly perceive as a representation of the European identity. The Great War documentation project is probably the first and more significant effort towards coordination and is leading to the surfacing on that platform of a shared historical and cultural identity.

2   BEIC Assessment

By no means has BeicDL dimensions, ambitions, scopes and resources in any way comparable to those implemented by the previous two projects. Nonetheless, the management has felt obliged to assess its own perspectives and to try and profit from any preexistent experience. To this purpose BeicDL was submitted to a SWOT analysis which provided the results shown in the table below (Table 1).

Table 1. SWOT analysis

INTERNAL ANALYSIS	
STRENGHTS	**WEAKNESSES**
• its quite recent history	• absence of a physical component
• knowledgeable staff engaged in key technical and bibliographic choices	• need for a severe adjustment of the DL model previously designed and of the collections and services development plan
• compliance with national and international standards	• weakness of the brand
• suitable technological equipment well supported by an excellent computer centre	• unbalanced bibliographic coverage of the knowledge fields involved
• flexibility and willingness to re-act promptly to evolving market trends	• uncertain availability of financial resources in the medium-long run
• low production costs	• understaffing even with respect to key roles
• partnerships with authoritative institutions from the various fields	
• bibliographic and documentary material of a good quality (as regards cultural interest, typological variety and coverage of knowledge fields)	
• financial resources adequate to carry out the project for a reasonable number of years	
OPPORTUNITIES	**THREATS**
• widespread existence of standards, protocols and models facilitating distribution, aggregation and reuse of data	• signs of great difficulty deriving from the Italian economic framework
• growing attention towards the availability of cultural contents in the public domain	• state of uncertainty in the Italian governmental initiatives in support of culture
• development of new promotion channels for collections and knowledge	• widespread incapacity on a national level to behave as a system and to develop medium-long term planning

(Continued)

Table 1. (*Continued*)

• subjects interested in the development of innovative services	• present fragility of the BeicDL in the absence of a supporting physical institution
• growing attention on the part of state, academic and private subjects, both in Italy and in Europe, towards the possibility of commercial exploitation of cultural objects to subsidize products and services in the public domain	• lack of contact with the current (contemporary) bibliographic production
• widespread interest towards the reuse of know-how and technologies developed within the project	• difficulty to predefine a specific target
EXTERNAL ANALYSIS	

Data offered by the SWOT analysis enable us to make some broad reflections, before proceeding to a description of the implemented strategies, along with more specific considerations [10].

3   Preliminary Reflections

In the first place, the recent history of BeicDL should be taken into account. Many libraries, some Italian ones in particular, find it difficult to combine efficiently their own history and their consolidated traditions with the perspectives opened by new services, renovated operating methods, and users still to be identified to whom to target their wealth of knowledge [7]. In several cases, this has led to the creation of digital libraries whose documents are treated as museum pieces, rather than published following criteria consistent with the digital environment within which they fall. This choice (or missed choice, if you prefer) can be explained in various ways: preference given to the text as the principal medium in transferring knowledge; difficulty in keeping separate the wealth of knowledge from the items hosting this knowledge (in regard to this, one could recall the difference between "bibliotheca", the bibliography, and "biblioteca", the actual library); granting the new search tools (Google, Wikipedia etc.) a lesser status than their printed equivalents; perceiving virtual exhibitions, educational tools and the alike, as trivial compared with the "high", professional service the library is bound to provide; last but not least, difficulties to implement new procedures and commitments given the hard times most libraries are currently facing, both in terms of cutbacks and falling staff turnover rates, the latter being of course a very critical issue [6].

BeicDL is therefore offered the opportunity of thinking in a native digital way, notwithstanding its commitment to be a library in the first place. The presence of young, strongly motivated staff, with a wide spectrum of work experience to get a feel for professional working environments and the taste for new means of expression in their background, provides BeicDL with a richness of opportunities. With their guidance, BeicDL is committed to experiment new ways, to secure alliances, to identify and implement data and service models coming from fields other than libraries and the cultural heritage whenever deemed strategical. In these cases conformity to national and international standards is obviously a basic requirement. Customizations that in the short term could be felt as shortcuts leading to taylor-made products, in the case of subjects the size of BeicDL turn after a short period to be way too expensive to maintain and upgrade, therefore contributing to the library's alienation from the web community.

4 Swimming in a Blue Ocean

Secondly, BeicDL should give special attention to identifying ways in which it can have its own identity, despite the absence of a physical library to rely upon. This has to do with going beyond the idea of an individual library and finding, instead, its own setting, its role within the digital ecosystem [17]. In order to explain the underlying philosophy of BeicDL's strategic choices, inasmuch as its physical component was becoming more and more remote, we should turn to the Blue Ocean Strategy (BOS) metaphor, an economic theory proposed by W. Chan Kim and Renée Mauborgne (2005). Its most successful implementation in the field of cultural heritage is probably the Cirque du Soleil case. Created in 1984 by a small group of underground street performers, the Cirque was seen thereafter by more than thirty-five million people all around the world. Due to the existence of a big leader as Ringling Bros and Barnum & Bailey, that set the benchmark, all the small competitors were only allowed to recreate that business model on a smaller and sometimes unprofitable scale. Cirque Du Soleil's huge achievement was that they were not competing on the same targets of the leader, but they created a new unchallenged market space. In other words, they made competition irrelevant. The implementation of BOS consists, therefore, in identifying opportunity for growth and potential for market spaces not yet or not adequately explored. This scenario stands opposite to the one in which the excess of players leads to a ruthless competition that "will turn the ocean bloody red".

In the case of BeicDL, the decision was not to compete on the same ground as the initiatives of Google Books or digital projects based on huge collections of large national institutions, such as the Bibliothèque Nationale de France (BNF) and the Bibliotheksverbund Bayern (BVB), but to choose as more desirable such criteria as selectivity and accuracy. Additionally, the search tools offered to the users were enhanced by integrating data and services provided by major bibliographic utilities.

Per se the decision to identify and fill a market niche is not one which would prove sufficient to define an identity and attract a good number of users. More strategic options are required in order to characterize data and services so as to make them distinguishable and attractive. In the first place comes quality, possibly the highest though bearing in mind the sustainability factor. Digital objects should be of good quality, metadata reliable and complete, descriptions of contents granular, navigational tools diverse and effective. In the second place comes the decision to put metadata and digital objects in the public domain, therefore freely harvestable and reusable in contexts even quite different. Agreements have been made with platforms and shared catalogues targeted to different users with the goal of making BeicDL data visible and active linking points. The third option was to take on editorial activities, focusing internally on virtual exhibitions, such as the Biblioteca idraulica, and externally on a set of entries in Wikipedia. Plans have been made to adopt linked open data to develop a digital reference service. In many ways, this is how BeicDL reacts to Karen Calhoun's suggestion that libraries should become digital *scriptoria*, so reevaluating a feature, which is inscribed into their DNA. The final option, in this summary recognition, is the relationship established with readers, which is not limited to the mere use of resources, but looks forward to collaborating in the creation of new contents, as well as implying the involvement of communities often quite apart from one another.

5   Strategies

The strategies implemented to avoid the risks and the weaknesses proceeded from the acknowledgment of the opportunities and exploitation of the strengths. As already pointed out, the main looming challenges are the loss of identity and the lack of visibility over the Internet. It is therefore important to ensure appeal to the collections, to enhance the services and to promote awareness among the public [18].

Several actions, resulting from a long period of studies with the goal of maximizing the outcomes given the limited amount of resources, were taken to tackle these challenges [19].

Firstly, partnerships with other institutions were established and metadata were released in the public domain to promote awareness among potential users. Secondly, multimedia technologies (online exhibitions and resource navigators) have been developed to ensure appeal to the collections. Eventually communities such as Wikimedia Italia and Material Evidence in Incunabola (MEI) were approached and involved in shared projects in order to boost the services. An evaluation plan was designed to monitor the achievements of these strategies and discuss future steps [20]. Indeed data provide the essential elements to understand the components of a digital library and the relations among them. Moreover they reveal the impact and effectiveness of the services. Finally the results of the analysis guide the planning of new projects and the allocation of resources. Data collection and analysis are not performed only at the end of specific tasks or projects, when it is crucial to identify the successful factors and compare the results with other experiences, but also when the activities are in progress, in order to track the evolvements and possibly to reassess the forthcoming steps [21].

BeicDL has embraced the constant users involvement model and highly value users' feedback since the very first day, believing that learning why some activities work and others fail should be the priority.

As recalled by Kyrillidou [16] in his article about assessment protocols published in 2005 "the project-oriented nature of digital libraries makes it difficult to evaluate them as a whole". To overcome this threat and collect qualitative and quantitative data, BeicDL employs tools both independent (Google Analytics) and dependent from the applications in use (Digitool and Primo from ExLibris). This approach, which has the advantage of setting flexible parameters, provides also more reliable results. Furthermore,

BeicDL follows a strict protocol based on a measurement plan and a rigid policy about data treatment drawn upon best practices and current data analysis landscape.

The following sections briefly describe the strategies and analyze their impact on pageviews and sessions statistics, where possible. The latter is accounted as sufficiently relevant and reliable although it cannot be considered exhaustive because the evaluation process must combine quantitative and qualitative data [11, 19].

5.1   User Communities Involvement

The first and most interesting strategy is the active involvement of users. BeicDL has recently partnered with one of the most influential communities on the web, wikipedians, and a small (compared to the previous one) proactive community of professionals, the incunabula specialists. A shared programme was signed in September 2014 to establish a relationship with the Wikipedia community and make BeicDL a potential reference for editors interested in topics covered by the digital library materials. Wiki- media Italia nominated a consultant[2] (a "wikipedian in residence") who has since been training BEIC staff and identifying interesting matches between the digital library items and various Wiki projects (Wikipedia, Wikimedia Commons, Wikibooks and Wiki-data)[3]. Activities are not limited to creating and editing articles. In fact, organization of edithatons, donations of books to Wikisource and editors engagement are also carried out[4]. The impact of the Wiki projects was beyond expectations, not only due to the linchpin role that Wikipedia plays in the Web, but because of the motivation and skills that staff (wikipedian and non) have put in these activities. By November 15th 2014, 2,044 articles written in more than 90 languages were revised and updated and 50 new entries were created. Accurately selected pictures of 50 works and 35 authors were loaded in Wikimedia Commons and are currently in use in more than 450 entries. As a result, references based on BeicDL were also added to each corresponding article.

5.2   Partnerships and Metadata Sharing

Partnerships have always been part of BeicDL priorities, in order to exploit resources, to benefit from team work and to ensure a local, national and international dimension to the digital library [14]. The edited articles have more than ten thousand monthly visits according to the Wikipedia statistics. The importance of this partnership is confirmed also by the BeicDL statistics: sessions beginning in Wiki environment generate approximately 20 % of the traffic[5].

---

[2] The wikipedian in residence is Nemo, wikipedian since 2006.

[3] http://wiki.wikimedia.it/wiki/Comunicati_stampa/Wikipediano_in_residenza_alla_BEIC.

[4] http://it.wikipedia.org/wiki/Progetto:GLAM/BEIC.

[5] http://it.wikipedia.org/wiki/Progetto:GLAM/BEIC/2014-11.

As for MEI[6], it is a database specifically designed to record and search copy specific evidence and provenance information of 15th-century printed books (i.e. incunabula) [9]. Data regarding ownership, decoration, binding, manuscript annotations, stamps, prices are formalized within a structured database linked to the Incunabula Short Title Catalogue (ISTC), provided by the British Library, thus allowing users to combine searches of bibliographical records (extracted from ISTC) with copy specific records (based on MEI data). Every element recorded is treated as a valuable clue for provenance. Ownership notes, whenever geographically localized and chronologically dated, enable tracking of the movement of books across Europe and through the centuries. Manuscript notes, equally valuable for understanding the readership of the early editions, allow for sophisticated social studies on the use of books, readership and reading [8].

Personal and institutional names of ownership are linked to the CERL Thesaurus, where further bio-bibliographical information can be found [4]. This provides links to other editions identified with the specified name, clarifying whether the owner was also an author, thus merging ownership and authorship information.

Over 50 editors in as many institutions (ranging from very small to very large) across Europe and North America are currently recording provenance in MEI, thereby contributing to the reconstruction of dispersed collections. This is where BeicDL comes in. Though some of the work needs a direct recognition of the original, a lot of information can be provided by integral good quality digital reproductions, such as those available in BeicDL. Scholars can use the DL in many ways: they can verify the existence of material evidence and identify its nature, use the digital reproduction as a source when recording data in MEI, handle it as a resource for identification queries. On the other hand, the links established in ISTC will direct users cross searching the two databases at CERL to copies available in digital format in BeicDL.

At the BeicDL's end, MEI records will be regularly downloaded for integration into the local discovery tool and more links and cross references will then be built, which will hopefully enhance the wealth of information at the disposal of the user. Since work is being currently carried out on this project, we are not yet in a position to provide figures on the use of this service. However, we can already provide the number of links from ISTC back to BeicDL documents, which is in the region of 200 per month.

Agreements on a local basis are well represented by the cooperation with the Braidense National Library[7] to support and manage the Archive of the Regional legal deposit of Lombardy[8]. On a national level, partnerships have been secured with several institutions such as the Istituto Storico Italiano per il Medioevo (ISIME)[9] and the Istituto Veneto di Scienze, Lettere ed Arti (IVSLA)[10] in order to provide a wider audience with relevant works that would have otherwise been available to a much more limited community. Additional collaborations are established to exchange materials or

---

[6] http://www.cerl.org/resources/mei/main.

[7] www.braidense.it.

[8] www.beic.it/en/articles/legal-deposit.

[9] www.isime.it/.

[10] www.istitutoveneto.it/.

participate in shared programmes, such as the one with Museo Galileo – Institute and Museum of the History of Science[11].

The BEIC Foundation is a member of the Consortium of European Research Libraries (CERL)[12] and The European Library[13]. The collaboration with CERL is aimed at sharing resources and expertise to improve access to European printed heritage. The European Library partnership allows exposure to the digital library resources on a global scale, through its own web portal, as well as through the affiliated portal of Europeana[14]. The traffic generated by national collaborations, which are typically based on projects, differs greatly and is relevant especially at the beginning and at the end of the project, when the impact peaks at 4–5 % before settling at 1.5 %. Another 4 % of the audience is guaranteed by international partnerships, in particular 1 % is generated by The European Library and 3 % by Europeana. These figures are constantly changing as they tend to be affected by initiatives and promotions (i.e. current events, virtual exhibitions, etc.). Data from CERL are not yet available. As a general policy, BeicDL provides descriptive metadata under the CC0 license[15], which includes the waiving of all rights to the extent permitted by law. Therefore, one is allowed to copy, modify, distribute and use, even for commercial purposes, all data without any limitation. This policy is in place to encourage and facilitate the reuse of BeicDL metadata which in general should be of a good quality [19]. An example of reuse is offered by the OPAC of the Biblioteche civiche torinesi[16], in which links to the BeicDL resources have been successfully established[17]. This approach provides crawlers with the chance to harvest the data and make BeicDL items available directly through major search engines such as Google and Yahoo. It is difficult to establish a quantitative value to this figure because results will only show in the long period. An estimated figure is 1 %, although it inevitably takes into account pipes that provide links back to BeicDL domains.

5.3   Resource Navigators and Online Exhibitions

As recalled by the Handbook on virtual exhibitions and virtual performances, an INDICATE [13] project publication, the creation of multimedia tools for the exploration of data and documents is considered one of the most important activities of cultural institutions because it encourages and strengthens the relationship with the users. The advantages of multimedia interfaces, although not entirely replacing the physical experience, are evident and include the possibility of browsing items following personal patterns and the chance to engage a greater number of users. This

---

[11] www.museogalileo.it/.

[12] www.cerl.org/.

[13] www.theeuropeanlibrary.org/.

[14] www.europeana.eu/.

[15] www.creativecommons.org/publicdomain/zero/1.0/.

[16] www.bct.comperio.it/.

[17] An example is: www.bct.comperio.it/opac/detail/view/sbct:catalog:44869.

approach also encourages feedbacks and gives visitors the possibility to cooperate in the development of the exhibition itself [12]. Furthermore, documents and valuable works can be enjoyed comfortably, without compromising their preservation. There are many typologies of multimedia tools and infinite combinations of resources, however BeicDL decided to focus on two of the most powerful: online exhibitions and resource navigators. An online exhibition is a hypermedia collection accessible on the web, which is made of digital objects linked accordingly to topics in a system architecture designed to deliver engaging and user-friendly experiences [12]. Museums such as MoMA[18] and Hermitage[19] have made successful online exhibitions for many years, and recently more libraries have ventured into this path as well, curating exhibitions such as "Discovering Literature: Romantics and Victorians"[20] by the British Library[21] and "l'Art du Livre Arabe"[22], a publication of the Bibliothèque Nationale de France[23].

BeicDL is currently implementing a virtual exhibition, which is part of a larger project named Biblioteca Idraulica. The latter, focusing on hydraulics, was created in collaboration with the department of Agricultural and Environmental Sciences - Production, Landscape, Agroenergy of the University of Milan[24] and sponsored by the Cariplo Foundation[25].

The project involves the digitization of 800 works, the publication of thematic monographs and the design of educational tools devised for use in secondary schools[26]. The topic was selected bearing in mind the undeniable role played in the European culture by water and to celebrate the great tradition of Italian hydraulics which is still little known. The programme "Vie d'Acqua"[27], included in the Expo 2015 event held in Milan, provided a further motivation. Its goal is to attract a well-defined audience who is looking for high-level content, but is not specialized, and to provide an interpretative and appealing key to a portion of the digital collection that was otherwise bound to have a small number of visitors. The exhibition went online in February 2015 and is constantly upgraded with new articles to keep it stimulating, enjoyable, and up to date. The BeicDL pageview estimate is around 3 %, a fairly high impact considering the specificity of the project.

Navigators are graphical representations of data, which allow users to access and interpret complex sets of data in a more user-friendly way. By cross-indexing descriptive and administrative metadata, BeicDL is providing new interpretative keys

---

[18] www.moma.org/.

[19] www.hermitagemuseum.org/.

[20] www.bl.uk/romantics-and-victorians.

[21] www.bl.uk/.

[22] www.expositions.bnf.fr/livrarab/.

[23] www.bnf.fr/.

[24] www.disaa.unimi.it/.

[25] www.fondazionecariplo.it/en/index.html.

[26] www.beic.it/it/articoli/biblioteca-idraulica.

[27] www.expo2015.org/it/cos-e/perche-milano-/vie-d-acqua.

allowing users to combine data in ways other than those provided by the OPAC. Two installations are currently available: the authors navigator and the Lombard publishers navigator.

The former[28] is based on the digital library metadata and aims at compensating for one of the most common deficiencies of catalogs, that is the ability to combine information based on authors rather than works. The navigator filters the authors' names by their date of birth and by the digital collection their works belong to. The Lombard publishers navigator[29], which is quite a unique development, is designed bearing in mind the specific feature of this database, engaging stakeholders like publishers, which usually have little or no contact with library services. Users are prompted with a map locating each of the publishers within the region and showing their annual production. Data were derived from the OPAC in combination with an administrative database constantly updated by the staff. The navigator has ended up being more accurate than ISTAT[30] (for instance in 2010, 535 publishers were tallied compared to the 331 notified by ISTAT).

6 Final Considerations

In total, the above mentioned traffic accounts for 25 % of BeicDL applications sessions. The remaining 75 % consists of direct queries (30 %) and search engine links (45 %).

It is also interesting to analyze the distribution of new visitors (35 %), returning visitors (20 %) and crawlers (45 %). Data have been calculated on the basis of a weighted arithmetic mean between BeicDL applications. However, these figures fluctuate depending on the application (web portal, discovery tool and repository).

References

1. Agree, P.E.: Information and institutional change: the case of digital libraries. In: Bishop, A.P., Van House, N.A., Buttenfield, B.P. (eds.) Digital Library Use: Social Practice in Design and Evaluation, pp. 85–118. MIT Press, Cambridge (2003)
2. Bertot, J. C.: Assessing digital library services: approaches, issues, and considerations. In: Papers Presented at the International Symposium on Digital Libraries and Knowledge Communities in Networked Information Society, Tsukuba, Japan (2004). http://citeseerx.ist. psu.edu/viewdoc/download?doi=10.1.1.114.7060&rep=rep1&type=pdf. Accessed on May 2011
3. Bishop, A.P., Van House, N.A., Buttenfield, B.P.: Digital Library Use: Social Practice in Design and Evaluation. MIT Press, Cambridge (2003)

---

[28] www.beic.it/it/autori.

[29] www.beic.it/it/content/gli-editori-lombardi.

[30] www.istat.it/it/archivio/64919.

4. CERL Papers VII: Imprints and owners. Recording the cultural geography of Europe. In: Shaw, D. (ed.) Papers Presented on 10 Nov. 2006 at the CERL Seminar Hosted by the National Széchényi Library, Budapest. Consortium of European Research Libraries, London (2007)

5. DELOS: Delos WP7 Evaluation Workpackage: Bibliography (2005). http://dlib.ionio.gr/wp7. Accessed on May 2011

6. Dempsey, L.: Thirteen ways of looking at libraries, discovery, and the catalog: scale, workflow, attention (2012). http://www.edu-cause.edu/ero/article/thirteen-ways-looking-libraries-discovery-and-catalog-scale-work-flow-attention. Accessed on Dec 2014

7. Di Domenico, G.: Fund raising e identità istituzionale della biblioteca: quale rapporto? Bollettino AIB **45**(4), 467–476 (2005). http://bollettino.aib.it/article/view/5573/5317

8. Dondi, C.: Provenance records in the CERL Thesaurus and in Material Evidence in Incunabula. Sborník Národního muzea / Acta Musei Nationalis Pragae, series C - Historia Litterarum **58**, 15–19 (2013)

9. Dondi, C., Ledda, A.: Material evidence in incunabula. La Bibliofilìa **113**, 375–381 (2011)

10. Ferri, F.: Biblioteca: una definizione non-pretecnica. L'importanza del Piano di comuni cazione. Biblioteche Oggi 2010(8) (2010). http://www.bibliotecheoggi.it/2010/201000804601.pdf. Accessed Dec 2014

11. Glenaffric Ltd: Six steps to effective evaluation: A handbook for programme and project managers (2007). http://www.jisc.ac.uk/media/documents/funding/project_management/evaluationhand-book0207.pdf. Accessed on May 2011

12. Gottardo, F., D'Amore A., Gasparotti, V., Raimondi Cominesi, A.: #Sveglia museo. Comunicare la cultura online: una guida pratica per i musei (2014). http://www.svegliamuseo.com/en. Accessed on Dec 2014

13. INDICATE: Handbook on virtual exhibitions and virtual performances (2012). http://www.digitalmeetsculture.net/article/handbook-on-virtual-exhibitions-and-virtual-performances/. Accessed on Dec 2014

14. JISC: Make your digital resources easier to discover (2014). http://www.jisc.ac.uk/guides/make-your-digital-resources-easier-to-discover. Accessed on Dec 2014

15. Kim, W.C., Mauborgne, R.: Blue Ocean Strategy: How to Create Uncontested Market Space and Make the Competition Irrelevant. Harvard Business School Press, Boston (2005)

16. Kyrillidou, M., Giersch, S.: Developing the DigiQUAL protocol for digital library evaluation. In: Proceedings of the 5th ACM/IEEE-CS Joint Conference on Digital Libraries (2005)

17. Lynch, C.: Colliding with the real world: heresies and unexplored questions about audience, economics, and control of digital libraries. In: Digital Library Use: Social Practice in Design and Evaluation, pp. 191–217. MIT Press, Cambridge (2003)

18. Marchionini, G., Plaisant, C., Komlodi, A.: The people in digital libraries: multifaceted approaches to assessing needs and impact. In: Digital Library Use: Social Practice in Design and Evaluation, pp. 119–160. MIT Press, Cambridge (2003)

19. MINERVA: Handbook on cultural Web user interaction (2008). http://www.minervaeurope.org/publications/handbookwebusers-firstdraft-june08.pdf. Accessed on May 2011

20. Saracevic, T.: How were digital libraries evaluated? In: Paper Presented at the DELOS WP7 Workshop on the Evaluation of Digital Libraries (2004). http://comminfo.rutgers.edu/~tefko/DL_evaluation_LIDA.pdf. Accessed on May 2011

21. Xie, H.I.: Users' evaluation of digital libraries (DLs): their uses, their criteria, and their assessment. Inf. Process. Manag. **44**(3), 1346–1373 (2008)

Author Index

Printed in the United States
By Bookmasters